Children of the Katyn Massacre

Children of the Katyn Massacre

Accounts of Life After the 1940 Soviet Murder of Polish POWs

TERESA KACZOROWSKA

Translated from the Polish by FRANK KUJAWINSKI
Foreword by WESLEY ADAMCZYK

Abridged from the original Polish
Kiedy Jesteście, mniej boli... (2003)

McFarland & Company, Inc., Publishers
Jefferson, North Carolina, and London

Library of Congress Cataloguing-in-Publication Data

Kaczorowska, Teresa.
　　Children of the Katyn Massacre : accounts of life after the 1940
Soviet murder of Polish POWs / Teresa Kaczorowska ; translated
from the Polish by Frank Kujawinski ; foreword by Wesley Adamczyk ;
abridged from the original Polish, Kiedy jestescie, mniej boli — (2003).
　　　　p.　　cm.
　　Includes index.

　　ISBN-13: 978-0-7864-2756-7
　　ISBN-10: 0-7864-2756-6
　　(softcover : 50# alkaline paper) ∞

　　1. Katyn Massacre, Katyn, Russia, 1940.　2. World War,
1939–1945—Children—Poland—Biography.　3. Children of war
casualties—Poland—Biography.
I. Title.
D804.S65K32813　2006
940.54'05094762—dc22　　　　　　　　　　　　　　2006020683

British Library cataloguing data are available

Cover photograph ©Design Pics.

Manufactured in the United States of America

McFarland & Company, Inc., Publishers
　Box 611, Jefferson, North Carolina 28640
　www.mcfarlandpub.com

TABLE OF CONTENTS

Foreword by Wesley Adamczyk   1
Author's Preface and Acknowledgments   5
Translator's Note   9

1. The Eleventh Urchin of Lvov   11
2. Construction Engineer/Publisher   23
3. A Participant in the Exhumation   33
4. American Professor   51
5. The Little Prince and the Fairy Tales   59
6. Little Ewa Always in Ribbons   81
7. Faithful to the Blue Uniform   91
8. In Love with the Land of His Birth   106
9. "When Tape Seals Our Lips"   118
10. Custodian of the House with the Turret   127
11. Witness to More Than One Crime   138
12. Stalwart from the Podkarpacie Region   150
13. Maja and the Cherries   162
14. Émigré Because of Martial Law   173
15. Devotee of Freedom   186
16. Fugitive from the Sailing Vessel "Dar Pomorza"   201
17. Child of Two Cultures   221
18. Katyn Pilgrims   233

Index   251

The Nazi-Soviet Partition of Poland in 1939

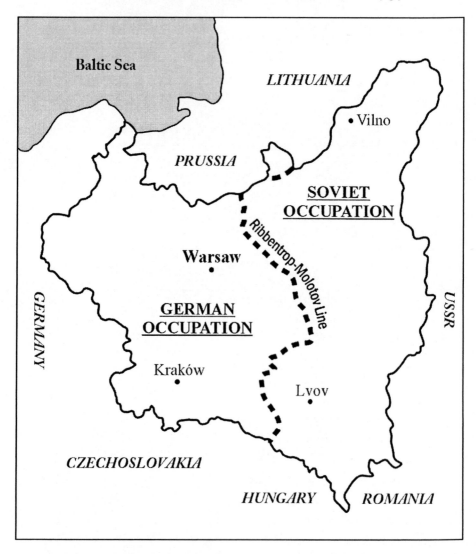

The Ribbentrop-Molotov Line shows the partition of Poland agreed to in secret by the Nazis and the Soviets in August, 1939. Courtesy Wesley Adamczyk.

FOREWORD BY
WESLEY ADAMCZYK

In the history of warfare, World War II ranks as one of the bloodiest on record. In Europe alone the war inflicted the highest number of casualties ever, causing incalculable suffering for millions of people. It was a time when man was wolf to man.

The evil began in September 1939, when the Germans attacked Poland from the west and the Soviets attacked from the east. Hitler swiftly turned the western part of Poland into a laboratory for testing the most efficient methods of mass murder. In the eastern part of Poland, meanwhile, the Soviets began their campaign with the extermination of Polish prisoners-of-war, mostly the military elite, and the intelligentsia. This genocide was promptly followed by mass deportations of Polish citizens to the depths of the Soviet Union with the intent of using them as slave labor. They were never to return to their homeland. The Soviets knew from experience that in due time most of the deportees would die from starvation, disease, exhaustion, or generally inhuman conditions.

Within a few weeks of the Soviet attack, the Red Army had taken about two hundred thousand Poles as prisoners-of-war. The army immediately sequestered the Polish officers and transported them to Kozelsk, Ostashkov, and Starobelsk, three preestablished camps located in the Soviet Union and guarded by the NKVD, the Soviet secret police. The camps held about 15,000 prisoners-of-war. More than half of the internees were Polish Army officers; the others included policemen, border guards, and some civilians, all of whom were considered individuals dangerous to the Soviet state. The prisoners were questioned around the clock about their political views, including their opinion of communism in general and the Soviet Union in particular. After six months of intensive interrogations by specially chosen NKVD interviewers, the prison-

1

THE KATYN MASSACRE

Courtesy of Wesley Adamczyk

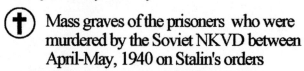

Mass graves of the prisoners who were murdered by the Soviet NKVD between April-May, 1940 on Stalin's orders

Three major camps where nearly 15,000 Polish POWs were interned, more than half of whom were army officers

ers were deemed of no use to the communist order. On March 5, 1940, Joseph Stalin and his top henchmen signed an execution order for 25,700 Polish prisoners-of-war, including the prisoners in the above-mentioned camps.

At the beginning of April 1940 the three camps began to empty, and by the middle of May, about 15,000 of their occupants had been murdered by a shot to the back of the head. The prisoners interned in Kozelsk were buried in mass graves in the Katyn Forest, those from Ostashkov were buried in Miednoye, and those from Starobelsk were buried in Kharkov. It should be noted that Katyn is often used to refer to the entire massacre. This is so because the first of the mass graves discovered was in the Katyn Forest, before the full extent of the massacre, including the other sites, was known.

On June 22, 1940, the Germans suddenly reneged on the eternal friendship agreement they had consummated with the Soviets only two years earlier and attacked them, quickly bringing them to their knees. Desperate, the Soviets now allied themselves with the West in a common effort to defeat the Germans.

By the spring of 1943 German troops reached the Katyn Forest area, where they discovered the mass graves of Polish officers who had been interned in the Kozelsk camp. Three commissions of forensic experts from twelve neutral European countries, as well as from Germany and the Polish Red Cross, were formed with the task of establishing the date and cause of the victims' death. Ultimately, more than 4,000 bodies were exhumed. Without assigning blame, the commissions concluded that the victims died in the spring of 1940, each killed by a shot to the back of the head. The Soviets accused the Germans of the crime even though they knew that the Germans were nowhere near the Katyn Forest when the crime was committed. At that time the Germans were still allied with the Soviets and remained in the western part of occupied Poland.

Allied leaders, particularly Franklin Delano Roosevelt and Winston Churchill, now faced a major dilemma. The Polish government requested that the International Red Cross investigate the crime. The Soviets became extremely belligerent and opposed the request. Shortly after, the Soviets broke relations with Poland, a country strongly allied with the West. Aware that the Soviets committed the Katyn genocide, the Polish government could have insisted that the requested investigation proceed, which would have confirmed the truth as to who was the guilty party. Not wanting to lose their important new ally, however, the Western Allies tacitly accepted the Soviet version that it was the Germans who had committed the crime. This set of circumstances constituted the beginning of the West's cover-up of the Katyn genocide.

After the war ended in 1945, the time came for the Allies to assign the responsibilities of charging individuals and countries with war crimes against humanity, in preparation for the upcoming Nuremburg trials. Conspicuously, only the Big Four (United States, Great Britain, France, and the Soviet Union) met in London for this purpose. They agreed to assign to the Soviets the area of responsibility that included the Katyn Forest massacre, despite indications strongly pointing to the Soviets as having committed the crime. The Western Allies also agreed with the Soviets that only the country with an assigned area of responsibility could charge the offenders in their assigned area. Thus, only the Soviets were responsible for handling the case of the Katyn massacre.

The Soviets ended up charging the Germans with the one crime they did not commit. The trial in 1946 lasted only three days. The United States and the British government, despite having enough incriminating evidence to indict and prosecute the Soviets, failed to submit this evidence to the court, knowing full well that by Western law failure to do so constituted a criminal offense in itself. The court, which included a Russian judge and a Russian prosecutor, did not allow the evidence held by the Poles to be submitted. The presiding judge, an American, dismissed the case for lack of evidence.

These sins of omission and commission by the West constituted a major cover-up. Not only did the Allies violate their own legal and moral codes of justice, but they also compounded the tragedy of Katyn—for the Polish nation and for the Polish people, particularly the families of the Katyn victims.

For nearly five decades the Soviet communist government kept their responsibility for the Katyn genocide a secret in order to protect the image of communism and the Soviet Communist Party. In communist Poland, on orders from the Kremlin, the very word *Katyn* was verboten. Children of the Katyn victims were forbidden from speaking publicly about their fathers' fate, and their own children were merely told that their grandfathers had "died during the war." Those who did talk about Katyn were spied on, deprived of their jobs, jailed, or worse. The children of the Katyn victims were forced to deny the truth in their own country and to suffer the indignity of being considered by their own government to be pariahs, or "enemies of the people." They lived in constant fear of the secret police. Those who escaped to freedom in the West soon found themselves again living with denial, as their adopted countries continued to perpetuate the cover-up of their fathers' murder.

In 1990, with the fall of communism, Russian president Mikhail Gorbachev admitted at last that it was the Soviet NKVD who committed the Katyn murder. Yet to this very day no one has been prosecuted or punished for either the Katyn genocide or its cover-up. Justice continues to elude the children of Katyn.

Wesley Adamczyk, author of
When God Looked the Other Way
September 2006

AUTHOR'S PREFACE AND ACKNOWLEDGMENTS

The problem of the Katyn crime had interested me from my youngest years. However I made the decision to write this book only in the year 2000 when the cemeteries at Katyn Forest, Kharkov and Miednoye were opened. It was during the solemnities dedicating these necropoli, in which lie more than 15,000 Polish prisoners-of-war, more than half of whom were officers executed by the NKVD, that I saw the children of the victims, sons and daughters who were scattered all over the world. I saw the pain of these now older people, the bitterness, and at the same time the relief that they could at last inter their fathers and speak of this massacre without fear. I decided then that I would contact some of them and describe their fates.

The idea turned out to be rather difficult to do. It was not easy to search them out, to get to the places where they lived, to exhort them to painful memories. Even so after two years work this book—factual, documentary, revealing a reality unknown because forbidden for half a century—came into being. It contains eighteen reports describing the fates of the children of the Polish officers.

Each of these biographies is unique. Eighteen of the heroes of this book, citizens of the Second Republic, live in the lands of six countries, Poland, Lithuania, Ukraine, Canada, the United States and Israel. They experienced various vicissitudes. Not only were they orphaned (sometimes completely, for very often their mothers were unable to bear the psychological burden and after the Katyn massacre quickly shared their husbands' fate), but from their earliest years they were condemned also to adversity and wandering, to Soviet and German prisons, and often to permanent exile from their country. Among them are deportees into the depths of the Soviet Union and those imprisoned in death camps and forced labor camps, whether in German territory or in that of the Soviet Union. They are members of the resistance: the Grey Ranks, the Union of Armed Struggle, the Home Army; there are participants among them of the national eruption that was the Warsaw Uprising. They are today people of various professions, with a rich baggage of experience, but always with the "scar" of Katyn.

This is the first reporter's book which describes, using the life-stories of yet living witnesses of history as its foundation, how extremely complicated and dramatic were their lives. Surely their fathers—later Soviet prisoners-of-war, the elite of the Polish nation, steadfast patriots, they who had after the long partitions built the new-born Second Republic—could not have foreseen such a destiny. Certainly they had believed in a better future for themselves and their children, never suspecting that life had prepared for them a true gehenna. These narratives are not only fascinating and true, they are also witness to the victory of truth over falsehood and good over evil. The children of the murdered officers have lived to see the crime brought to light, though not the judgment, punishment and condemnation of the guilty. But they can even so go to the graves of their fathers, render them homage, place flowers. And what is most important: they need no longer hide the truth.

The initiative for the publication of this book into English began early in 2004 at the Polish Museum of America in Chicago where I first presented the Polish text to the Polish American community. I am especially grateful to the then exhibit curator of the museum Bohdan Górczyński who organized the presentation. Indeed, I would not have been able to come to the United States at all had I not received a grant from the Kościuszko Foundation in New York; to the members of this organization I am deeply grateful.

Special thanks go to Jacek Kawczynski who graciously proposed financing the translation of this book into English, to Frank Kujawinski who prepared the English version, and to Wesley Adamczyk and Maria Zakrzewska who spared no effort in preparing the prospectus for the book and subsequent editing. Without their patient and diligent efforts, the publication of this English version would not have been possible.

I am indebted to Kazimiera and Janusz Lange for gathering together many of the photographs in the book, some from their own private collection and others received from the Katyn Family Association of Łódź, Poland. Personal photographs were given by four of the interviewees, namely, Wesley Adamczyk, Janusz Lange, Ewa Leśnik and Stefan Nastarowicz. I am likewise indebted to Wesley Adamczyk for preparing the maps that appear in the book.

Lastly, I would like my words of gratitude to extend to all individuals who not only contributed available documents and pictures for this book, but opened up their hearts as well and shared publicly their pain and their haunting memories.

Teresa Kaczorowska
September 2006

Translator's Note

All Polish names of individuals and cities retain their Polish spelling, except for the following. *Warsaw,* Poland's capital, is given its English spelling whereas *Vilno* (in Polish "Wilno," in Lithuanian "Vilnius") and *Lvov* (in Polish "Lwów," in Ukrainian "Lviv") appear as shown. These two latter transliterations reflect the fact that, before World War II, Vilno and Lvov were part of the Polish state. The name of *Kraków* appears in its Polish spelling, as is now more common in English texts.

Three specifically Polish words appear in their original spelling in order to indicate the special reference these words have to the Polish situation. *Kresy* refers to the pre-war lands which included the cities of Vilno and Lvov. Literally, the word *kresy* indicates "borderlands" but the emotional content is so much stronger in context. The two major cities of the *kresy,* Vilno and Lvov, were considered integral and inseparable parts of the historical and cultural life of Poland.

Gimnazjum at this time was a secondary school equivalent to American grades seven through ten. *Liceum* corresponded to the last two years of American high school, namely grades eleven and twelve.

Lastly, the Polish spelling "Kozielsk" is retained in the title "Our Lady of Kozielsk" as a proper name. The Russian transliteration, Kozelsk, is used in all other instances.

1

The Eleventh Urchin of Lvov

Lvov, Ukraine, July 2001

The Katyn massacre took from him his father, Władysław Antoni Sidor. As an only son, he must have many of this father's characteristics, among them elegance and style.

"Please count to twenty, wait another five seconds, and then come in. I have to put my tie on!" he shouts through the door.

I had come a quarter hour earlier than we had agreed.

"Better earlier than later. I hate late-comers. I cross them off my list of acquaintances right away!" He opens the door dashingly. He is now quite elegant: hair combed upwards, a white shirt, dark pants, a brownish green tie. Roman Sidor has worn only white shirts his entire sixty-nine years of life. He washes, presses and folds them himself. They are arranged orderly on a shelf in his apartment in the tenement on Dnietowska Street.

"Women aren't able to do this, just as they don't know how to cook potatoes either. That's why I have lived alone for seventeen years, eleven months and twenty-five days." His humor is typical for Lvov, as is his accent.

And alluding slightly to his two former wives, he adds with the charm of old Lvov: "I love both my freedom and my independence."

Radio Lvov is on at this moment and, unlike its famed broadcasts from before the war, is now heard only two days a week, for two hours on Wednesdays and three on Saturdays. It's been like that for the last ten years.

A song is coming over by the legendary Jerzy Michotek, actor, bard, prisoner of Vorkuta. He died six years ago in July 1995, yet his songs and ballads about Lvov live on. The radio announcer has just dedicated one of them, "The Ballad of the Ten Urchins," to Roman Sidor on his birthday, calling him the eleventh urchin.

"I've never been anyone's flunky," he says. Roman Sidor is proud of the moniker his friends have given him.

He serves "the best coffee in the world," brewed in an Italian expresso pot. He has several, all of different sizes, using the one appropriate to the number of his guests. He serves the coffee with water and ice. The water of course comes from the tap but it had been boiled earlier for a few hours. The cups are tiny, porcelain, and the glasses are crystal clear. He keeps such order in his bachelor apartment as many an experienced homemaker might envy. The tub in his bathroom is filled with water, as everywhere in Lvov, since the flow is cut for eighteen hours each day.

A thick, red ribbon binds all the important documents relevant to his father. Some are damaged, yellowed, glued with care. Others are new, photocopies. The best preserved items are the black and white photographs.

Władysław Antoni Sidor was the same height as his son. He stood five feet seven inches tall, was likewise similarly slim and brown-eyed. He was born in Lvov, in the Zamarstynów district, as his Austrian birth certificate attests, on June 9, 1903, into a family of manufacturers. His father Józef (Roman's grandfather) owned a contemporary furniture-making shop in Lvov at 6 Sienna Street. He had seven children.

"My grandfather died young, almost at the same time as his wife Maria, my grandmother, in 1923." Roman Sidor goes about his story quite colorfully. He interrupts his narrative by reaching into the family archives because there is a "lot on this family, almost too much." His memory is excellent.

A series of calamities befell the seven children, orphaned and cheated by an "unscrupulous" uncle. The fourth of the seven, Władysław (Roman's father), was forced after the death of his parents to interrupt his only just begun medical studies at Jan Kazimierz University in Lvov. He took various jobs in order to help his siblings. He managed also to pass the examinations for teacher in the public schools. In 1925, as a corporal in the Officer Cadets, he completed his half-year training in the infantry reserves. He attained the rank of reserve-lieutenant in August 1935, and of lieutenant in March 1939.

It was only years later that his only son, Roman, thanks to copies of documents from the archives of the Polish Ministry of National Defense, learned that his father, as a seventeen-year-old boy, wanted to fight for Lvov. On July 12, 1920, without telling his still living parents, he enlisted in the Małopolska Division of the Infantry. On July 20, 1920, he was assigned as a private to the reserve battalion.

"He had never mentioned that to me, though I knew he had always had a special spot in his heart for those killed by the bolsheviks," says the eleventh urchin of Lvov. "My father's friends, those who defended Lvov, lie today in the Cemetery of the Lvovian Eaglet-Cadets. I always place a candle there."

I am shown a large beige business card in a red folder, "Władysław Sidor, Teacher." In Podlesiejki, he met Olga Mendykówna, also a teacher and a graduate of a teacher's college, who was then the director of the school. They were married in Vilno, in the church of St. Anne, on July 11, 1930.

"I've safeguarded my mother's wedding ring," Roman Sidor says as he brings out the only gold item which remained to him from his parents. "I went once, 25 years ago, to the church in Vilno. It was December, hideous weather. Drifting snow, and later rain."

Roman Sidor came into the world February 15, 1932 in Podlesiejki. He spent the first years of his life in village schools—the two rooms to the left of the entrance were rented out to the teachers. The manor, the buildings of the schools and the fences surrounding them, all constructed of wood, are visible in the pictures kept in the red folder...

Twenty-five years ago, during a sentimental journey, Roman visited the sites remembered from his childhood. He even brought back from his Aunt Janka a painting made by his father. Especially as it is the only saved canvas of his father who used to enjoy painting with water-colors in his free time. The other place most dear to his heart, Lvov, he has here before him. He opens wide the windows and the balcony of his bachelor flat...

What was the childhood of this only child like?

"It could not have been more wonderful!" he says even more energetically. "I don't remember Podlesiejki too well. I know that my mother was sick for a long time after giving birth, for over six months. She made her confession and was anointed as if on her deathbed. Afterwards throughout her life she was always sickly."

When he was one year old, the family moved to nearby Swojatycze. He remembered the look of this town, almost entirely Polish. He closes his eyes:

"The peat, the tree, the well, the wooden building of the six-class school (it is still there), the garden, the presbytery, the church (also there), the palace of the Polish counts of the Plater family (destroyed by the bolsheviks), the fire-brigade, and the paved small market place with its three streets leading away from it." As a child he learned to speak a number of languages: Polish, White Russian, Russian, Ukrainian, and then German.

Even today he holds dear the image of love and harmony from those first years of childhood, remembering the simple, ideal marriage of his parents. He never heard them quarrel or fight, but recalls instead most of all his mother singing or his father playing the mandolin.

On his fifth birthday, February 15, 1937, little Roman was officially enrolled in the first grade at school. "I sat near my mother. I was able to finish two classes before the outbreak of the war." He shows me his official certificates.

As a seven-year-old, he visited the capital of the Polish Republic. It happened that one year before the war, the Vilno school authorities sent his father for higher studies in pedagogy to the Polish Free University in Warsaw. His father was homesick, often sent letters, and in the spring of 1939 requested that Roman and his mother come for an Easter visit. Together they went to the theater, zoo, movies. He remembered best of all the movie they saw entitled "Letter to Mother," about the tragic fate of a Jewish family. Likewise, he keeps in his possession pictures of the whole family from those days in beautiful, pre-war Warsaw. A happy, plump boy with bright, tussled hair, his mother serious and elegant. His father handsome, gallant, wearing glasses and a hat, shiny shoes and a long overcoat. Would anyone have guessed that his father would be executed a year later in the Katyn massacre?

A final photograph from August 1939 remains. It shows a serious, Polish reserve officer in a full dress uniform with two stars. "My son, Andrzej, is the one who looks most like him today. He even wears the same kind of glasses," comments Roman.

He and his mother bade farewell to his father at the large main train station on August 26, 1939. As his father left for the war with the Germans, he was wearing his field uniform; this Roman remembers "in detail," though he was barely seven years old.

A few days later his lieutenant father came back on a military bicycle. "He was somehow taller, changed. I know only that he had pedaled the 15 miles so he could see his wife and child for a half an hour." He remembers that his father was in an enormous hurry.

Now the recollections are beginning to tire him.

"Let's rest a bit. I'll make some coffee," he says as he breaks off the difficult conversation. He opens the windows even wider. The green from the tenement's outdoors, the ripening cherry tree, are now almost inside the bachelor flat on the first floor.

He still remembers the smell of the first Russian soldiers. "Word of honor!" says the eleventh urchin striking his breast. "What kind of smell was it? Of anti-lice preparations! Perhaps you know that the Soviet army was the most infected with lice of any army in the world. Understandable as it came out of the most 'licentious' state of all!"

This smell stands out from thousands of others. It is like the smell of burned human bones.

On September 17, 1939, the bolsheviks marched and drove their tanks through Swojatycze, merely to make a show of strength. They didn't fire on any of the inhabitants who were watching them though they did murder local Polish petty gentry and burn their properties. Local helpers of the NKVD, with red bands on their sleeves, helped with the deportations to Siberia. In the space of the first few months of Soviet aggression and the planned partition of Poland up to January 1940, a great number of people, something no one knows about, were arrested and murdered in this part of the *kresy.*

"Among them were friends of my parents: land-owners and clerks. I remember how they would whisper with terror at home: 'They killed this one, took away that one.'"

At first they left the teachers alone, but they did send in a school director from Russia. He took over their living area and they were resettled into the recently built, brick building of the new school, J. Piłsudski School (his father had been instrumental in the new construction). There they received "community quarters."

One night at the end of September, his father returned from the war. He was on his bike, famished, tired, wearing civilian clothes. He had fled German capture.

"He had a volvulus," the son remembers. "He had to heal himself and hide. He didn't leave the house."

The day of October 18, 1939 imbedded itself in every detail in the seven-year-old's memory. His mother had been summoned to the regional school board headquartered in Darewo in order to clarify her work situation in the new, meaning Soviet, school in Swojatycze. She went there by farm wagon early in the morning when it was still dark.

"I stayed home alone with my father," he said as he began to fill in the details. "All of a sudden there was pounding on the doors and windows. My father had to open. One of the assailants was from the NKVD, had a red star. The others, about ten of them, White Russian helpers, had red bands. They shouted: '*Sobiraysya!*' ('Get out of here!') Mr. Ciula, the chief official in Swojatycze was already in the wagon where, under the threat of their rifles, my father and I were made to sit. My father wasn't allowed to take anything at all, not even warmer clothes. It was years later that I found out that my father was given up by a White Russian, more or less a neighbor."

After reaching Darewo, some fifteen or so kilometers away, they locked up Mr. Ciula, seventeen-year-old Roman and his father in a room with a grated window and a steel bed. Roman Sidor remembered that there was no mattress on it and that he could not sit on the wire-spring because his backside hurt. There were two buckets also, one with water, the other for relieving oneself.

He goes on intensely, with sadness:

"When it got dark, they brought my mother to the cell only to get me and to say good-bye to my father. I'll remember the return trip to Swojatycze to the end of my life. I still hear the sobs of my mother and feel the pain in my heart! I had a foreboding that I would never see my father again. It would have been better for me to be one of the arrested than to have felt that! It was horrible! I'm not exaggerating!

"About two months later a letter came from my father. He had written the address: Kozelsk, Post Box 12. There were a few more letters. All of them brief, sometimes with a request for biscuits. Mom sent them, wrote..."

Roman brings from the kitchen a poster board covered with large numerals. These are the numbers of those POWs who were shot: in Kozie Góry, that is in the Katyn Forest (the Kozelsk camp) 4421, in the basement of the NKVD offices at Kharkov (the Starobelsk camp) 3820, in the basement of the NKVD offices at Tver (the Ostashkov camp) 6311. All together: 14, 552. These were the career and reserve officers of the Polish Army as well as officials of the National Police, secret service, Border Patrol, judiciary, prison personnel, members of the clergy. At other camps and prisons in the Polish *kresy*, 3435 Poles were murdered on territory now part of Ukraine, 3870 on territory now part of Belarus (together: 7305). "Which adds up to a total of 21, 857 victims," comments Roman Sidor, who "imbibed" all the available literature on this "crime of crimes." Every now and then he reaches onto his shelves for books, looking for corroboration of facts and particulars of the events.

I check these numbers on my return to Poland. The figures are identical with those given in the secret report of the head of the Committee for State Security of the USSR, A. Shelepin, in 1959. Only the report of P. Soprunienko of December 3, 1941 gives a somewhat higher figure of the POWs put to death in the three camps, 15, 131. He also asserts that the commission of the crime in the spring of 1940 was the work of the Russian NKVD. The proposal to shoot the POWs was made by the People's Commissar of Internal Affairs, Lavrenti Beria. The decision came on March 5, 1940. Besides Stalin, the highest functionaries of the Soviet Government and the Communist Party of the Soviet Union signed the order: Molotov, Voroshilov, and Mikoyan. The POWs of the Polish Army were placed under the supervision and jurisdiction of the political police, namely the NKVD, and not of the army, an action not in accord with the Geneva Conventions concerning military prisoners-of-war. From the beginning of 1940 in the three camps, Kozelsk, Starobelsk and Ostashkov, interrogations took place, personal files were opened, attempts were made to link the POWs to espionage. Outside of a few exceptions the attempts were not successful. Which is why, to his conclusion that the POWs must be shot, Beria added: "All of them are hardened, irreconcilable enemies of the Soviet government."

Roman Sidor presents a dramatic comparison:

"Had my father in September 1939 not fled from German captivity, surely he would have survived. Ninety-seven percent of the Polish officers imprisoned in the German camps were saved, whereas only three percent of those in Soviet camps. It is a tragic ratio."

Sidor is now today reconstructing his father's life. He was taken to be shot, as other prisoners of the camp, from the Kozelsk monastery. First by rail to Gniezdowo near Smoleńsk, and from there to the Katyn Forest by car (the first transport was on April 3, the last about the middle of May 1940). He imagines to himself his father standing over the open pit with a band over his eyes, his hands tied behind his back. It was night. A bullet in the back of the head. He doesn't know if his father shouted out. Perhaps the trees remember. Every night the Soviet genocide killers made about 530 such firings. Then they would drink. They were given cases of vodka every day. Many of the executioners later shot themselves. A great many went blind. There are no executioners now. Only 405 prisoners from the three camps managed to survive in one way or another.

"My mother and I learned about my father on Thursday, May 30, 1943 from the newspaper 'Gazeta Lwowska.'" He shows me in his red file the yellowed, glued "sacred item." "The Germans broadcast that the NKVD had murdered him. However my mother didn't entirely believe the news. We continued to wait." I see tears in his eyes. We had to break off our conversation.

Before the tragic information reached them, they themselves passed through a hell of their own...

On the postboard Roman Sidor has also written down data concerning the planned extermination of the Polish families from territories of Poland occupied by the Soviets. There were four great deportations into the depths of the USSR, the so-called "cleansing of anti–Soviet elements." On February 10, 1940, 220,000 were transported; on April 13, 1940, 320,000; in June of 1940, 240,000; and near the end of July and the beginning of August 200,000. Further "cleansing" was interrupted by the German aggression against the USSR. It is difficult to establish the exact number of deportees. The majority of emigration sources puts the number at about 2 million people. They were transported always at night, in cattle cars. All members of families were taken, irrespective of age or health. A great many, how many isn't clear, were unable to survive the trials of the journey.

Roman Sidor and his mother were taken in the second deportation, during the night of April 13, 1940. Perhaps his father, teacher and reserve lieutenant, was no longer alive. Now they had to make their way to northern Kazakhstan.

"They came for us too at night, in a group similar in size to that during my father's arrest." Roman was now eight years old. "They gathered us up in farm wagons. The weather was rainy. We traveled along muddy tracts, in an unknown direction."

It was an ordinary, dirty, two-axle cattle car. It held about twenty people, men, women, and children of various ages. Besides the wooden bunks and a latrine slot for physical needs. They managed to get a bunk at the very top, on the right side. They had a little bedding, some clothing and food.

Roman remembers those next to them in the cattle car. Twins who were only a few weeks old, always crying, with a young mother. It isn't clear how long they traveled, one or two days. In the dark, without getting up, without food, with unbearable noise, the rumbling of the train and the crying of children.

"It was a nightmare! But I didn't put up any fuss though I almost suffocated. I did everything my mother told me to do. Everything in order to live through it," he says, rolling a cigarette from his tobacco and paper. He doesn't throw out the unburned butt, but makes use of all the remains to roll the following one. "I don't really smoke too many, but I need one now!" he explains the next time we take a break.

It was Providence, even more than a miracle, that in Baranowicze, when they were let out to get their allocation of bread, they succeeded in escaping. They took with them only a small briefcase, the one with the silver tableware. They had friends and acquaintances in the city. However they were in Baranowicze just a few days... "when Mom went out to the store," Roman sighs.

She didn't admit to the NKVD that they were escapees. They would have killed them. They ended up at an estate in Równopole, three miles from Baranowicze. There were no healthy men in the five-room house surrounded by barbed wire, with a single turret and guard. Merely women, children and a few old men.

"In the empty rooms there was only some straw on the floor," recalls Roman Sidor. "Do what you want, lie down where you wish, sleep on whatever you want. And wherever Moscow is in charge, there are always lice and bedbugs. We slept like cattle."

Seventy or eighty people were being held in this camp. There was a field kitchen in the yard outside, where barley was cooked every day. The only flavoring was some kind of bitter oil.

"Which is why I haven't put barley in my mouth ever since," he jokes.

"Later, after getting a letter from Mom, her sister Aunt Janka, also a teacher, paid us a visit," he says. "She came in a farm wagon. She brought honey and some other foodstuffs. And some liquor for the guards. We were already preparing ourselves for the next escape..."

On May 18, 1940, they found themselves in a dense forest. It was night, humid, the mosquitoes were a nightmare. "I can still feel their bites because I didn't have anything to cover my head. Somehow we made our way to the tracks. For the first time in my life I slept while I was walking along."

At daybreak they were in Baranowicze. The parish priest didn't want to take them in. They then went by some kind of carriage, and then a village wagon, to the railroad station where they boarded a train for Lvov. They were warmly welcomed by distant relatives in a village outside Lvov.

"They were themselves dirt poor, but they gave us milk to drink and fed us real bread. There had been no kolkhoz there yet. The worst thing for us was that we had no documents," Roman Sidor says in a voice now hoarse, yet amazing me with his excellent memory.

His mother eventually took a risk. She went to the authorities with a request for a passport. She wanted to teach in school. She knew that, since so many of the Polish intelligentsia had been exiled, there was a lack of teachers for the Soviet occupants. She knew four languages, Polish, Russian, Ukrainian, and White Russian.

"And she did get a passport, for a half year, in her maiden name. So on September 6, 1940, we came to Zagórze, eight and a half miles to the south of Lvov, to a village school. I would refer to my Mom as 'aunt,' pretending to be her orphaned nephew."

On June 22, 1941, the nine-year-old Romek heard bombs over Lvov in the night. He woke up and called out: "Mom! Dad's coming; I hear the war!"

The Soviets were not prepared for the invasion. The Germans quickly occupied Lvov and the surrounding area. Olga Sidor, the wife of a Polish officer, began using her husband's name again. She began to be better treated. She was made the director of the school and the only teacher in the neighboring village of Kuhaje.

"It was there that we learned from the newspaper 'Gazeta Lwowska' that my father had died in Katyn." He repeats, lowering his head, that despite the fact that the bolsheviks broke all laws on their arrival, it was still hard for them to believe in the annihilation of the Polish nation. There always remained the hope that perhaps it was a mistake.

On July 22, 1944, the Soviets once again returned to Lvov. He says:

"There were Polish families everywhere in the area. The Soviets displaced them, took them into exile, put them in prison. They destroyed the churches, exiled the Polish priests. But they didn't move our Mom. She remained a teacher."

Olga Sidor however lived in extreme poverty. Besides her work in the village school, she tended a garden, raised a goat and some fifteen or so chickens. Roman, now going to the seventh grade, that is as of September 1945, studied in schools in Lvov. It was difficult for his mother to care for him. He was brought up in an orphanage, then moved on to boarding school. Two months before the end of middle school—now a pupil in the ninth class— he was once again stopped by the NKVD. He was arrested on April 2, 1949, at the Armenian cathedral in Lvov. For what reason? He answers with the words of a song by Jerzy Michotek: "The world's gone mad. And everything's collapsed..."

"They hadn't forgotten that my father was an officer of the Polish Army and a prisoner at Kozelsk. Too, that during the German occupation we hadn't concealed the fact that we had twice fled from the unvanquished, heroic NKVD guards," he explains seriously. "They knew also that I knew the truth, that the perpetrators of Katyn had not been the Germans but rather them. And that in my trunk I had Polish books."

As Roman walks along the streets of Lvov, he shows me where he had been imprisoned, where interrogated, where sentenced, where severely beaten... He shows me too where the ghetto in Lvov had been. "I was there with my mother. My father's best friend from the time of his medical studies, Dr. Kohn, was there. We would bring him chickens, eggs. He cured me of severe angina during the time of the Soviets, in the winter of 1940."

Roman Sidor was sentenced on July 13, 1949, in the district courtroom on Halicki Square. The sentence: ten years imprisonment in distant camps of the USSR.

"Even then I wore a white shirt," he smiles bitterly. "Even though in prison number 1 on Łącki Street I sat with twenty-eight men in a space of ten square yards. Mine was the only one. There was a barrel for excrement: foul-smelling, lacerating one's backside. Next to it there was a bucket with drinking water, also stinking."

Roman speaks only reluctantly about the gulag.

"There's too much chatter about it. Everything that Solzhenitsyn wrote in *Gulag Archipelago* is true. You didn't know where you were or what would happen to you ten minutes later. And how come they hadn't killed you yet, you didn't know that either," he repeats.

At first he served his sentence in prison no. 2 in Lvov. From there he was taken by special train to Kolyma, as far as the Sea of Okhotsk. He spent exactly five years, three months and eleven days in the camps. He was released early, thanks to Krushchev's amnesty, on July 19, 1954. He was then twenty-two years old.

Before he reached Lvov he fell ill from a serious case of jaundice.

"I remember that I passed red urine and white stool. I lived through it by a miracle. O, how many miracles have there been in my life? I can't count them all. You know that only one out of ten lived through Kolyma."

He returned to Lvov exactly on his mother's birthday, October 17, 1954. Olga Sidor had been ailing, often hospitalized, and transferred from school to school.

"We could have left for Poland in 1956. We had an official invitation from Aunt Misia," he says, continuing his narrative. "But what would we have done there? I had just come from Kolyma, without any schooling. And mother, the wife of an officer lost in the Katyn massacre, was almost on a stretcher. And Poland then was not the same as Poland today! The only thing possible was to remain in Lvov."

Roman loves Lvov. Today it is becoming beautiful again, being restored, regaining its brilliance.

"I used to dream of it even in Kolyma. Especially during the transports, which were the most difficult to bear," he adds.

He had to repeat the ninth and tenth grades of middle school. It was only in the subject "Constitution" that he has a B on the report card he still has. All the other grades were A's. It was in 1956 that he received his longed-for diploma.

His mother, after she had ceased teaching, received neither a pension nor an apartment. She lived out her last days in an old people's home for teachers. She died at age 53, in 1960. She is at rest in the Lewandowski cemetery in Lvov, as she had wished.

Roman Sidor, despite all the adversity he suffered, completed the Institute of Technology in Lvov. In 1967 he received the desired diploma with honors of chemical engineer. While working in a chemical plant, and then later for ten years in the Institute of Experimental Technology, he raised two children, each of them born of a different wife. His son Andrzej, born in 1957, completed Lvov University, and now teaches English in Lvov. Ola, ten years younger than Andrzej, studied German and is today a successful translator.

His children know the full truth. There was no way they couldn't know: the reality emotionally undergone by their father, a witness of Katyn, accompanied them their entire life. Even though one could speak openly of it only for the last ten years. In May of 1989 Roman Sidor went to Katyn Forest. Alone.

"I felt that it was only then that I buried my father," he says. He brought back with him some earth. A portion of it he has poured into shiny, metal commemorative containers engraved with the words: "Katyn 1940." He gives these out as a gift to others, even though he himself struggles daily with his own material needs.

He dreams of seeing the Polish military cemetery in Katyn Forest, which opened in 2000.

"How can I possibly go on the money I get?" he asks. He shows me his pension payment: 116 hryvnya, which is 21 dollars monthly. "In Poland everyone complains about their low earnings. I myself would love to get that tiny supplement, that 500 zloties, that many Polish veterans get."

Then he announces that it's time for lunch. It all happens quickly. He serves it even more beautifully than in a restaurant. First course: soybean soup with potatoes and vegetables. Second course: four whole potatoes artistically arranged and sprinkled with dill in the middle of which is asparagus in sauce and homemade pickles. For dessert, "a spot of coffee."

"I haven't bought meat for ten years. I don't have the money for it. But I never borrow anything from anyone." Though he has "passed through a kind of grinding-mill" and suffered daily poverty, he has kept up his spirits. "I never lie, not even to my dog," he jokes as he again rolls himself a cigarette.

The eleventh urchin of Lvov has been spreading the truth about Katyn for many years. He founded the Lvov Katyn Family. And even though, after having gathered together eighteen descendents of the victims of Katyn, the organization does not officially exist (there is no money to register it), he directs it out of his own apartment.

"After so many years of silence and lies, it is imperative to keep alive the memory of this tragedy of the Polish nation, this violation of human rights." He repeats that he is a witness to this crime.

He spreads the truth about Katyn through lectures and a documentary exhibition "Crime of Crimes." Since 1993 he has traveled from city to city, presenting documents, maps, and showing a documentary film "Thou shalt not kill" in museums, churches, military retirement homes for officers, cultural centers. He has already traveled around six Ukrainian districts. He last showed his exhibition in 2000 in Lvov.

"We had a full complex of guests, including the Polish consul. But since that last time I haven't been traveling much; I don't have the means to pay for transporting anything," he says sadly as he points to the materials of his exhibition now sidelined in his bachelor's apartment. The racks, posters and documents lie along the walls.

"I wasn't successful in finalizing the building of the monument, the Katyn Cross, at the renovated Cemetery of the Eaglet-Cadets of Lvov. I didn't get any help anywhere. And the monument was almost completely ready. All that was lacking was few hundred dollars."

2

CONSTRUCTION ENGINEER/PUBLISHER

Gdynia, Poland, August 2001

He meets with a journalist somewhat unwillingly. Only after I called him another time that I was vacationing here on the Baltic did he agree I could visit him in his home near the beach in Gdynia.

His house is large, built high up, with a beautiful view of the Gdynia neighborhoods. An August summer. The flowers in his garden are all blossoming, cats are warming themselves on the large terrace decked with red geraniums and luxuriant grapevines. He is cautious.

"I wrote my recollections about my mother, wife of the reserve second-lieutenant of the Polish Army, forester, a prisoner-of-war at Starobelsk, in 1999, in my book *Written with Love*. Have you read it?" he asks me on the porch. Heavy-set, somewhat stocky, but good-natured, with cheerful blue eyes.

"But I am writing about the children of the POWs...," I mutter.

"Please come in," he says, yet with some reserve, inviting me into his spacious villa. In the living room there is an exceptionally beautiful fireplace made of green granite, which looks even better than marble. From the doors which open widely onto the garden there spreads out a beautiful view of summer in Gdynia.

Andrzej Spanily of Gdynia did not know his father. He was barely a month and a half old when the reserve second-lieutenant, the forester Zdzisław Spanily went off to war, and then immediately ended up in Starobelsk. An only child, today sixty-six, he was raised only by his mother Karolina Maria Spanily. He searched for a long time for a refuge for himself until he settled finally in Gdynia. A construction engineer by profession, today he is a publisher, the editor of the monthly "Rodowód" and president of the Katyn Family of Gdynia. He recalls sadly:

"It was on a beautiful September afternoon in 1997, at the Junikowski cemetery in Poznań, that I bade farewell to my mother. She was eighty-nine years old. She had remained alone and always lived with the memories of her husband who had been murdered at Kharkov. She passed away on September 18, the day after the anniversary of the Soviet army's invasion of Poland. It is they who destroyed her happy, only just beginning, married life. And my own world as well, as I was still crawling on all fours."

Karolina Maria Spanily, born Rymszewicz, came from the region of Nowogródek. She was born in Berdówka, some 15 kilometers from Nowogródek. Her father Piotr Rymszewicz, the son of an insurgent in the uprising of 1863 who was imprisoned in Siberia, was the forest inspector of the private forests of Count Karol O'Rourke. He was in charge of over twenty thousand acres of forested areas.

"The wooden forestry buildings in Berdówka are still standing, even the house in which my mother was born," says Andrzej Spanily. His mother had instilled in him her love for the extremely beautiful lands around Nowogródek, for the enchanting forests and woods, for the lands of her birth. He went there for the first time only several years ago. His face becomes radiant whenever he talks about the lands of his birth.

"It may seem improbable, but the old building for husking the hops, designed back in the 1920's by my grandfather Rymszewicz, still stands. It was there in its loft that my mother would hide in her youth with her books and her cats. It was her own private sanctuary."

Andrzej Spanily read in the parish books of the Catholic church in Wsielubie that his mother was sponsored for baptism in 1914 by the owners of the estate. Karolina Maria Rymszewicz's godfather was Count Karol O'Rourke, who had come over from Ireland and her godmother was his wife Maria, herself of the old *kresy* family Tyszkiewicz.

"The combination of my mother's first names was no accident. Because of the great respect my grandfather had for the count's family, he named his daughter Karolina Maria," Andrzej Spanily concludes. He also knows from family stories that the count loved her a lot and pampered his godchild. This was due in large measure to the fact that Count and Countess O'Rourke did not have children of their own.

As he described the country of his forebears, stories told him by his mother and encoded in his childhood imagination began coming back to him. Stories about the severe, snowy and cruel winters in the *kresy*, of starving wolves, of her grandfather's hunts. How vivid to him remain his mother's narratives about the house being tightly closed before Easter "so that the yeast cakes would rise," about impenetrable forests full of wild animals, mushrooms, blackberries, blueberries and raspberries. About the enchanted countryside, famous in legend, simply flowing with milk and honey. His mother, as many of the young people from Wsielubie, went to the high school in Nowogródek named after Adam Mickiewicz .

"Immediately after high school, direct from the wild backlands of the forests of Nowogródek, my mother stepped out into the world," says Andrzej as he recreates his mother's youth. "She came to Poznań, and began her agricultural studies at Poznań University. She lived under the guardianship of her father's friend, the dean of the agricultural and forestry department, professor Biehler. It was in Poznań that she met her husband, my father."

Zdzisław Spanily came from the southeastern part of the Polish Republic. He was born in 1910 in Hryniawo. When he met his future wife in Poznań, he had been working as a young academic in the university institute for the management of forests. His advisor and mentor, professor Biehler, wrote of him: "He is endowed with true passion, conscientiousness and an all-embracing knowledge as regards the management and care of forests. I see in Mr. Zdzisław Spanily an excellent responsible young forester."

After receiving her diploma as an agronomist, Karolina Maria Rymszewicz returned in May 1938 to the eastern *kresy*. They were married that same year, precisely on September 10, in the church at Wsielubie. Her father, Piotr Rymszewicz, died two months later. And thus the newly become son-in-law, Zdzisław Spanily, employed at the time in the headquarters of the state forests in Łuck, took over his father-in-law's job. Just like him, he became the overseer of the forest complex of Count Karol O'Rourke in Wsielubie.

Andrzej, their first and only son, came into the world ten months later, on July 17, 1939.

Life had begun to get better for the young and very much in love couple. The Spanilys bought a car.... Then, however, September 1939 intervened.

Second-lieutenant Zdzisław Spanily soon found himself in the 24th Infantry Division in Łuck. The invaders, first those from the West and then on Sept. 17 those too from the East with equal cruelty, destroyed the people and land of Nowogródek. The Soviet occupiers were especially brutal. The women, children and aged who remained alone were thrown out of their homes, robbed, imprisoned, reviled and cruelly beaten. The Soviets subjected them, unarmed and trusting in a civilized world, to a barbaric system of hypocrisy and lies.

The Soviets behaved most cruelly toward the families of Polish military officers and police.

"They expelled my family from their home," says Andrzej Spanily. "Father Kuczyński took my grandmother Rymszewicz to the presbytery with her youngest daughter Hala. My mother's sister Teresa from Nowogródek took in my mother and me."

A Soviet administration took over in Wsielubie. The few local communists assisted them. The head position at the estate of Count Karol O'Rourke was given to a cartwright at the estate. He put on a red band, was given an old rifle by the new regime and one day went and arrested the count as well as the count's guest Brzozowski and the local district leader Augustowski. He seated them demonstrably on the wooden seats of a large farm rack (belonging to the count), with their legs tied. He transported them ostentatiously to the prison in Nowogródek. There the count, now an old man, was severely mistreated by the Soviets. However, thanks to the intervention of the Irish government, he was soon turned over to the Germans.

"The cartwright's administration in Wsielubie was short and grotesque." This Andrzej Spanily knows from the stories of the inhabitants. "He butchered the estate; everything got stolen. Even the bolsheviks couldn't tolerate such devastation. They eventually sentenced him to hard labor in the camps, which he did not survive."

The intelligentsia of Wsielubie was either exiled to Siberia or murdered. A number of officers were murdered in Kharkov, just like Lieutenant Zdzisław Spanily who himself had been captured after the September campaign by the Soviets in unknown circumstances and imprisoned in Starobelsk. It was from Starobelsk that he sent a postcard in December of 1939. And again in early April 1940, in a telegram paid for by his wife, he wrote: "Don't think about the future. Take care of the child and yourself. With deepest affection. Zdzich." The family learned only fifty years later that he had been murdered in Kharkov. He was number 3128 on the NKVD list.

Andrzej Spanily is unable to remember the dramatic circumstances in which his mother took him from Nowogródek. Even so he is grateful to her today. In those terrible times, during which his father was not returning, when every next day was uncertain—his mother was informed that she and her son were to be exiled to Siberia on February 10, 1940. As a result, she immediately made the decision to flee. It was on the very day before the first Soviet transports. She took her son in her arms and crossed, illegally, two borders, that between Russia and the General Government and that between the General Government and the German Reich.

"I marvel at her courage," says Andrzej, noting that at the time he was only seven months old. "The escape from the *kresy* protected us from the penal camps and a sure death."

Karolina Maria Spanily and her son ended up first of all in Warsaw, and then in Nowe Miasto Lubawskie in Pomorze, where her husband's family lived.

Life in this city, now incorporated into the German Reich, was extraordinarily difficult. Karolina Maria Spanily had to work extremely hard. She was called up for forced labor, digging ditches on neighboring German estates. The occupying power destroyed all external signs of Polishness and required people to register on German nationality rolls. For speaking Polish one could be sent to a concentration camp.

"My mother had much trouble with me," laughs Andrzej Spanily. "I was a very active child. When I began to talk, there was always a lot of it, loudly and of course in Polish."

He remembers the agreement he had with his mother. Whenever they would be going along a street and had to pass Germans, his mother would squeeze his hand hard. That was the sign that they couldn't speak together at all. He suspects however that his talkativeness one time saved his life. The head of the Gestapo, a certain Zulauf, was the terror of Poles, especially of small children. He would kill them by hitting them many times against a wall.

"One day while I was playing with some Polish kids all of a sudden I found myself alone. When I turned around there before me stood Zulauf and he was yelling. It seems that I, not at all disturbed by this, answered him in Polish. The whole street held its breath. And Zulauf, he let me go. I think that he was taken back by the sheer audacity of it."

Despite everything, little Andrzej learned to sing the national anthem and to draw the Polish eagle symbol during the occupation, though under secret, conspiratorial circumstances. They would listen in great secrecy at neighbors' basements to Radio London and he would look through colorful picture books of the Polish Army.

"I was brought up on the annals of pre-war 'Płomyk.'" Now many years later, he recalls with affection his mother's continual efforts to raise him. She also gave secret lessons to others, helping individual students to pass their high school exams.

The young child took away his impression of the Red Army from the final stages of the occupation and the approaching front lines of the Russians. He and his mother had by then moved to a village near Nowe Miasto, to one of the houses abandoned by German settlers. These homes stood perpendicular to the main road and he watched as the Red Army soldiers marched down. Those of the first wave behaved quite properly; he remembers that they were cultured and that his mother offered them tea. The second wave of approaching Soviets were already stealing and plundering. The third wave, however, the ranks of the NKVD, were in his opinion professional bandits. They destroyed whatever they could, robbed the inhabitants, raped the women and killed.

"I still have before my eyes the time when a Soviet soldier aimed his gun at my mother. He ordered her to undress. Then I began to cry, shout and wail hysterically. That probably deterred him. He only shot and killed the dog of a neighbor who shared our dilemma, saying: '*Tvaya pula na sabaku!*' ('Your bullet I give to the dog.')"

Other women were less fortunate. Once during a return visit to Nowe Miasto, despite the fact that his mother wouldn't allow him to look at the half-naked bodies of murdered women, he saw more than enough.

"The devastation was dreadful. Everywhere there were ruins and blood." He remarks that the Red Army soldiers destroyed everything with exceptional hatred. During the nights they would bang on the houses with their rifle-butts.

"All wet with perspiration, clutching my mother, I continually trembled from fear," he remembers. "They used to catch fish with hand grenades in the Drwęca River near our home."

After the war his mother began to teach natural history and geography in the *gimnazjum* and *liceum* in Nowe Miasto Lubawskie. But before the devastated schools could begin their work, they had to be cleared of rubble, cleaned of refuse and of mud mixed with excrement after the departure of the Soviet headquarters in place there. Andrzej reads movingly a document that he has kept from the first postwar years. It is an affidavit from July 4, 1946, signed by the mayor of Nowe Miasto Lubawskie, Mr. Grześkowiak: "Let it be attested that citizen Karolina Spanily was a Pole throughout the time of occupation and was not included on the German nationality listing."

In 1947, his mother and he moved to the Poznań area. Karolina Spanily found work in her profession; she took over the supervision of a 400-hectare experimental farm near Konin.

The next stop in their wandering was Wolsztyn, a small town in the Poznań area. There his mother organized and guided an agricultural learning center together with an educational farm in Powodowo. In Poland this was at the beginning of the worst period of the Stalin years.

Little Andrzej, not realizing that he was putting his mother in difficult situations by his boyish, ill-considered antics, loved to listen to Radio Free Europe. Since the broadcasts were jammed, it occurred to him to string speaker wires from his mother's office where their "Stolica" radio was kept to his bed. Lying there, and with the help of headphones, he could listen as he wished to the forbidden broadcast, avoiding the buzz of the jamming because he was able to escape the noise in the radio. It was there, on Radio Free Europe, that he heard for the first time that the NKVD had eliminated wartime POWs. Names were not given however...

He thought up another invention. When his mother was at one of her conferences, he and a friend set up a telephone connection between the neighboring buildings in which they lived. The wires were taken from the dynamo of a bike; the other materials came from railroad telephone apparatuses since his friend's father was a railroad worker.

"When Mom returned from her course and in the morning our phone rang, she almost got a heart attack. In those times personal telephone connections were a serious crime." He tries to excuse their foolishness as the carefree attitude of young people.

"A particular provocation on my part was also that I later wrote in my background file that my father had been murdered in Katyn, in defiance of the generally obligatory formula that he died in wartime." Again he emphasizes that as a young man he hadn't really realized that the times were so strange.

His mother safeguarded her son as best she could. She didn't acquaint him with the political situation that existed or her own troubles, including those that she had with the Office of Security (UB).

"When I was in my final year of elementary school, the director of the school called me into the teacher's lounge. A dour-looking person was waiting there for me. He took out some notes and turning some over some pages said: 'On such and such day you told some friends that American cars were far superior to ours.' When I said that that was true, he asked: 'Did you get this from your mother?' I then understood the situation. I answered that my mother didn't know anything at all about cars. And that American cars were better, I had learned this from a certain tall guy with a beard who used to pass by our school..."

That surrealistic dialogue made him realize that the well-known security people were gathering material against his mother. It was only years later that he learned that his father's brother, living in Warsaw, had many unpleasant moments being often interrogated only because a draftswoman where he worked had informed the Office of Security (UB) that Zdzisław Spanily died in Katyn.

In 1954 Karolina Maria Spanily and her son moved to Poznań. She worked there until retirement as an inspector of agricultural education.

Her son Andrzej did not follow either in her or his father's footsteps. In 1963 he became a construction engineer, a graduate of the Poznań Institute of Technology.

"I most regret that I was unable to participate in the memorable events in Poznań in 1956. I was an athlete, in field events, the javelin throw, and at the time I was in Łódź for the Polish Youth Championships. When I returned to Poznań, it was all over."

Despite many proposals, Karolina Maria Spanily never again married. She was always waiting for the return of her husband Zdzisław whose company she had enjoyed only so briefly. Her son remembers how she would repeat: "Your father is not on the London list. Perhaps then the Soviets sent him to Siberia. After all he is a forester and that's what they need..."

She waited even to the downfall of communism and the admission of the Soviets in 1990 to the terrible crime... Perhaps it was as a reward for her integrity in a difficult life that in 1997 she had a very gentle death. She didn't suffer. She passed away suddenly, during breakfast, with the gentle countenance of her eighty-three-year-old face.

"After September 17, 1939, Polish society was divided into two parts. Into those, not very numerous, who had betrayed Poland and those who had given their lives for their country, those like our fathers. Unfortunately, many of our present political activists, both from the communist left and from the right, emerged from the ranks of the betrayers. Which is why the bulletin of the Katyn Families, which has been published in Gdynia since 1996 by the Katyn Family Association, is called 'Rodowód,' meaning 'Genealogy,' in order to make known the patriotic bearing of the Poles of the Second Republic and to stigmatize the betrayal of the nation."

"I founded this publishing house because the Katyn Family does not engage in financial activities." He explains that the name of the publishing house comes from his grandfather Rymszewicz's name. "And so I have transformed myself from a construction engineer to a publisher. I run it at my own expense, without earning anything from it, but the truth about Katyn must be told."

"ASP Rymsza" can already take credit for other publications besides the monthly "Rodowód," including such colorful, hard-cover books as: *Written With Love. The Fates of Katyn Widows (Pisane miłością. Losy wdów katyńskich)* (two volumes), *Generation 2000 About Katyn (Pokolenie 2000 o Katyniu)* (writings of young people), *The Green Years: Nowogródek 1921–1934 (Zielone lata: Nowogródek 1921–1934)* the album *Kharkov, Katyn, Miednoye (Charków, Katyń, Miednoje)* (from the military cemeteries opened in 2000). Most recently he has prepared an album dedicated to the families of Katyn. He is also printing bulletins, for those from Nowogródek among others, as well as postcards with the Our Lady of the Victims of Katyn.

"This most recent effort is quite simply a cultural one!" he says with enthusiasm. "On these postcards we are disseminating an image of Our Lady of Ostra Brama sculptured by a POW of Kozelsk."

The creator of the original Madonna, Henryk Gorzechowski (1892–1940) was a lieutenant. He carved it with a pen-knife on a piece of wood from a prison bed slab. He gave it to his son, also Henryk (1921–1989), in the Kozelsk camp on February 28, 1940. It was a present on the nineteenth birthday of his son and at the same time a committing of him to the protection of Our Lady. The lieutenant died at the hands of the NKVD in April 1940, but his son, also a POW at Kozelsk, was saved as one of only a few. And the sculpture was saved with him. The holy relic from his father, carried in his uniform on his chest, safeguarded him a number of times. During his service in the English navy, in the anti-aircraft artillery in England and in the difficult combat under General Maczek. After the war the younger Henryk Gorzechowski returned to Gdynia. He took great care to protect his exceedingly powerful Advocate, a remembrance and heirloom from his father.

"Not long ago we handed it over to Bishop Sławój Leszek Głódź, chaplain of the Polish Army." Andrzej Spanily shows me a cast made from the original, a faithful copy of Our Lady of the Victims of Katyn. "The original will be put in the Katyn chapel of the Military Cathedral of the Polish Army in Warsaw. The grandson of the sculpture's maker, also named Henryk Gorzechowski, who lives in Gdynia presented it to us. It will be placed on the altar with ashes brought from the military cemetery in Katyn Forest, Kharkov and Miednoye, there to be again among its soldiers."

Andrzej says with admiration: "It's quite amazing that someone who never had artistic training could sculpt such a miraculous Madonna!"

It is thanks to the efforts of the Gdynia Katyn Family that a Katyn Monument was placed in the military cemetery of the Defenders of Gdynia in Redłowo in 1992. Ceremonies take place there every year on International Katyn Day, namely April 13. Likewise a Katyn Chapel has been opened in the church of Our Most Holy Lady, Queen of Poland. A bas-relief of the Madonna of Katyn has been placed there over a most precious relic, earth from the Katyn Forest cemetery. On both sides of her are found the epitaphs of those officers and policemen who were lost.

Andrzej, president of the Katyn Family, summarizes the activities of the Katyn Family of Gdynia:

"We are very pleased that we have a Katyn Monument, annual Katyn competitions throughout Poland, a Katyn Chapel and the epitaphs of our fathers. Thanks to these things we can unite with them during our prayers and meditations."

He has been several times at the military cemeteries opened in 2000. "Wonderful designs were chosen, beautifully presented necropoli, the wooded areas preserved." He points out that "all that is lacking now is historical information concerning these sites."

He recalls John Paul II's words spoken to the Katyn Families in Rome in 1996. They were gathered in the chapel, beneath its own bas-relief of the Madonna of Katyn: "You are here as a family so that you will not forget but likewise so that you will forgive."

Andrzej Spanily admits that as he gets older he returns more often to the *kresy*.

"I have become more and more dependent on the place of my birth. I have already been to the Nowogródek area five times to know better and more closely the family homestead; it somehow eases things, brings relief."

He has become a member of the Association of the Friends of Nowogródek and of the Nowogródek area. Every year they visit the family homesteads. They went to Rome on the occasion of the beatification of eleven nuns of the Holy Family of Nazareth order who were executed by the Germans in August 1943. The fruit of this trip was the bulletins. In one of the bulletins, Andrzej

Spanily wrote a description of Wsielubie, and included contemporary photographs. A few landmarks have been saved in his family's village: the church, a twenty-five acre park. But it is all devastated, seriously despoiled. The estate of Count O'Rourke has been changed into a hospital and looks like a barrack.

"In the former Rymszewicz holdings, there is an ancient pine where storks used to weave their nest. I was told that efforts have been made many times to expel them but they have always returned. I checked myself; it is the only nest in Wsielubie. There is no other!" laughs Andrzej whole-heartedly.

Andrzej has a small copy of the Wsielubie church, made of wood and painted white, in his home. He acquired it from a local folk artist two months before the artist's death. Nearby not far from the small shrine there hangs a portrait of his mother, then a portrait of his father, grandfather... Also there is Our Lady of Katyn and the Katyn Madonna of Gdynia...

Andrzej Spanily repeats that he must yet preserve the memory of the patriotic bearing of the Poles of Nowogródek during the Second Polish Republic as well as during the Second World War.

"I feel that it is a kind of debt which I should pay back, to these fine, wise people." He adds almost in secret that he has "big plans" for the Nowogródek area. "I feel myself there at home. The people treat me well and many of them remember warmly my grandparents."

3

A Participant in the Exhumation

Szczecin, Poland, September 2001

We found in the excavations even leg prostheses and artificial eyeballs... The orthopedic shoes were a great shock for me; they were the kind worn by those suffering from Heine-Medina disease, for deformed legs of different lengths. It was evidence that the Soviets murdered invalids as well as the old.

Indeed, for them it wasn't a question merely of destroying the Polish military. For what was little Poland compared to enormous Russia? Or to the powerful Germans? Both of these countries neighboring the Polish Republic had the same goal: to deprive the Polish nation of its leaders, of its educated and learned people. These neighbors wanted to "decapitate" and "debrain" the country so that Poland would never be reborn. They had been dedicated to the same goals in the 18th century when they partitioned Poland and subsequently laid claim to her as their own for more than 120 years. They weren't successful then. Which is why during the last war the invaders murdered the Polish elites out of forethought and bestiality, making use of truly barbarous methods in the camps.

I proclaim this truth so obvious to me even though there is little of Polish blood in my veins.

My father came from a German family of barons; his name was Julian Gruner. One of his ancestors, still having the surname "von," a military officer, had at sometime married a Polish woman and in this way a part of the family was polonized. They settled at first in Inflanty and later at property in Mariampol not far from Vilno.

In turn my mother Maria, from the house of Mittelstaedt, descended from a Germanized Swedish family. Her ancestors settled on Polish territory

The cemetery bell is part of the monuments dedicated to the murdered Polish officers; it is present in all three cemeteries of the Katyn Forest, Kharkov, and Miednoye (previously USSR), 2002. Courtesy of Kazimiera and Janusz Lange, Katyn Family Łódź, Poland.

probably during the Swedish invasion. My mother's father had married a German woman whence arose the mix of Swedish and German blood.

My father was born in 1898 and my mother was ten years younger than him. She was still a child when he was studying medicine in Kazań. She was raised on the Biernatki estate near Kalisz.

During his second year of medical studies my father learned that a Polish army was being formed. He dressed himself in a bolshevik uniform and wended his way through and out of the revolution that was embroiling all of Russia. In January 1919, he enlisted as a volunteer in the 3rd Reconnaissance Unit of the 10th Squadron of the Lithuanian Uhlan Regiment where he fought against the bolsheviks until the very end. Oh! I still have in my possession a wartime medal of his, a few other decorations, and even his gorget. He started off as a private but in March 1921 was discharged with the rank of Second Lieutenant.

In the independent Second Polish Republic he continued his medical studies in Warsaw. In 1925 he received his diploma as doctor of general medicine. I still have that diploma.

A cast of the VIRTUTI MILITARI medal, the highest honor bestowed by the Polish government for military bravery. The same cast is present in the three cemeteries of Katyn Forest, Kharkov, Miednoye (previously USSR), 2002. Courtesy of Kazimiera and Janusz Lange, Katyn Family, Łódź Poland.

My mother then was seventeen. She was living in Biernatki. The family estate was large and counted about thirty-seven thousand acres. Within its confines there were seven residences, a distillery and a tannery. Mother had just finished her high school studies and, not working, was an eligible young woman.

My parents met in Kalisz where my father had begun work after his studies. He started in a company clinic; later in the Kalisz hospital he organized the pediatric unit of which he became the head.

They were married in 1931 in the church of St. James. I, Ewa, their only daughter, was born in Kalisz three years later.

I was recruited for the exhumation at Kharkov for two sessions: 1995 and 1996. All together for eight weeks. Together with my team, I was to examine the fourth quadrant of the Forest Park: it was there that the burial place of the murdered prisoners-of-war from Starobelsk had come to light. I was also the team's doctor.

As a matter of fact something warned me not to go there. Never in my life had I imagined, however, that it would be such a difficult assignment. I hadn't considered the enormity of the cruelty of the crime. I had thought: after all I'm a doctor, a surgeon and an anesthesiologist; I have known many people in the course of 40 years' practice, close friends and acquaintances, who have died. It had seemed to me, after all, that I was prepared for the work of exhumation, especially 60 years after the crime. I overestimated my strength.

The exhumation was like a mental illness. I came to experience a split personality...

I boarded a bus full of laughing, boisterous young people. The students from the Nicholas Copernicus University in Toruń were going on an archeological practicum. I however was going to my father's funeral... I knew with certainty that it wasn't rational but I couldn't divest myself of a strange tenseness. From the outset I felt as if my feet were fastened to the ground...

We went to the site of exhumation. Traces of earlier excavations were evident in the bones protruding from the ground; here a jaw, there a segment of skull, elsewhere a tibia. I was fearful that I was walking over remains, perhaps over my father's bones. I walked on tiptoe... The feeling of the profanation of this place was deepened by the sight of scattered bottles and trash as well as traces of campfires and recreational foot-paths; after all, this had been a rest-area for the KGB.

I wanted to crowd out all these thoughts with hard work. I worked as a machine: I dug, I extracted from the earth each least remains, I checked over the already examined heaps lest there remain in them yet some particle. My energy was contagious. The young people became more serious with each passing day; they worked almost ceaselessly, as if in a fury so as not to overlook the least fragment, to find every shred of evidence of the crime. I think that the young people, just as I, were conscious that they were touching not only objects which had accompanied these marvelous people to their very end but their remains as well. And my father's too... All the found remnants were for us nothing less than sacred...

Work conditions were incredibly difficult. It's hard enough to imagine let alone to describe. In the deep excavations, often filled with a cadaverous fluid which splashed on us, pieces of bodies would tumble down...

In this picture (Ewa shows a photograph) one can see the so-called "wet" grave, three meters deep. We are standing in it up to our knees in a greasy substance arising from the decomposition of the soft parts of corpses. To get to the remains it was necessary to transfer out 300–400 buckets of a thick, cadaverous, terribly smelling, greasy substance. Only then could we extract the remains, pass them above out of the excavation; there they were scrupulously washed, cleaned, counted, described and packed. The stench was such that the local health officials wanted to interrupt the exhumation...

And in this photograph (here she shows the next picture) there are the so-called "dry" graves. In the largest of these, corpses were preserved in their entirety, with hands, legs, toes, nails, faces. They lay in disorder as if thrown from vehicles. Some had their hands tied behind their backs by a rope having two characteristic knots, or by barbed wire. We found complete bodies, but only where the large drills, the so-called "meat-grinders," had not passed over. For in the years 1970–1980, here in this cemetery, as it seems in other cemeteries in the Soviet Union, gigantic industrial machines destroyed the traces of Soviet crimes. In some graves in Kharkov sixty to seventy percent of the skulls had been crushed. Traces of these "meat-grinding" machines exist to this day; oh, here cameras caught them. In one of the holes of death we uncovered also a corpse crushed by a huge stone. In another—one partially burned.

The disjuncture in my mind grew all the time. When we would go for dinner I would joke and laugh, but the fear kept growing in me...

During the work of exhumation I wanted so much to find my father's remains or some object belonging to him. I knew that he could have had on himself a gold ring, an ancestral signet, a watch, a cigarette case with the monogram "JG" as well as photographs of a thirty-year-old brunette with long hair and of a five-year-old girl with short light hair...

Yet I was afraid at the same time that I might really find them...

Working like a madwoman I would summon up images from childhood. His portrait... Really what was my father like? I wasn't able to recall him at all! He was for me a "blank" ...Even so I should have remembered him at least a little! When we were separated I was already five years old!

However there rattled around in my head only the shreds of images from a pre-war childhood: a dachshund in some kind of yard, steps leading to a garden, boys from Kalisz walking on their hands at the Prosna River. The only thing connecting me with my father was his short, sharp mustache. I remembered how the hairs pricked. And also the knickers he wore and his thick socks. That was the extent of my awareness of the world in those days. Nothing more...

Already as a child I had amputated him from my memory. He was like an annoying, painful memory. All the time he was someone we were forbidden to talk about as if he has been a criminal of sorts. Even Mom was unwilling to talk about him, fearing that I would "blurt" something out...

As I grew older, I began more and more to gather information about him on my own. I would browse through documents, pictures, would read articles from before the war, listen to the stories from family and acquaintances. And suddenly I discovered that his life had been unusual, beautiful, heroic.

He had distinguished himself everywhere. He had written into his life-history beautiful pages not only during the war with the bolsheviks but also during his studies, in his professional work, in his family life.

During his medical studies at Warsaw University he was the first one there to lecture on physical education. In the years 1921–1928 he himself actively participated in sports. He was a frequent winner and runner-up in the high jump and the javelin throw; he also ran the hurdles, jumped the pole vault, swam, rowed, skied, participated in the motorcycle rallies. Unfortunately, after the war his name was withdrawn from all the sporting annals. He ceased officially to exist because ... he had died as the victim of a crime wrapped in a conspiracy of silence.

He had been also universally esteemed and respected as a doctor. I learned from his former patients, today already sixty, seventy years old, that as children they would often feign illness in order to get to see him. To this day his portrait hangs in the pediatric unit of the hospital in Kalisz, my father, who had founded the unit, though until recently no one had known who he really was and where he had died.

When I would ask Mom who my father was, she would answer tersely:

"Very tall, stood over six feet tall, was well built, energetic. And had a sense of humor. When you were born he came into the hospital room on the first floor by way of the window. He was carrying an enormous bouquet of flowers..."

It was later I learned that after the mobilization he had turned up at an emergency hospital in Lublin. He was taken into Soviet captivity on Sept. 19, 1939, together with the personnel of the field hospital in Stanisławów. He had been wounded in the head as he was attempting to protect the wounded lying in the street in front of the hospital as a Soviet tank drove down toward them.

I know also that he could have saved himself. He could have claimed German ancestry and demanded an exchange with the Germans or pledged to remain in the USSR and change citizenship, to which he had been urged. But such disloyalty was for him evidently too high a price for his life.

Everything I know about him, I know from strangers. The powerful personality looming from these testimonies captivated me to such a degree that time and again I had the impression that he was guiding me from beyond the grave. In the most important moments of my life I would always pose this question to myself: "What would my father say if he came back?" And then, when for a long time he hadn't returned, I would ask: "What would my father say if now he arrived?"

I am convinced that my spiritual contact with him kept me from many errors. And it was now after over fifty years that I had come to him, to Kharkov...

Never had I been so close to my father as during the intense exhumation work. I had the impression always that I was touching his body, touching ground mixed with his own very blood... After removing another body I would think: perhaps it's him. And while cleaning objects, I would feel that I was washing away his ashes together with the clay adhering to each small item...

I was unable also to cease thinking of facts already known to me. I knew that they had been taken first of all from Starobelsk to the Kharkov prison. Those who actually did the executing of the several thousand prisoners-of-war were not many, probably less than twenty. First, in one of the cells, three of them would tie the prisoners' hands behind their backs. Then they would lead them to a special inner section of the prison where the walls were thick. An official prosecutor would be sitting behind a table, he would check over the personal data and say: you can go. When the prisoner would turn in the direction of the exit, the NKVD officer attached to the procurator would shoot him in the back of the head. No prisoner of Starobelsk would have expected death at that moment. They would have assumed that they were being exiled to Siberia...

In Kharkov I was trembling all the time. I would ask in my thoughts: Was my father afraid then? What was he thinking before his death? Did he sense it coming...?

The executed were dragged across the ground outside the cell and loaded on a truck. The interiors were lined with sheet metal so that no blood would drip out of them. On the side panels was the lettering: "bread," "milk"...

The basic method of the crime was always being refined, the details fine-tuned. For example, initially they threw a piece of canvas over the body. However, it was difficult to clean—cleaning cost five rubles, spirit alcohol and sausage or fish. They then hit upon removing the prisoners' overcoats and throwing them over their bodies. That explains why that during the exhumation we found one grave full of officers' overcoats. Only a brutalized people could behave in this way... And yet it wasn't all that easy to bear up under the enormity of the crime since the majority of the seventeen or eighteen executioners drank themselves to death and some committed suicide...

Soprunienko died only a few years ago but no one was given access to him before. They said only: "He is old and sick..." Though he was the one who signed the death sentences of thousands of the best sons of the Polish nation...

The effect of these reflections of mine? Well, I didn't make it through to the end of the session ... I who had never had trouble with sleep or digestion began to have regular nightmares. I would dream for example that I was sleeping with my dachshund in a grave and I felt that we were lying on human remains. In order not to crush them I would carefully lift the dog, then myself ... and I would wake up... Each day became progressively more difficult. Every day in the morning before the departure to the cemetery, I had to break through ever greater resistance.

I had to leave before my time was up. Actually I ran away. I thought that if I didn't get myself away from there I would go mad.

I left my business card only with three people. Also particulars about my father and details concerning objects which he might have had in his possession at the final moments of his life. And that was my solace!

A few days after my return to Szczecin where I was living, I received the news: a signet had been found with the monogram "JG" and a watch!

To this day I don't know whether I would have been able to endure it had I been there ...

A year passed by and I went again to the exhumations. And this time I stayed in Kharkov until the end of the session. I felt that I ought to even though I was as deeply terrified as before. Others also had experienced moments of weakness. One of the professors underwent such a severe nervous breakdown that he suddenly fled into the forest and cried...

I was more composed this time. I explained to myself that my father's grave had already been uncovered, that his remains had already been buried. Now at the common grave in which his remains too were at rest, I could light a candle, place a flower...

I did find the living conditions to be as difficult as during my first stay. We lived in one of the Kharkov sanatoriums. The toilets there consisted of latrine holes. Of course there was one toilet bowl but without a seat. And the toilet bowl had to be partially bricked up because it was always being stolen. And despite the one hundred plus heat waves in July and August, there was no water in Kharkov for entire weeks.

Also, the meals we received were horrid, for example a bowl of field millet with suet. The charges for our stay were high; we were even required to pay in dollars. It was lucky for us that those from Toruń had brought with them a lot of food. Too, we would buy some items at the marketplace.

There was no running water at the cemetery. We would transport it in canisters from a nearby spring. This time those in charge of the exhumation noticed my difficulties and transferred me from the death-holes to work at the center, where the cleaning took place. But I worked just as intensely as ever.

As for that so did the others. The first group would dig morning and evening in the cemetery. In the afternoon and evening they would deliver to us, the second group, what they had found. We would clean it all and write descriptions. A third group would do the final documentation and enter the particulars into the computer, photograph documents and revise records. The day's work would end about three or four in the morning. Shouts would often break out: Here it is! But more and more often names were found which did not appear on any list. It turned out that in the graves there were several hundred bodies more than there had been prisoners-of-war from the Starobelsk camp. The local KGB was very reluctant to address this topic.

"Yes, there is one other list, about 900 names...," they would mutter.

We were completely taken aback by the skulls. They were intact, without traces of a bullet, in those areas where the "meat-grinder"drills had not passed over. This was different from Katyn Forest and Miednoye where the skulls had clear traces of entrance and exit of bullets. In the beginning we didn't know the manner by which the prisoners-of-war at Kharkov had been murdered. It was only after thorough examination that the archeologists discovered that the skulls were damaged in a different way: either upper and lower teeth were smashed or eyeball sockets shattered. It turned out that the bullet had passed through the large occipital opening and gone out through the mouth or the eye. It wasn't by accident that the shots were so very precise. The criminals, with their knowledge of human anatomy, knew that by aiming that way the blood would remain in the sinuses. And as a result they wouldn't have to clean up often...

However, the blood would often run onto the parquet. In some skulls we would find traces of an axe; the prisoners must have been dispatched by a crushing blow...

We found also traces of the desecration of corpses after the war. The local population began to find bones, Polish buttons, and military decorations when they, in need of fuel, were demolishing the fence that, during the war, had still bordered the burial areas. They would dig through this place in pursuit of military accessories and valuables. They destroyed a lot of remains.

Though in the second session I worked on the cleaning of the exhibits, I was unable to break off from thinking about my father. Remembrances from my youth, from my whole life, would come back. Of a life without him and in waiting for him...

Before the mobilization, in September 1939, my father didn't imagine that the Soviets would likewise invade Poland. He sent me and my mother eastward. We stopped in Tomaszów Mazowiecki at my mother's brother's, he also a doctor. Later we escaped to Warsaw. I remember from that time some sort of hospital, the lack of food, the awful bombardment.

After the major war engagements had ended, we returned back to Kalisz, but our home was already occupied. However, the German officer turned out to be decent; he allowed us to gather up all our documents, warm clothing and told us:

"Get away immediately. You are on the German list for transport to work duty."

During that very night, in a crackling frost, Mom and I returned by sleigh to Tomaszów. But here too we soon found ourselves on transport lists.

There were already official lists. The Germans had exchanged with the Soviets information as to who ought to be eliminated. The Polish nation had to perish, had to be deprived of its educated class. The Germans and Soviets worked together with each other, shared data, names.

The arrests of reserve Polish officers and their families, under various pretences, lasted throughout the period of 1939–1940. They were taken to extermination camps from the occupied territories both by the Germans and by the Soviets. I believe that it had been thought out in great detail and agreed to by the leaders of these countries a long time before their aggression against Poland. After all, Beria had already on September 19 published a list of extermination camps for Poles, precisely noting locations, number of prisoners, and even commanding officers, commissars and the amount of their salaries!

For example, my father's entire family from Mariampol were sent to Siberia or locked up in prisons. And the uncle from Tomaszów, the doctor, at whose place Mom and I hid, was soon arrested by the Germans. He spent five years in the death camp at Auschwitz.

From Tomaszów we fled to Częstochowa, to Mom's sister. There we remained until the end of the war.

From Częstochowa I remembered how the holy painting was covered, the prayers to the Black Madonna ... and sliding down sleds on Jasna Góra. The sledding was marvelous. Straight down to Holy Virgin Mary Boulevard!

Our hunger was terrible. We used to eat noodles made of buckwheat, a dark moist bread with marmalade made from rutabaga, and horse meat. I won't ever forget the holidays during which plates would be set on a beautifully covered table, and on each of them one slice of tomato with a small piece of horse meat. And my first sin: I was so monstrously hungry that I stole from a common serving plate one small sausage...

Initially my mother was the only working person in the house. She knew German and got work as a saleslady in a lamp store. But the family increased: one of my mother's sisters joined up with us, there were three children in the house, and also two orphans from a bombed train. And me...

One time the Gestapo took my Mom away. She returned after several days in a state of severe depression, with persecution delusions. A young normal woman to that moment, she had now to be tied to the bed because she kept wanting to jump through the window. I remember that later a psychiatric doctor came to see her. Mom would never again get back to her healthy state. Of course, there were periods of improvement but to the end of her life she had relapses of depression. She would close herself up, live in her own world. I lost any deep human contact with her.

After the war we left Częstochowa for Poznań, to the second of Mom's sisters, widowed in the course of the war. There I completed my high school studies in 1951. I was interested in sports. Just like my father I swam well, skied, was even on the national volleyball team. On documents I would write:

"my father died during the war." Thanks to this I was accepted for studies at the Medical Academy.

Mom worked as a secretary at the Poznań Philharmonia. When I was in my second year she became completely incapacitated. I was at that time living through my own youthful trials: I had married early and infelicitously. Wanting to free myself from this relationship I transferred in 1955 to the Medical Academy in Szczecin. I took up residence with my father's family, also from Mariampol, because some of them had returned from Siberian exile and settled there in Szczecin. My father's spirit was perhaps watching over me. His friends, doctors and pharmacists from Kalisz, funded my scholarship. Every month they would of their own accord gather up money and send it to me. If it weren't for them, for sure I would not have completed my studies. But I was already working a little by then in the sports clinic and as a medical assistant in a superphosphate factory near Szczecin.

I received my doctor's degree in 1957. I went to a hospital for children, and then on to the children's surgical ward—I worked there for twenty years, added two areas of specialty and a further academic doctoral degree, after which... I transferred to anesthesiology. I spent the following two years on the intensive therapy ward. At the same time I worked in the emergency room for more than thirty years and taught academic courses for forty-three years.

I never signed on with any party.

I don't have children, though my second marriage has worked out. I have been with Andrzej Zarnoch, a ship's engineer, now for thirty-five years. I never intended to have children; the crime at Katyn had greatly influenced my decision. Already as a young girl, in a moment of weakness, I had told myself:

"I'll never give birth to a child. For sure there will be another war to follow and my children will be treated as badly as I was... I don't want that!"

Besides all my wanderings and flights, I had been given over, already in Częstochowa, for a number of years to the Sisters of Nazareth. And later, in Poznań, when Mom fell sick and my father didn't return, again I had to go to the locked boarding-school at the cloister Sacré Coeur. The school was at that time under the personal patronage of Stefan Wyszyński, the Primate of Poland, who would often come to us. I remember his teachings and charisma; we were the Primate's special young people. I have to admit that the level of education was high. And too it was an excellent school at developing character. But even so a boarding-school is not the best place for a child. It exerts a life-long influence...

I don't know how to cry. In my childhood I had no one with whom to shed my tears. I had learned that crying helped nothing. And so I have never cried, either as a child or as a grown person. But at the exhumations, for one only time, I burst into unexpected tears...

We had uncovered in the Kharkov forest, about eighty meters from the road leading to Moscow, seventy-five mass graves. Fifteen of the largest were the graves of Poles. In one of these we found as many as 1050 corpses. About 8500 in total of these were exhumed, and of these 4302 Polish officers. Likewise 60 graves of Soviet citizens were uncovered presumably of different national backgrounds, sex and age. The graves were all completely mixed together, which is why it wasn't possible to apportion either a Polish or a Ukrainian part of the cemetery. The distance between them amounted to barely 20 centimeters. The actual place of burial turned out to be not too large: 100 by 50 meters. Identification of bodies was altogether impossible.

The Poles had been buried in uniforms and shoes. The Ukrainians had been left without any items of clothing or identifying objects, by and large naked. The plunder of clothes and footwear from Polish victims was severely prohibited so that murder would not be suspected. But Polish shoes were for Russians something marvelous which is why we would find shoes with the leather cut off in front.

What did we recover besides human remains?

Over ten thousand various objects belonging to those murdered: documents, money, decorations, military equipment, mess kits, canteens, cigarette cases. A good many books: Kraszewski, Sienkiewicz, textbooks. In addition many buttons, watches, holy medals, rings, family signet rings. On some of these there were names or initials. All of them have made their way to the Katyn Museum in Warsaw.

I remember a well preserved backpack with handkerchiefs. Also I'll never forget the shoe, the so-called "apelówka," with the sole carved from wood, so that the disintegrating footwear would be warmer and protect against the cold during the daily assembly. Among the prisoners-of-war at Starobelsk there were 300 doctors—that's why we would find during the exhumations ampoules, needles, medicine, medical instruments and stethoscopes, thermometers, bandaging material. I often wondered if they might have belonged to my father? Because he had worked in the Starobelsk camp in the infirmary.

In Kharkov I realized anew that I had been waiting a long time for my father! Mom would cut off any conversation on this topic, and simply forbid me to talk about him. Up to her death in 1968 she didn't even tell me that there existed a valise full of my father's photographs, letters, family documents and articles clipped from pre-war newspapers about his international sporting success. It was by chance one day that I found them. I had some difficulty opening it and almost threw the whole thing out!

Mom also never showed herself at the pediatric ward of the hospital in Kalisz though she did agree to the installation there of a large portrait of my father, which she did without telling me. She also forbade me to go there. She said:

"If you go there, they'll take your father's picture down..."

Even so I succeeded in holding on to two cards sent by my father from Starobelsk. He had sent them, probably to inform us, by way of a private whom he had treated in the infirmary at the Starobelsk camp. The Soviets had released this soldier but then he was taken to a German camp.

After Mom received these cards she started writing to father. She made efforts to find him, she importuned the embassy in Moscow that he was of German descent. But by that time he was probably no longer alive...

Already in 1943 we felt that he could have been murdered. True, his name didn't appear on the lists printed up by the Germans, but he didn't write, gave no sign of life. In its place a number of strange people, primarily privates, came by the home, with improbable information:

"Julian Gruner is a doctor somewhere in the Omsk region; it is very difficult for him...," they would say.

These were most likely informers recruited by the Soviets. Their visits lodged in my memory.

When Krushchev took power, it seemed to me then that I might go to the Soviet Union and work for my father's release. The fact was that I always had the hope that he was still living. I wrote to Krushchev but he didn't answer. I was by then a doctor, so I got together some money and bought a ticket on an excursion. And though the excursion guide didn't let anyone out of her sight, I was able to meet with the Polish ambassador in Moscow. He told me:

"Officially I can tell you that in the territory of the Soviet Union there isn't one Pole who would care to return to Poland. But unofficially there are about two million Poles but they don't have citizenship and not one of them will return..."

The ambassador didn't say to me however that I couldn't go to Omsk. From the embassy I made my way right to the train station in Moscow to buy a ticket. And there they very nearly locked me up! Because for every trip to a different republic of the Soviet Union you had to have a special permit...

And the money I had scraped together to look for my father I had to spend on large Russian rings because it wasn't permitted to carry rubles back out. Later I couldn't believe in my own naiveté! But honestly I still trusted that my father was living. The conversation with the ambassador also did not deprive me of hope for his return...

The truth came out only and finally in 1990. It was then that I saw my father's name on the lists presented to Jaruzelski by Gorbachev... At entry 627, in Russian letters, there appeared: Julian Lucjanowicz, 1898 *god...*

It was a blow... I felt just as if they had killed him right then, at that very moment...

This happened at the main office of our Szczecin Katyn Family. The crying was universal. And not simply crying, but rather a huge shout, sobbing... Widows, children, grandchildren, entire families of those in Katyn sobbing... It's hard to convey the grief and despair. The reaction of all those present was similar to my own: they felt that their close ones had died just at that moment...

They too had still been waiting for them...

The exhumation was conducted under extremely difficult conditions in the years 1991–1996. There were many exhumation teams; they changed every four weeks, from May to November. Among the workers were students (Ukrainian also), academics, doctors, journalists, members of the Polish Red Cross. The young people were especially admirable. There aren't words sufficient to appreciate their work and express gratitude. Everyone worked selflessly. I think that none of us will ever forget it...

Unfortunately, there was no representative of the Polish justice system present during the exhumation. Until 1995, in view of the Polish-Russian investigation/inquiry begun in 1990 relative to the crime at Katyn, Polish prosecutors had always taken part. Prosecutor Stefan Śnieżko had initially taken charge of the Katyn issue quite admirably, but then suddenly he gave it up. He dispersed all the 17 or 18 volumes of materials and documents. He stopped the investigation.

We, the children of Katyn, grieve over the fact that this crime remains not only unpunished but also not even adjudicated. The fact of the matter is that the Soviet authorities have admitted to nothing, have asked pardon of no one...

True, the Russians did hand over to Poland lists of the prisoners-of-war and the sentence, but didn't go as far as acknowledging that they were the ones who carried it out. To this day we don't have the files of individual prisoners-of-war, lists of those transported, or any documents corroborating that the crime was committed by the NKVD. Too, we don't know the fates or personal information concerning those murdered who appear on the Ukrainian and Belarussian lists.

The inquiry of the Chief Military Prosecutor of Russia did not clarify anything, and in the summation I read that the investigations on the basis of the materials of the exhumation in the Katyn Forest authenticated only the fact that a crime had taken place, but left open the question of time, guilty parties, motives and circumstances...

There are also no final results as to Kharkov and Miednoye, though the Russian commission has already completed its work. In Russia, both in the Duma and in the universities, untruthful publications and printed materials have been spread widely not merely accusing the Germans of guilt but casting mud on Poland and Poles. The Russian bolsheviks have time and again profaned the Polish flag, threatened to revive the Ribbentrop-Molotov pact, to profane the cemetery in Katyn, to destroy Poland... What does that betoken?

The worst is that the inquiry has also been stopped in Poland. Our letters and appeals don't help.

"One could say that the inquiry is dormant," Prosecutor Stefan Śnieżko told us tersely, when once we were successful in having him appear at one of our meetings. My opinion is that he personally is responsible for the constraint placed on opening up and resolving the Katyn issue. The Polish commission, just like the Russian one, ceased investigating. Again the archives have been closed, documents concealed. Therefore there won't be any legal proceedings, anyone found guilty, sentenced, punished.

So far only one of the perpetrators of the extermination of our nation has been sentenced and punished. It's the Germans. To this day they feel responsibility for the crime of the Second World War, and many of Hilter's criminals were hanged. This is why a rapprochement between Poland and the Germans is possible.

But the Soviets? Though they likewise murdered us, they were after the war proclaimed as "friends" of Poland. Deceit and the distortion of history has continued for half a century together with the relativist slogan that there is no such thing as good and evil, only some grey in-between. The same thing continues today. And that is the worst of all because it eliminates the application of the fundamental moral principles contained in the Decalogue. It is a transgression of a basic tenet of justice, it corrupts people and introduces the morality of the proverb: if someone steals Kali's cow, it's wrong; but let him steal someone else's, that's very good...

The inauguration in 2000 of three Katyn cemeteries was the authentic funeral of our close ones. We can thank only the enormous effort of the Council for the Preservation of the Memory of Struggle and Suffering led by Andrzej Przewoźnik and the goodwill of Jerzy Buzek's administration for the establishment of these necropoli.

A joint, Polish-Ukrainian cemetery for the victims of totalitarianism has been opened in Kharkov. Its appearance is horrifying. But the effect is intended. It calls to mind the eruption of a volcano throwing forth human remains, a land ridding itself of a murky secret. The fifteen largest of the burials sites are the Polish tombs. The remainder are not identified; Orthodox crosses have been placed there. Jews died here as well. They constituted probably about two percent of those murdered, though no one really knows exactly how many, since many had Polish names.

I was at the opening of the cemetery at Kharkov. I was to have spoken but... I experienced a breakdown. I thought that I was then leaving this world. Just before I was to say a few words in the name of the families of the murdered, I suddenly lost touch with my surroundings. Standing next to Premier Jerzy Buzek I suddenly slipped to the ground.

As the scouts lifted me onto a stretcher, I could hear voices coming to me: "Ewa, what's happening?"

I responded that I was strong, a doctor: "Nothing is happening! I'll be alright and deliver my speech..."

I awoke in a tent; everyone thought I was dying. I remember how an ambulance arrived, how I explained to the Ukrainian doctor that it was an infarct, how I told him to give me oxygen and morphine. I spent ten days in the hospital at Kharkov. A marvelous doctor cared for me. Despite the extensive infarct which I experienced in Kharkov and the trials of the exhumation, I am glad that the necropolis has at last been established. Now none will be allowed to destroy it, or at least erase it from memory. Reverence will return to those who were murdered, and to all others the knowledge of a terrible crime perpetrated on this small patch of ground. Today it is visited not only by Poles from all over the world but also by people who live nearby.

I have lived in Szczecin since 1955. It's a beautiful city. It isn't at all parochial; tolerance and openness prevail.

The Szczecin Association of Katyn Families is one of the most active organizations in the country. It started as one of the first; its first meeting was to have taken place already in December 1981, meaning two days after the declaration of martial law. We were finally able to meet in 1989. We are our own support, being completely apolitical. I am the president of this organization.

There are more than 400 families living in Szczecin who have lost relatives in the Soviet extermination camps. Undoubtedly not all of them have come forth. We would have to go through innumerable war-time cemeteries in the East.

Certainly we will leave some trace of the 18 or so thousand unarmed, bound prisoners-of-war murdered in the course of a few weeks. There have already risen two Katyn monuments and six remembrance plaques in churches in Szczecin. There is now a Plaza of the Victims of Katyn and name plates of the murdered, and, too, earth taken from the three Katyn necropoli has been carried to several places. All our anniversary remembrances take place at the foot of the enormous Katyn Cross, built through communal effort in the main cemetery. We have organized seven exhibitions on Katyn and published five books on the topic. A commemorative stamp with envelope has been issued and we have had medals and coins struck. At our request the Holy Father crowned in Kraków the picture of Our Lady of Kozielsk.

We promote also a wide educational program in the Schools of Pomorze. I myself have up to now met with thousands of young people. I have traveled ceaselessly to meetings, no matter how difficult and exhausting and no matter how few wish to talk about this crime. One school in Pomorze—in Świerzna—has taken the name of Dr. Julian Gruner.

It is painful to us, however, that the Katyn Family, namely the association of the children of those murdered, will end with us. For us freedom and truth came too late. We are now sick, old and more and more of us are dying. Only a few of us know how to make use of the internet or know foreign languages in order that we might present to the world the full truth. And there are none willing to replace us.

I think that it's only our grandchildren, that is, the great-grandchildren of Katyn, who will be interested more in this crime. Even today I see how they absorb knowledge of it, take part in meetings. In the publicized competition "Golgotha of the East" more than 200 young students gave evidence of broad knowledge and wrote essays on a very high literary level. The competition bore its fruit in the book published by us *Truth and Memory*. I have been edified and have such hope that the young people will not allow the world to forget about this crime.

"Why didn't you talk to us about this earlier?" they ask with reproach and sadness during meetings with us.

They don't understand that I wouldn't have been allowed to finish before being taken off to prison... But this only testifies to their normalcy.

I'm not withdrawing yet from the work at the Association of Katyn Families. During the last years I have felt that I owe something to my father. I have had the impression that he is constantly placing on me new duties to fulfill. The first time that I felt at peace for any length of time was only in 2001, after writing the book *Starobelsk in the Eyes of Rescued Prisoners-of-War (Starobielsk w oczach ocalałych jeńców)*. But now I have further plans. I want to write an appendix for it...

I also hope that I'll still live to see the time when historians undertake in a solid and serious way research studies on the Katyn crime. It is possible today to assess it accurately, to research whether it was part of the plan to exterminate the Polish nation and why the Allies participated in the conspiracy of silence surrounding it.

In my opinion this yet unadjudicated and inadequately researched crime has made it difficult for us as a nation to undergo rebirth. Poland would today be a different country if the Soviets together with the Germans had not deprived it of its most enlightened citizens. Their extermination resulted in the next generation being taught and raised by opportunists, traitors and betrayers. The liquidation of Poland's elite is permanent and irreversible. Murder, fear and terror are inscribed to this day in the fates of Poles. These have made us unable to rise from our knees. At present not many wise and steadfast people remain...

My husband Andrzej, a normal everyday Szczecin shipyard worker, doesn't understand at all my commitment to the Katyn cause. He comes from Pomorze, his family had to deal with only one occupant—the German one. He is tolerant, but even so he came to me when after my infarct I was lying in the hospital at Kharkov and said:

"Promise that you won't set foot here again for the next five years..."

But I want to go again this year to Kharkov. And most likely my husband will accompany me. I've already reserved the tickets...

4

AMERICAN PROFESSOR

Chicago, Illinois, USA, October 2001

His mother had died several months before he lost his father at Katyn. From thirteen years of age on he had to manage for himself. For a long time he wandered across the world without any documents or citizenship. The orphan's relatives had been scattered throughout different countries. Ultimately he became an American academic.

The professor's house is spacious and orderly. It sparkles with pictures and knick-knacks. Lined up on the tables are elephants ("for good luck'). The plump faces of three grandchildren smile from three evenly spaced photographs. The light-colored carpets are so soft and springy that they sink under the least load.

"We have lived here already thirty-seven years." He speaks Polish slowly, calmly, enunciating perfectly each word. He has a high forehead, grey hair and beard together with a dignified face. He's rather thin. "For forty-one years I have been lecturing here at the university," he adds.

Professor Edward Kamiński descends from a Toruń family that was well-to-do before the war. "I rode to my first communion in a carriage with decorated horses and a coachman in a silk-hat," recalls this learned American who was born in 1926 at 10 Mostowa Street in Toruń.

His father, Marcin Kamiński, an officer in World War I and the bolshevik war of 1920, a participant of the Battle of the Vistula, a reserve captain, decorated with among others the Virtuti Militari, had worked in Toruń in a bank as well as been treasurer of the Toruń section of the Polish Red Cross. He earned about 450 zloties at the bank and 150 zloties at the Red Cross, whereas the average pay in inter-war Poland was not much more than 100 zloties.

His mother Jadwiga, four years younger than his father, was the daughter of Jan and Konstancja Ruchniewicz, owners of the first Polish factory of gingerbread in Toruń. "Torunian Gingerbreads" was the largest of the three business establishments in Toruń, and the only Polish one. The firm had three company confectionery stores: in Toruń, Warsaw and Grudziądz. His mother, who did not work professionally, raised three children, Halina, Jerzy, and the youngest Edward, and was active in social work. She was president of the Vincent de Paul Home for the poor.

"She worked there a lot, especially in the kitchen." The professor recalls that he too was there often, as his mother wanted him to be sensitive to the needs of the poor.

All three Kamiński children were educated in a private elementary school at the teacher's college. They frequented the conservatory where they took piano lessons.

"We were very well educated," reminisces professor Kamiński. I loved classical music very much, especially Chopin. Already as a child I would play the piano in public, on stage, most often at the school festivities concluding the academic year.

They would spend vacations together as a family, primarily at the Baltic Sea near Sopot. Though the Kamiński's didn't lack for anything, from their earliest years the offspring had been inculcated with a respect for work. The children would help in their grandfather's store, and the boys, Jerzy and Edward, after they were six years old, had to leave for one month every year to work in the village presbytery at Łążyń outside of Toruń.

"There we would begin the day by serving at Mass and then until evening we would do all the things that village work entails. First, as young boys, we would take the geese and cows out to pasture. Later we would spend our time with the most simple village workers. The presbytery had nearly 700 acres of land so there was a lot of work to do."

After a pensive moment the professor commented: "Those were the best lessons in learning respect for human work."

Edward's father, Marcin Kamiński, was called up to the army two months before the war's outbreak. He was then forty-five years old. He was assigned to manage the office of counter-espionage of the Pomorze armies, first in Toruń, then in Wrocławek.

"I didn't even say good-bye because as in every July my brother and I were working in the village. But I did see my father just for a little while on the next to the last day of August 1939." The professor adds that before the war he was 13 years old and had finished his first year of *gimnazjum*. They were then living in Toruń at 41 Bydgoska Street, just across from the German consulate.

Then the gehenna of war started. The Kamiński's had to leave their house immediately. The Germans seized their family savings and gold. They tried to leave for Wrocławek, taking with them their mother who had been suffering from breast cancer for some months and the domestic staff, to be closer to their father. The winds of war forced them, however, to break off in a small village. Miraculously there they met their grandparents and returned with them to Toruń but with their mother already on a stretcher. In October 1939 in Toruń their mother underwent a serious operation. Nevertheless she died three days later...

"Our father didn't even know about it as we had had no news from him at all," the professor said, measuring his words and emotion. "My sister Halina was then one year from graduation; she was eighteen years old. Jurek, who was two years older than me, was fifteen. From that moment on we had to make do for ourselves."

His brother left for the village and was officially registered as a farmhand. It helped that he had had some training at the presbytery.

Halina and Edward, both orphans, remained in Toruń, trying their hand at different things. They started with work in the gingerbread factory. It no longer belonged to their grandparents but to Germans because their grandfather Ruchniewicz was now merely a baker. They packaged cakes and delivered them around to stores for six marks a week. "I was then living with my grandparents," the professor said.

A letter from their father came before Christmas 1939 from Kozelsk. It was the only one they ever got. The professor goes to the mezzanine, to his library. He brings back this letter. Partially glued together, damaged, written somewhat illegibly in black ink. Marcin Kamiński had written it on November 27, 1939. In it he tells how he has been in the USSR since September 18. He expresses concern over the health of his wife, "Dearest Jadzia," wishes his children well, gives the names of some friends who are co-prisoners-of-war, among whom are several acquaintances from Toruń as well as his godson, the dentist Marcin Hirsh from Kościerzyna. He asks them to send some warm clothes. He laments that he is writing with some difficulty but he doesn't have his glasses.

Unfortunately, his wife, "Dearest Jadzia," wouldn't be able to read the letter...

"But we did send him some clothes. Only we don't know whether he got them or not," his son says.

In a Toruń now attached to the Reich, the occupation forces introduced a complete ban on the use of the Polish language. One day his sister Halina was walking down one side of the street and Edward with his friend the other. They had just cautioned each other in their native language absolutely not to speak in Polish today, just as the Germans were conducting round-ups. And a moment later all three were apprehended... The Gestapo released Halina that same day in the evening. Edward, together with a group of 400 others, was led off to the camp at Sztutowo.

"I was the youngest in this transport, being hardly fifteen years old," says the professor. "Perhaps I caused some pity to awaken in one of the German officers because after a short exchange of words he pulled me out of the wagon and put in someone else, just grabbed off the street, in my place.

His grandmother Ruchniewicz, terrified by this event, wanted to send him at once to work in the countryside of East Prussia. But Edward didn't want to be a farmhand. He made up his mind to procure in Toruń a driver's license. As a chauffeur he received work in the military automobile depots. Later he became the driver for a Polish doctor. He would drive with him to the homes of the sick until early 1944.

The year 1943 was for him especially tragic. The Germans discovered the graves at Katyn. During the exhumation of remains, they straight away identified the body of Captain Marcin Kamiński. He had his ID in his pocket and a Toruń trolley ticket. The hope that his father would return vanished...

"We learned about it from the 'Warsaw Courier' in April 1943," recalls the professor.

Today he has an entire bookshelf of books about Katyn, the largest collection in Chicago. He shows copy number 30 of an edition numbering only 100 copies entitled, *Katyn. Cemetery Ledger.* He had marked off with bookmarks the short biography of his father as well as that of his godson from Kościerzyna, Antony Marcin Hirsh. "It turns out from the transport that my father was shot on April 15, 1940," he says almost to himself.

In 1943 Edward also lost two of the middle fingers of his right hand. It happened at his grandfather's place as they cut a tree with an electric saw.

"For me that was a real tragedy. I had to give up forever playing my beloved piano. Even during the occupation I had practiced at least an hour a day," he says quietly.

In 1944 the Germans attached him as chauffeur to a military person stationed in western Germany. At first he was a driver in Munich, but later at the western front after he had completed a course on driving caterpillar-treaded vehicles. One day the tread broke and he was captured by the American army. As a German soldier he was placed in an Allied prison camp.

" I survived thanks only to a thief who recognized me. He used to steal flour and sugar even from my grandfather's sugar factory. In prison too he stole. Everything. But that turned out to be an advantage because it kept us alive. There weren't enough things to eat, whereas the prisoners-of-war were in the thousands, and he would share with me almost every morsel."

After a month of prison and the submission of a declaration that he was a Pole (now in French territory), Edward was transferred to northern Scotland. There he made his way finally to the Polish Army and on March 19, 1945 was sworn in as a private. He became a writer in the information office of the First Corps commanded by General Kopański. He began at once an intensive study of English. He took advantage of this every free moment, evenings, and even dinner breaks. Particularly in Edinburgh, to which he was transferred in April of 1945.

At the same time he graduated from secondary school in Edinburgh. In 1951 he also received, the first Pole to do so, a diploma from the Institute of Medical Laboratories in the local university. He was drawn to research work.

In this same time period, after a year and a half acquaintance, he married Krystyna Karpińska, a nurse, the daughter of Major Władysław Karpiński who was the officer in charge of the repair section of General Maczek's 1st Division. That same year Edward Kamiński received a job offer at a university in London. He and his wife left Edinburgh and he became the head of a radiation therapy laboratory in the English capital.

"I liked London, but, just as in Edinburgh, I felt very much a stranger there. At every step the English made it clear to me that I was a foreigner. For example, my technical assistants, English women, were invited to various holiday celebrations and social events. But I, never."

However, he was warned by his grandparents not to return to Poland. They wrote to him from Toruń of the repression in the country, of Stalinism and of the occupation, this time Soviet.

The newly married couple considered leaving for North America.

In 1953 they arrived in Toronto, Canada. There Edward Kamiński was to direct a radiology laboratory and at the same time study medicine. As he was not permitted to begin studies, after three years as a specialist in laboratory work in a Jewish hospital, he decided to depart for Chicago. Thanks to his considerable scientific output he and his wife received an immigration visa without much of a wait.

Through the help of an acquaintance from Edinburgh who was then a lecturer at Northwestern Medical and Dental Schools of Chicago, Edward found work there. He was likewise admitted for studies in the Department of Chemistry.

"I studied and at the same time worked as a lecturer, day and night, three separate shifts, since I had to support my family," he recalls.

They rented their first apartment. Their son Norbert was born in 1956 in Chicago, then seven years later their daughter Ivone. After raising the children, Edward's wife, Krystyna, worked until age 62 as a salesperson in a large department store.

In 1964 Edward Kamiński defended his doctoral thesis in chemistry. He continued on at the university. In 1979 he became professor, and in 1981 a professor of toxicology. For forty-one years, he lectured on pathology, toxicology and nutrition.

"It was my job to supervise these aspects of training in the graduate schools of dentistry," he notes.

He retired when he was seventy-one, lecturing on into the year 2000. Even now he is a forensic expert in the field of toxicology. His professional career includes about 150 scientific publications, articles and papers as well as visiting lectures; he has trained three doctors, 50 master degree students in various specialties of dentistry as well as a large number of students, occasionally of two generations, fathers and sons.

He is proud of his professional and familial accomplishments. Notwithstanding his academic work he always endeavored to be involved in raising his children.

"I would take my son camping, together we would go fishing, hiking. We would play hockey in our backyard which I flooded in winter to make an ice rink."

That his son Norbert, today a professor of pharmacology and toxicology at the University of Michigan would write to him recently that his father has been his best friend, gives him great satisfaction. His son is married to an American woman who doesn't speak Polish but yet understands everything.

His daughter Ivone works as a federal agent in Wisconsin, in the narcotics division. Her husband is a federal prosecutor, the son of a Polish father, a parachutist during the war.

"And in this year we are celebrating our golden wedding anniversary," warmly smiles Krystyna Kamińska.

As he points to a photograph on display in the living room, he adds: "We have three wonderful grandchildren. But their generation doesn't even understand Polish."

"All the while that I have been living in foreign countries I have never had Polish citizenship or passport. I was taken to Germany by train, without any identity. In 1946 the government of the Polish Peoples Republic withdrew the citizenship of everyone who had refused repatriation. That's why even today we can't participate in the elections."

He has been in Poland seven times, in 1971, 1977, 1989, 1995, 1996, 1999 and 2000. He recalls most bitterly the first visit.

The Kamiński family home still stands on Most Street in Toruń. Some kind of Catholic office is installed there now. After the war only a sister, Halina, remained in the family home, and she died ten years ago. His brother, an electrician, emigrated to Toronto. He is still living but was widowed in 1976.

And Toruń has remained the beautiful city it was, having been spared the worst of the war.

In 1993 Professor Kamiński founded in Chicago the Katyn Family. It is the only Katyn organization registered as a non-profit organization and so tax-exempt. As president he now travels often to Poland since the organization belongs to the Federation of Katyn Families in Poland.

"There's always some kind of matter to take care of in Warsaw," Prof. Kamiński smiles.

In the beginning the Katyn Family gathered together over fifty people. And today? Professor Kamiński shows the list. Most of it is crossed out; there remain hardly ten names.

"We are the last Mohicans. But we want yet to educate the Poles as well as Americans here concerning the Katyn matter. That's our chief goal," he says with enthusiasm.

Together with three friends from the Chicago Katyn Family, he was at the unveiling of the Katyn memorial in Baltimore in 2000. In Chicago they honor the memory of the murdered in Katyn every year with a Mass at Holy Trinity Church. And, too, at the monument dedicated to the Polish soldiers at the Catholic cemetery of Maryhill where Professor Kamiński has placed earth from Katyn.

He spent four days in Katyn Forest, during the Communist era. He recalled from childhood the image of his father and felt that he had at last given him burial.

"I had preserved in my memory the image of my father as being a conscientious man, loving, dedicated to family and work. In the last weeks of his life he had been fearful over the health of my mother."

His visit in Katyn bore fruit in the shooting of the first documentary on the Katyn crime. Professor Kamiński co-produced the new film in 1991 together with a Polish television station from Chicago, Polvision. They delivered 100 copies to all the Polish Saturday schools in the United States and Canada.

"You have to see the film." Professor Kamiński led me downstairs to a lower level of the house, to a small room in rustic style where there was a TV.

The film lasts 45 minutes and is accompanied by the music of Józef Czajkowski, "For the Siberian exiles." It recalls the background of "the intellectual Holocaust of the elite of the young country," tragic Polish history, the ignominious genocide, the deeds at the cemetery. Professor Kamiński emphasized as in a lecture that Russia and Germany had attempted over the centuries to prevent the intellectual development of Poland which despite eveything endured and would never allow itself to be erased from the world map.

Krystyna Kamińska had herself been with her husband twice to Katyn.

"Each time it was extremely moving and shocking. How good it is that, under the Polish government of Premier Buzek, cemeteries were established not only at Katyn but also at Kharkov and Miednoye," she comments with satisfaction.

The professor underscores the general lack of knowledge in the United States about this great genocide of the last century, which had its beginning even in Lenin's time. It is for this reason that he organizes for the students of medicine, dentistry and law (especially those of Polish ancestry) meetings on the topic of Katyn. He shows his film, and leads discussions among the students together with members of the Katyn Family.

You don't find books about Katyn in American libraries. And in the Holocaust Museum in Washington, it was only in the last year that the word "Poles" was added whereas initially it was written that the museum arose "to the memory of murdered Jews, Gypsies, homosexuals and others."

Professor Kamiński reproaches Americans also that they know so little of the contribution of Poles to the defeat of Hitler, even though there was not one great battle in which Poles did not fight.

Would he want to be buried in Poland?

"I have thought of it," he answers. "In 1989 I brought some earth from Katyn to the cemetery of Święty Jerzy in Toruń. I transformed my mother's single grave into two. Now Captain Marcin Kamiński, murdered on April 15, 1940, in the Katyn Forest lies next to Jadwiga Kamińska, deceased on October 20, 1939. It may be that I will rest next to them..."

5

THE LITTLE PRINCE
AND THE FAIRY TALES

Deerfield, Illinois, USA, November 2001

He was unable to find his father's grave until 1990. He had hoped that somewhere he might still be alive. When eight years later in the Piatichatki cemetery at Kharkov he buried Jan Franciszek Adamczyk, a captain of the Polish Army, he then had to accept it.

"I lost my country, my home, my parents. Can a person lose more?" asks his son Wiesław, now Wesley Adamczyk, an American chemist and one of the more accomplished bridge players in the United States.

He greets me with open arms in his modern, elegant and quiet condominium in the northern suburbs of Chicago. His chief occupation in the course of the last few years has been the writing of the dramatic fates of his family.

"I have everything fresh before my eyes. I have dedicated thousands of hours to this issue. I don't read other books or media, almost never watch television, don't have time even for bridge. I've been writing out the effects of this horrible crime based on the experience of my family. I am doing it in English so that America will finally come to know about it," he explains while still standing at the front door. He is well-proportioned, bearded, wearing a flowery shirt and elegant pants. He looks carefully at the reporter from Poland, scrutinizing, as if to ask whether I believe his story or not...

He is sixty-eight years old, talkative and buoyant, yet serious, at times even somber. Young in spirit, he is open to people, frank, has his greying hair tied in a pony tail. He narrates his strange story, the deeds of "a little Polish prince," as if reading a musical score. He recalls the tiniest details from childhood, supports them with rich documentation, and dazzles with his perfect memory. Without a doubt playing bridge has helped in this; Wesley Adamczyk is well known in competitive bridge circles in the United States.

Ever since the death of his wife, he lives alone in a large condominium not many miles from Lake Michigan. An enormous table in the living room almost sags under the books and documents connected with Katyn. Many materials are piled up on the floor. A glass coffee table next to the leather sofa and chairs serves as a place to display relevant maps. A television and VCR occupy one large segment of the room together with a collection of casettes, records and films many of which are related to the work of these last few years. Even the bedroom does double duty as a work room. There he has put his computer at which he works before going to bed.

"The Katyn massacre is intertwined with the tragedy of Poles deported by the Soviets to Siberia. The Siberian tragedy has been my primary preoccupation all my life," says Wesley who is himself connected both to Katyn and to the Polish Siberian deportation experience. This is why he took on the difficult job of coordinating the large project of promoting the documentary, *A Forgotten Odyssey*, about the tragedy of Poles deported to Siberia. "It's the first film on this topic in English," he mentions with feeling. "It's already had its premiere in Great Britain; we will show it in a few months in Chicago, New York, Washington, Toronto, Montreal and other cities in North America. Because we want to educate Americans, preserve the memory of this deportation and insure that this period of Stalin's repression not be passed over in history.

Wesley Adamczyk speaks in Polish but with a strong American accent. He often apologizes and asks for the Polish words he lacks. Sometimes he speaks with eyes filled with tears.

He is from the pre-war southeastern area of Poland though his parents came from the region of Małopolska.

His father, Jan Franciszek Adamczyk, was born on January 21, 1893 in Ciężkowice, in the district of Grybów, into the family of a railroad man, one of eight children. Four of them emigrated to the United States in the years 1906–1912. Documents sent to Wesley Adamczyk at his request from the Central Military Archives in Warsaw attest to his father being a commissioned officer. After passing his secondary school examinations in Nowy Sącz, he was drafted in August 1914 into the Austro-Hungarian army. He completed officer school in Judenburg, fought in World War I, and was wounded several times and decorated. He knew a number of languages, namely Polish, German, Italian and French.

When the Polish state was being reborn, the young lieutenant joined Piłsudski's Legion on November 7, 1918 as a volunteer. He was made the commander of a company of infantry and fought against the bolsheviks. "He often told us that during the bolshevik war he made use of his experience in the Austrian army." In the light of a lamp Wesley shows an old, somewhat darkened black and white photograph of his father and his company.

After Poland regained its independence, Jan Franciszek Adamczyk received land that had been attached to the Polish Republic in western Wołyń, in the environs of Sarny not far from Łuck. He was assigned there in April 1921 to act as representative of the Małopolska Military Staff responsible for soldier settlement. Similar to other officers of this time, he participated in creating the structures of the new state. He divided up the estates of the magnates, shared in organizing the agricultural infrastructure, and helped the newly arrived in taking possession of their farms as well as in receiving loans and allowances.

"He had two adjutants to help him. They lived on the same estate, but separately, in a little house in the garden." Wesley indicates on the map that Sarny is now within the borders of Ukraine.

Jan Franciszek was married on July 5, 1921 to Anna Schinagiel, four years younger than he was and the daughter of a lawyer.

In Sarny the Adamczyks welcomed three children. Wesley was the youngest, being born in Warsaw on January 14, 1933; his brother Jerzy (1922) and his sister Zofia (1926) had come before him into the world.

"We were raised in a traditional, patriotic and comfortable home." Wesley strokes his grey, thick, short cut beard. "We had a servant and a beloved nanny, our teacher. We called her 'Professor Winiarska.'"

It is amazing how the American Wesley remembers details from his childhood in that part of Poland. Even though he had to leave those lands at age seven, he dedicated many pages to those years in the book he has written.

When he returns in remembrance to that home and that childhood it is hard for him to hold back the tears. Although he is embarrassed by them, he talked about the Christmas Eves and the Christmas trees, the holiday poppy-seed cakes, the gingerbread cakes, and the yeast cakes, the hand-painted Easter eggs and the Easter table, and the many house guests. Too, about the tall, tiled room-stoves that radiated heat all around, the kitchen stove with its iron lids, the storage rooms below where they kept potatoes, canning jars of food, fruit and piles of vegetables. Too, about the roses in front of the house as well as other flowers and bushes. Through his tears he could see the garden and the orchard, and deer coming right up to the fence; he could see the nearby forests and in them the abundance of berries, mushrooms and forest animals. He could see too his father's hunting.

"That was my kingdom! When I was six years old my father took me for the first time on a rabbit hunt," he recalls nostalgically.

Most of all he loved the fairy tales.

"As the youngest I listened to a great many of them," he says movingly. "About gnomes, elves and storks. I simply adored books of fairy tales!"

He was entranced also by his father's study. There his father had his uniforms, swords, various guns and rifles. Portraits and pictures of battles hung on the walls; Piłsudski, Kościuszko and Pułaski gazed out from behind the desk. His father would tell him about the history of Poland, about its kings, heroes and enemies. "Even as a five year old boy I knew that the Tartars and Mongols had struck Poland from one side and the Teutonic Knights and the Germans from the other," he smiled with pride.

At table, proper etiquette was required and not merely during the holidays. Even so, not one of the children was ever struck.

"My parents never quarreled in our presence," he says as he dries the tears with a batiste, white kerchief. "When they had a falling out over something, they would speak with each other in French. I once even brought it up to them that it wasn't proper because I didn't understand anything... My mother promised me that it wouldn't happen again..."

And Wesley goes on in a strong voice:

"My childhood has turned out to be the elixir of my life, my source of strength in the most difficult of times. Childhood is the foundation, one's identity, one's roots. It's that which determines what kind of individual we become. I draw from its energy even to this day."

His condominium connects directly to the outside. The tall glass doors of his living room open on an extensive, wavy lawn that looks much like a carpet. Marvelously trimmed bushes and trees complete the picture. Each tree, bush and flower is individually cared for, weeded, pruned, and watered. There is even a small pond with wild duck swimming beneath the window, geese from Canada landing and snow white swans. This private luxurious apartment complex spreads out some distance. There are a number of multiple family dwellings, as well as some large wealthy villas, often enclosed by walls.

"It is a fine place to live," Wesley says almost reading my mind. The day is sunny. The landscape paintings which hang in gold frames on the walls of his living room are illuminated by lights and coordinate perfectly with the view outside through large, glass doors that extend upward the full height of the room.

In 1938 the Adamczyks had moved to the city, to Łuck along the Styr River. His father had begun to work in the agricultural bank, though he continued to travel out to the Wołyń area monitoring the settlements.

Christmas of 1938 holds a prominent place in Wesley's memory. Then Gerry Siepak, the twenty-year old daughter of his Aunt Maria, one of his father's sisters, who had emigrated to Chicago, came from America. Having visited different places of the country, she also spent a month at the Adamczyks. She spoke Polish very well.

"She told me stories about American cowboys and Indians as well as many different fairy tales. And I told her many Polish fairy tales, and described our customs and traditions. We built snowmen together and went down to the river. We agreed that in the fall of 1939 we, the entire family, would go to America on the ocean liner the *Stefan Batory* just as she had. My father had not seen his three sisters and brother for almost thirty years," Wesley says of those times.

Even then there was talk about the possibility of war breaking out with the Germans. Six-year-old Wesley had overheard his parents speaking together; it appeared to him from their conversation that it had already taken place. "I thought that it was another fairy tale," Wesley said removing his glasses. "But then one evening my father came to my bed. He was in uniform. He said in farewell: 'Wesley, I love you. But I have to go to the army. Take care of mother...'"

As a six-year-old boy Wesley didn't know what it meant. Even so he felt uneasy. It turned out that he had seen his father for the last time.

The bombing began soon after. The bombs would fall quite close often enough. The family took cover in a trench near the Styr River. One time he could feel dirt in his mouth. "This was for me the taste of war. And of fear. For the first time I realized the difference between a fairy tale and reality," he says with gravity.

The Adamczyk family moved back to Sarny. A second, unexpected offensive opened up after the German one. The Soviets invaded Poland from the east. Pillaging by the bolsheviks and the removal of the population began everywhere. His mother began to bake dry biscuits and pack them in bags. And she sewed her jewelry into the underwear.

Letters came from his father. He wrote that he was in Soviet captivity in Starobelsk. They received his last letter in March of 1940.

It was May 14, 1940, the day before Zofia's namesday. Mom had baked a cake for her then thirteen-year-old daughter. Suddenly, in the middle of the night, they heard loud blows on the door. Before his older brother, seventeen-year-old Jurek, was able to open it, the NKVD broke it open violently. The door hit him so forcefully that he streamed with blood.

Wesley remembered that the captain of the NKVD had a dark blue uniform and a red stripe down his pants. He ordered the family who had come from their beds in pajamas to wait below by the door while his people plundered the house. The boy would keep lodged in his memory that at each window he saw the face of a Soviet soldier with a rifle.

"They were dead, stony faces, without feeling." Wesley takes from his documents a revealing, dark drawing. A small boy looks at them through the window. Drawing back the curtains, he saw dark masks—faces of soldiers with red stars on the caps. The drawing had been done by his cousin in Kraków and would be found on the cover of Wesley's coming book.

Wesley Adamczyk, son of Captain Jan Adamczyk, laying a wreath at a mass grave of Polish officers. On the left are three unknown pilgrims and on the right part of the Polish-Ukrainian Honor Guard. Kharkov cemetery, Kharkov, Ukraine (previous USSR), June 27, 1998. Courtesy of Wesley Adamczyk.

The NKVD captain amazed them with his detailed knowledge of each one of the members of the Adamczyk family. He called them Polish bourgeoisie and enemies of the people. He announced sharply that they were being arrested and had only an hour to get their essential things together. Wesley went then to his room to pack his favorite fairy tales and toys. At sight of this the captain turned red with rage; foam formed at his lips. He called Wesley a small Polish prince and wouldn't allow him to take anything. He ordered his men to burn the boy's books too, just like his father's.

"That was a shock. To this point in my life I had seen only cultured and calm people. Now I saw someone raging mad, furious, full of hatred. I had met *homo sovieticus*. I had met the barbarians who my father had told me had invaded Poland hundreds of years ago," Wesley was telling me now.

Mother and three children were loaded onto a truck. Under the cover of night, amidst bayonets and rifles, in the fading glow of burning Polish books they were being taken to prison in Równe. They would spend almost three weeks there.

"We stayed in one large room together with others and we slept on the bare floor. There were women and children as well as a few old men," he remembers as a seven-year-old.

Soon after they found themselves on a deportation train, in one of the cattle cars. Wesley takes out the next drawing done by his Polish cousin. At the front and back of the cattle cars there were three levels of wooden shelves with straw. In the middle was a foul-smelling latrine as well as a thick crowd of tired, tormented and perspiring people.

"I had been properly raised and so for a number of days I couldn't bring myself to take care of my physical necessities in front of everyone. I could still hear the words of my mother telling us to close the door of the bathroom, to wash our hands... For the first time in my life I came to the realization that something was not right with mankind. I began to doubt God's existence," he confesses.

That nightmare of a journey in the June heat, mostly without water and food, lasted about three weeks. "To this day at the word Russia I hear the clattering of wheels on the rails and I see an expanse slipping by," says Wesley.

They were unloaded from the train in northeast Kazakhstan, not far from the city of Kustanai, at the very border of Siberia. The sovkhoz of Sharmamulzak was one of the 2600 places in the USSR to which Polish families were deported. Kazakhstan was the place of exile for the intelligentsia and especially for the families of Polish officers.

There the Adamczyks met primarily Kazakhs. They lived in mud huts lacking floors and windows, without water, crowded together like sardines. In hunger, stench and terrible poverty. With millions of lice and fleas which one had to kill between one's finger nails hours on end. In the summer the heat was terrible, and in the winter there was penetrating cold and the Siberian snow gales, the so-called *"burany."*

"When I first caught sight of the Kazakhs, I connected them right off with the Tartars from the fairy tales. I thought that they would kill us right away," Wesley says, describing his first impression of Kazakhstan. He takes out the next drawing of his Polish cousin: a small boy standing on the steppe; behind him one sees only the earth cracked from the sun, limitless grass, a horizon blending into this wasteland...

"How I longed to be then far away, to be at home and to read my fairy tales," sighs Wesley with tears in his eyes.

The NKVD informed them that in the Soviet Union certain rules were to be followed: *"net panov,"* "no Mister or Madam," and *"kto ne rabotayet tot ne kushayet,"* "who doesn't work doesn't eat." His brother Jurek was assigned to primitive brickmaking, his mother and sister Zosia had various duties in the sovkhoz. Seven-year-old Wesley also received a job; he had to round up the *"kizyak,"* which was cow dung. "This was the dung of cattle and horses which after drying was used in winter for heat," he explains today with a smile. "We gathered it up on the steppes and carried it to piles. That was a real trick! The '*kizyak*' couldn't be too moist because then it would fall apart. It couldn't be too dry either!"

One day their sister had a nasty experience. The hot, dry wind on the steppe would make a huge, moving ball made of dried grass and weeds. The children were to gather them up too because the local people used them as kindling. They didn't know, however, that they should protect their bodies from it. At the very first contact with these they were painfully pricked with sharp stickers so much so that only a dark lotion brought by an old Kazakh woman who lived in the same mud hut healed the wounds all over the body." Zosia called those balls, "steppe devils."

"The Kazakhs were very good people. More than once we escaped death because of their great hearts," Wesley emphasizes.

He remembers how the steppe burned. It was a miracle, the way they escaped death. He asked his mother then: "Mom, has hell come to earth?"

And in winter the "*burany*" came. An eerie, blinding, snowstorm. Burying the mud huts up to their roofs, changing people into white dead snowmen.

After a few months the Adamczyk family was transferred to the nearby town of Semiozersk, where there was a felt boot factory. Even though they changed mud huts four times, the lice never gave them rest. They had even laid their eggs in Wesley's eyelashes; his eyes were inflamed from them. There was no medicine, not even soap.

"During our stay in Kazakhstan I never saw any soap items except for sand." He describes vividly how his mother would remove the nits from his eyelashes with a needle and he howled from the pain.

The older children had to work in the forest. His mother, however, fought for the right of her older children to attend school, saving them in that manner from heavier work. "She made up her mind to educate me at home. Even though she esteemed education highly, she said that I was too young for the Soviet school as it would poison my mind," and then he quotes other words of his mother which he has remembered his entire life: "No one can ever take your learning away from you."

He would go fishing often with an older Russian. "I remember how he did not permit himself to be called Mister. He was afraid that if someone had heard it there might be a lot of trouble. He couldn't believe either my descriptions of how people lived in Poland. This Russian had had inculcated in him that Poles were bourgeoisie sucking the blood of the poor."

He remembers distinctly a winter expedition he made to the forest for wood with his brother Jurek. They went by sled, had two axes and a shotgun hidden in the hay. Even today he can hear the profound quiet of that forest. It was so terribly quiet as to seem that spirits were hiding behind the trees. And in the deep silence all of a sudden they heard an explosion. It happened that a tree had exploded from the cold... And when they were returning with the wood, wolves followed them. They howled but they didn't attack. Wesley sat in the back with the shotgun and protected the sled. His cousin has also memorialized that scene in one of her black and white drawings.

After the Germans attacked the Soviets, the hunger grew more severe. The supplies of hard biscuits and jewelry had been exhausted. What saved them from death was black flour and the paste prepared from it.

On an August night in 1941 the NKVD came and took Jurek. They wanted to conscript him into the Russian army. He refused even though they had promised him an officer's commission after two months. That was already the time of the Polish-Soviet amnesty. In October of that year, Jurek had made up his mind to enlist in the Polish Army forming in the USSR. Mother didn't especially oppose it. She believed that her son would meet up there with his father from whom they had not received any word.

In the winter of 1941–42 the hunger grew still more severe. The cold as well. Getting fuel was difficult. Wesley remembers how he was unable to sleep because of the hunger. The remaining biscuits were used sparingly.

"Had it not been for the fact that the Germans attacked the Soviet Union in June of 1941, we wouldn't be sitting here today at this table. The Soviets would have finished off all the deported Poles," Wesley asserts.

In the spring, summer and fall of 1942 those deported Poles who had not yet died and had sufficient courage traveled to southern USSR in order to save themselves together with General Anders' army as it exited to Persia.

Anna Adamczyk gathered together her two children and decided to risk escaping from enslavement in Kazakhstan. On a day in July, after two years and two months of exile, she took her children in hand, without any suitcases, but with the remaining jewelry, and left their mud hut on foot. Without permission from the NKVD, because the formalities connected with the departure were taking too long. "It was scorching hot, we wandered on for a long time. Blood was flowing from my feet." Wesley remembers the overwhelming weariness during the escape.

By some miracle they got on a train going first south to Alma-Ata and then westward. His heart fills with pain when today he remembers the two-week long, murderous trip (not far from the borders of China and Afghanistan) through Kazakhstan, Uzbekistan, and Turkmenistan.

"I still feel the press of the crowd on the train, the terrible heat and stench. I see the sick. Some of the passengers had dysentery and relieved themselves wherever. On the myriad platforms of the railroad stations I saw many sick children more or less my age lying side by side. Starving, with pus oozing from their eyes, with sunken ribcages. Bald. Vermin were crawling up and down their legs. The boys stood out from the girls simply by their huge, disease infected genitalia."

As a nine-year old boy he then asked God how He permitted such human straits.

"All of this had an effect on my faith. I asked my mother: 'Is God blind?'" He could not make sense of God's silence in the face of such misfortune.

After two weeks they came to the camp in the port of Krasnovodsk in Turkmenistan. They renewed their search for their father and brother. His mother went daily from one person to another; no one had heard of the Adamczyks. At last she found Jurek in one of the Soviet hospitals. He was near death, exhausted from hunger. She was able to get hold of a chicken and nursed her son with soup. She spent several days with him until the ship Kaganovich arrived, on which they were to get to Pahlevi on the Caspian Sea in Persia. They were on the list of passengers so they had to say goodbye to Jurek. His mother bore heavily the fact that she was leaving her sick son behind and that she had not found her husband. And then the first indications appeared of Polish officers murdered by the Soviets ...

Wesley shuts his eyes:

"On board the *Kaganovich* there were four and a half thousand civilians and soldiers. Impossible heat! Crowded, so that it wasn't possible to lie down or to reach the cordoned-off toileting area. We took care of our physiological needs overboard. We sailed for two days without water and food. The Persians feared letting us into port since the ship was coated terribly with the excrement of the passengers. They brought us ashore on little boats."

Under the supervision of the British, those newly arrived from the USSR were at first disinfected in order to prevent the spread of disease, lice and other vermin. Quarantine lasted two weeks. "My mother could no longer endure this hell. She fell gravely ill, and was taken to the hospital." He adds that during the delousing they lay on mats on the beach. "After a few days I too fell ill with something. I know that I lost consciousness and was taken to the hospital. It was a tent reserved exclusively for sick children."

When he regained consciousness he looked for his mother and sister. But on the beach, where they had been together, there remained only sand and palm leaves. He learned that the camp had already been moved to Tehran in Persia (now Iran). Then his own orphan tragedy began.

"I suddenly realized that I was alone in a foreign country." He points out that he was only 9 years old. "I cried and I looked into the sky. I called on God and I saw only sea-gulls. I once again came to the conclusion that God was deaf and blind."

An enormous animosity rose up in the nine-year-old on this Persian sand, equally toward God as toward humanity.

Craggy mountains and precipices separate Pahlevi from Tehran. Even today he remembers the truck-trek through them. "When I looked out I saw the many bones of those who had tumbled down."

After the tortuous journey, Wesley and a small group of other escapees were given quarters in a hangar. "I felt horribly alone. Without relatives, without love, without my fairy tales," he recalls. It was only days later that he came upon Zosia near an evening bonfire.

For weeks on end they looked for their mother until one day Zosia found her... She came back terribly sad, carrying a pair of shoes, and said: "Wesley, our mother has died. Nothing remains of her but these shoes. They had gone with us thousands of miles, they had led us out of prison into freedom..."

Zosia had found their mother in a hospital, barely an hour after her death.

"Why couldn't God have granted her at least that one hour?" Wesley wept. Besides the shoes, Zosia was given also her mother's gold earrings and wedding ring. The family cherishes them to this day.

It was October 1942. The two orphans buried their mother on Persian soil the following day. Wesley, despite begging and tearful insistence, wasn't allowed to view her again. Because of the heat and the prevailing epidemic which was effecting a huge rate of mortality among the Poles, it was forbidden to open the casket already sealed with nails.

"I didn't want to leave my mother in the Persian sand... I remembered how my father had instructed me as he left for the war to watch over my mother! And here I didn't even say goodbye to her, I didn't have anything with which to buy flowers." Wesley weeps without embarrassment.

He hasn't been at his mother's gravesite since the time of her burial in the Polish part of the Dulap cemetery in Tehran. In getting a visa to go, first there was his difficult financial situation, then the unfavorable American-Arab relations, wars.

"Next year the Polish embassy in Tehran is going to prepare an anniversary dedication of all the restored Polish cemeteries in Persia," he says spiritedly. "I have already signed up to go with a group from London that is organizing a trip for the occasion. I want very much to see her grave before I die. Though I don't know if the war in Afghanistan won't make such a trip impossible."

His brother Jurek didn't know of their mother's death and wasn't at her funeral. He was serving with the Polish Army in Iraq, in the Second Armored Corps of General Władysław Anders, which in the years 1942–44 was protecting the oil fields of Mosul-Kirkuk. He learned of his mother's death in 1943, during the only time the young children gathered together in Tehran.

In the lamplight we look over the pictures taken during that visit. It turned out that Jurek had sailed from Krasnovodsk to Pahlevi on the same ship they had...

Later, after leaving the Far East, Jurek fought on the Italian front, at Monte Cassino and Piedemonte among others. He was wounded several times and carried a fragment in his face the rest of his life. After his demobilization in 1951 he emigrated from Great Britain to Chicago where Wesley had gone two years earlier.

"After the war my older brother became an entirely different, psychologically handicapped, person," Wesley ruminates. "He couldn't come to terms with the fact that he had fought on many fronts for a free country, had undergone so much, and, though Poland had been among the victorious, had lost his homeland. This was the first such case where an army which had won the war was then unable to return to its own country. It was a crime! The Americans and the British betrayed us!" Wesley said in his brother's sharp tone.

Wesley looks through the collage of black and white photographs of the Adamczyk family, starting with the great-grandparents. Most members of the family are at rest today in cemeteries of various countries: Poland, Czechoslovakia, Ukraine, Iran, the United States...

We continue our difficult conversation the next day. I have the impression that Wesley is hurting emotionally because of the memories yet he feels an obligation to lay open the events of his ordeal.

Zosia was sixteen when their mother died in Persia. Wesley was almost ten.

Zosia looked much like her mother. She had the very same black hair, clear complexion, loving eyes. On the day of their mother's death, she said to Wesley: "I'll be your adoptive mother now."

Wesley says: "And indeed she was. We have almost never been apart."

Their mother's death nevertheless weakened Zosia. She fell ill from typhus as did so many hundreds of others among the exiles. She ended up in the hospital. Once again Wesley found himself in barracks among people he didn't know. "Don't drink water after meals, especially after eating mutton with barley," she enjoined him when they took her off to the hospital.

Zosia and Wesley attended school in the camp for refugees near Tehran. One summer day in 1943 someone called them out of class because of an unexpected visit by an important guest. They were convinced that it was their father.

"Zosia had me wash and put on a green shirt and we were off to the

Polish camp headquarters," Wesley says, remembering himself as a ten-year-old. "A woman we didn't know, wearing the elegant uniform of an American officer, stood in the doorway. We felt let down but at the same time curious as to who she was."

She spoke to them in Polish. She hugged them. It was Jean, the sister of Gerry who had visited their family in 1938. She was the daughter of Aunt Maria, their father's sister. She was working as a nurse assisting at operations in the 113th American military hospital near Ahvaz, on the Persian Gulf. She had found them through the Red Cross. The children considered it a miracle and counted on their cousin to save them from this hell on earth.

"But she was only on a short furlough. She spent a few days with us, took us to Tehran, supplied us with food and clothing. It was hard for her to believe our descriptions of what we had endured." Wesley shows me the souvenir photograph from those days: their cousin in an American uniform, a growing teenage Zosia and a small thin boy, standing next to an American Red Cross vehicle. The photograph later appeared in the Chicago "Dziennik Związkowy" together with their cousin's article. Wesley has it today among his archival material.

Jean promised that she would do all possible to have the children transferred to Ahvaz from which she could more easily get them to America. It was the summer of 1943. Thanks to her mediation they were to have set out by ship from Ahvaz, together with other orphans, for Santa Rosa in Mexico. Unfortunately Wesley at that moment fell ill from scarlet fever and Zosia would not leave him alone. "Instead of getting to America I ended up in a hospital for four weeks," Wesley remembers sadly.

Cousin Jean then brought Wesley and Zosia closer to where she was, to the transit camp for refugees in Ahvaz. He remembered the terrible heat of those times, the scorching desert, the Arabs and the muddy river Karun. They lived in a camel stable which had formerly served an Arabian cavalry.

"The stable was incredibly high, four times higher than this condominium." Wesley smiles as he makes the comparison. We slept on boards. Men, women, children, all together. Families were separated only by hanging blankets.

Jean would often take the children to the hospital where she worked. There they would see wounded soldiers, without legs, without hands, with disfigured faces. Many of them were of Polish heritage, and spoke Polish. They took warmly to the kids. It was difficult for them to believe what these two orphans had undergone in making their way to this Persian desert. "Inasmuch as we were children we reminded them somewhat of their own family homes. We became mascots of the hospital," smiles Adamczyk.

One of the wounded officers, an American major, whose name Wesley no longer remembers fell in love with the boy. He was himself childless and after a serious operation was about to return to America. He offered to adopt Wesley, promised that he would take him to his own home and later send him to a university.

"He told me that he lived in the western part of the United States. That there were marvelous rivers there, forests, animals, that he had a lot of horses and cattle, that we would go hunting. My heart began to beat faster, thoughts of my family life in Wołyń came to me. But, despite the urging of my sister and my cousin, I hesitated."

The major gave him a month to consider it. It was already 1944. Wesley was eleven. The proposition was enervating; he would get out of this hell. But he couldn't leave his sister, his adoptive mother, behind. Too, he still counted on finding his father. He declined the major's offer.

Wesley Adamczyk relates a lot about his life in the desert. The thousands of bats and scorpions, the numerous vultures which he and his friends went out after on hunting jaunts. The most threatening of all were the sandstorms. First, in the distance there were dark clouds. They would approach quickly, change their color to grey, then to grey-gold, then an orange almost red. The sun would be shining without letup and affected the colors. A strong wind blew. As the wind drove the sandstorms away, the clouds would again change their colors, but this time in the opposite order. And sand would squeeze in everywhere. Every bodily orifice had to be securely covered.

Another problem were the winds from the Persian Gulf. Disturbingly salty, clinging all over one's body. Frequent showers were necessary.

Zosia and Wesley stayed in Persia until the end of 1945. Even though their Chicago family made every effort to have the children come, the American immigration authorities were in no hurry.

The war was ending, and the orphan children didn't know what would become of them. Wesley went for a time to an orphanage in Tehran. One day during a visit to her brother, Zosia went to the British Embassy in order to ask—as she did everywhere—about their father. She had heard there that the Soviets had murdered Polish officers in Katyn and that her father was listed among the victims.

"I however continued to refuse to believe it," says Wesley. In Katyn over four thousand officers perished, but what about the others? What about the remaining eleven thousand prisoners of war? I kept on thinking that my father was alive somewhere, maybe on the steppes, maybe in Siberia. I thought this with my heart, not my mind..."

Zosia and Wesley wandered in the Near East until January, 1948. They spent two years in Lebanon. The boy always and everywhere lived through his memories of home.

"I often didn't know any more what was dream and what reality," he says, approaching the map and tracing out his wanderings.

Near the end of 1947 the opportunity came to return to Poland together with other Poles. After a lot of thought they decided not to go. As it was, their home, land, loved ones no longer existed and they had already learned enough about the Soviet system. In January, 1948, they decided that they would sail on an English transport from Egypt to Liverpool. On their way to the port in Egypt they had then to trek through Palestine.

In England a few weeks later they met their brother Jurek, war-ravaged and life-weary.

Wesley began to study in a Polish school located near Cambridge University; he lived in a camp and during vacation worked on a farm. However the hostile treatment by the English, the terrible cold and inadequate portions of food did not bring about his adjustment to life in the British Isles.

"In the barracks where we lived, the water was frozen in the morning," he says in a strong voice. "Because of the cold I suffered from infected sinuses. The English weren't eager to secure us decent accommodations or to help the families of the soldiers who had won the war. To get extra food, my friends and I trapped pigeons and prepared a soup from them and stole supplies from storerooms."

In November of 1949 his Aunt Maria in the United States sent him documents and a ticket to Chicago. He decided to leave England despite the fact that Zosia and Jurek had already made a home for themselves there. Zosia had married a Polish officer who also had been an exile in Semiozersk. He had served during the war, been awarded the medal Virtuti Militari. Their first child was born in England. Jurek at first worked as a clerk then later cleaned train wagons.

Wesley sailed from England to Halifax in Canada on the last cruise of the ship Aquitania with five dollars in his pocket. He knew hardly thirty English words. In transit for ten days, he took account of the fact that in the course of ten years of childhood wanderings he had roamed over twelve countries and three continents and now he was aiming for a fourth. And he asked of God that this would be the final stage of his homeless roaming, that in America he would finally find a home for himself... "Even old ships make their final voyage," he had thought, hungry, with severe sea-sickness, a boy not quite sixteen.

He traveled two days by train from Nova Scotia to Chicago. He remembers how shocked he was when he boarded the train to see good food, a beautiful tablecloth, elegant service, reminding him of Poland... He sat himself down, ordered breakfast for himself, but ... he had to give up two and half dollars for it, which was half of all he had. Afterwards to the end of his trip he would buy bread and milk only sparingly in the station shops...

The train station in Chicago swept him off his feet. He was astounded by its airy brightness, its beauty, the diversity of people, the pulsating life of it all. With his last thirty cents, he used the telephone for the first time in his life... And for the first time he heard the voice of his Aunt Maria... About twelve people all came for him in their cars. He remembers their joy, the tears and his own shock at this abundant world. It happened to be Thanksgiving Day, 1949.

He discovered that his Aunt Maria's living room resembled that of his own family's back in Poland. On the table there was an embroidered linen tablecloth, table settings, everywhere things Polish, on the walls portraits of figures known to him: Piłsudski, Kościuszko and Pułaski. Bathing in a tub completely astonished him, this the first time since he had left his home.

"I entered the bathroom and what did I see but decorations, scented soap, a stack of towels and clean underwear. And in addition my aunt asked: 'Wesley, the water's not too hot for you, is it?'" Wesley is moved by the memory of it.

"Whereas I for so many years of my odyssey had not even seen soap! Or a tub, or a toothbrush! And here my aunt is asking me if the water is too hot..."

He was terrified, felt almost uncivilized. He was fearful lest he not behave appropriately at table. He dreaded questions about his life during the war, about his parents. The family exercised great tact, however, and posed only a few questions.

Wesley finished St. Bonaventure High School, a boarding school in Wisconsin, in two and a half years with excellent grades even though the instruction was rigorous and intense.

In the fall of 1952 he began studies in the department of chemistry at DePaul University in Chicago. At the same time he took a job as a locomotive mechanic; a year's tuition cost $850 and average monthly expenses at the time were about $100. Wesley was now living on his own and providing for his own support. It was also his desire to become a military officer and so he completed ROTC training and received a commission as a lieutenant.

"A lot of studying and forty hours of work besides. It was a weight around the neck. But I managed it," Wesley says, recalling those exhausting university years.

In 1957 after graduating in chemistry and philosophy, with a lieutenant's commission as well, he spent a half-year at a base in New Jersey. Then he was hired as a chemist in the Lever Brothers Co. where he worked for thirty-eight years right up to his retirement in 1995.

His life's great passion was bridge. "Man doesn't live by bread alone," he says with a strong, determined voice.

Wesley learned to play bridge on his own. For two years he pored over books on tournament bridge and mastered the game to such a degree that he received mention in the "Who's Who" section of the official encyclopedia of bridge; he has frequently played with the best bridge players in America.

He hasn't played bridge now for three years. From the moment in 1990 when the Russians acknowledged that the NKVD murdered the Polish officers and released the documents of the crime, Wesley felt on a mission to describe his childhood in Poland, his experience in exile and the search for his father's grave...

"My heart had been locked in chains," he repeats. "I wanted to break them in the process of narrating our fates. For almost half a century I had lived with the hope that my father was alive somewhere since I could never find his grave. Even though I had often heard the treading of the executioners' feet, the thousands of gunshots, the cries of those killed..."

His book is to be entitled *When God Looked the Other Way*, with the dedication: "FOR MOTHER AND FATHER, who died so their children could live. And for all the proud Polish people who endured the Inhuman Land with the hope that their children might one day live in freedom."

He insists moreover: "I can't wait until it's released. I hope to be freed of this torment and return to some semblance of normal living."

He belongs to the Katyn Family in Chicago. In 1998, on June 21, which was precisely Father's Day, Wesley Adamczyk left with his son George for Poland. After visiting Kraków, he left by train from Olkusz for Kharkov. A Polish military band played for the more than 200 pilgrims, chiefly children of murdered officers. The trip going lasted two days.

"My son wanted to honor his grandfather with his presence. He was the only grandchild from America and one of three who were present at the ceremonies opening the cemetery," Wesley noted with pride.

We sit on the thick sofa upholstered with black leather. Wesley puts on a BBC documentary filmed during this excursion organized by the Polish government. It has already been shown throughout the world; its producer, who accompanied the pilgrimage, was Olenka Frenkiel, a journalist from London. The first officer to be shown in the film was the Starobelsk prisoner of war Jan Franciszek Adamczyk, executed in Kharkov. And the central figure in the film is his son Wesley Adamczyk from Chicago.

The film recalls the events of the Second World War, the known facts surrounding Katyn, the 50 years of lies connected to this crime. It shows the new cemetery in Kharkov and the emotions of the children, today already advanced in years, scattered over the world, whose fathers died there. None of them knew exactly where the bones of their parents lay; they said prayers, then placed red and white flags, candles and flowers on the common graves. Many, including Wesley, took from that place a handful of earth, branches, pine cones, leaves from the trees...

American born George Adamczyk, grandson of Captain Jan Adamczyk, standing in front of the largest mass grave at the Kharkov cemetery, Kharkov, Ukraine (previously USSR), June 27, 1998. Courtesy of Wesley Adamczyk.

"That pilgrimage did not obliterate our tragedy and pain. Yet thanks to it we were able to honor our fathers. I wasn't the only one who had dreamt all his life of finding the grave of a parent who died during the war," Wesley says.

The film reveals the Soviet reality that continues unabated today: the statue of Lenin in Kharkov, Ukrainian poverty, old people and children begging on the train platforms. The most shocking of all is the conversation between the film's journalist and a Ukrainian journalist in that section of the film when responding to the question who murdered the Polish officers in 1940. We heard the response, given with complete personal certainty: Hitler!

Stirred by the commentary, Wesley takes from a chest of drawers a glazed, ebony box. He removes, among other things, a small plaque embossed with "Wiesław Adamczyk, Charków, 27 czerwca 1998 r." [Wesley Adamczyk, Kharkov, June 27, 1998], a carved statue of Our Lady of Katyn, earth and a cartridge case brought home by his son from the honorary salvo at the opening ceremony of the cemetery at Kharkov. In this way something of history remains for the descendents...

An inscribed commemorative tablet dedicated by the Polish Nation to the murdered Polish officers. The same tablet appears in the cemeteries of Katyn Forest, Kharkov, and Miednoye (previously USSR), 2002. Courtesy of Kazimiera and Janusz Lange, Katyn Family, Łódź, Poland.

**The original Katyn Forest cemetery constructed after the 1943 exhumation.
Two Polish generals were buried sparately in two small graves. Courtesy of
Kazimiera and Janusz Lange, Katyn Family Łódź, Poland.**

Wesley Adamczyk married twice; the first marriage was a premature
one and didn't work out. The second was wonderful, mature, lasting thirty
years.

In 1957 he married Józefina Żebrowska, the daughter of an exile from
the eastern section of pre-war Poland. Though their marriage lasted only
three years, it resulted in two sons. The older, George, a businessman,
lives not far from Chicago, where he has an American wife, four children
and a construction company of high-end luxury homes. The younger, Eric,
died in 1992.

In 2000, Wesley lost his second wife, his beloved Barbara, of Italian
descent. "She was my angel," he says, motioning to a beautiful woman in
paintings and photographs around the apartment. "Someone like her happens along rarely, one out of ten thousand. Elegant, always smiling. She was
a school teacher. Her spirit is always with me."

Today his close family consists of his son and four grandchildren. His
sister Zosia died in 1990, his brother Jurek eight years later. His sister Zosia's
home was open to the entire family; they used to spend all the holidays
and anniversaries at her place. That function is taken over now by his son's

General view of the Katyn Forest cemetery in 2002 with the Memorial Wall to the left and to the right tablets depicting symbols of various religions of the murdered Polish officers. Courtesy of Ka-zimiera and Janusz Lange, Katyn Family Łódź, Poland.

large home outside Chicago. Now his son's family keeps many of the Polish traditions, especially those of Christmas and Easter. His beloved Aunt Maria is still alive and living in a home for the aged. She is one hundred and five.

Before leaving Chicago I could not pass up a visit with one whose life had spanned three centuries. We are traveling with Wesley Adamczyk to a modest home for the aged where his Aunt Maria has been living for several years. Her daughter Gerry, she who had visited the Adamczyk family in Łuck in 1938, the sister of the military nurse Jean, is herself over 80 years old.

Aunt Maria has blue eyes, is wearing an outfit with sky blue flowers and she has a blue dressing-gown. She is well groomed and smiling.

"The hair-dresser came yesterday and gave me a permanent. I don't have to comb it now," she says in her beautiful Polish. We found her in a group activity with an activities director.

She left Poland when she was 15. She jokes: "Have I helped you at all in your life or rather have I taken from you more than I gave?" Wesley explains that she had always helped Poles, sent packages even to the Italian front.

A memorial tablet in the Katyn Forest dedicated to Lt. Janina Antonia Lewandowska, a pilot, the only female murdered during the Katyn genocide. Courtesy of Kazimiera and Janusz Lange, Katyn Family, Łódź, Poland.

Aunt Maria is glad to recall Poland: the family village of Zaryte, her father in the railroad uniform, her brother Janek who "was an excellent student but died during the war." She recognizes without any mistakes the photographs of the Adamczyk family on her mantel. Seven generations: from Austria, inter-war Poland, America. She recalls all their first names, their faces, little things about each. She links together all the pieces of the Adamczyk family's history... And three centuries...

"God directs everything," Wesley says to me in parting. Despite the hell through which he had passed, he hasn't lost his faith in God. He has something to be thankful for, though he has only been to church in America a few times.

"I am moreover certain that God and my family are watching me," he asserts in a strong voice. "That's why I will not allow myself to break. I need for them to be proud of me."

6

LITTLE EWA ALWAYS IN RIBBONS

Warsaw, Poland, December 2001

Ewa Leśnik is always working. Though it was already getting dark at four o'clock of a November evening, still I didn't find her at home. Her husband Marian was the one to greet me, warmly, at their Warsaw neighborhood of Brodno. He was the first to have experienced the consequences of his wife's situation.

"When I married Ewa, I had no inkling of the consequences for me of my wife's family's patriotic past, especially as regards its impact within the Polish People's Republic." Marian Leśnik is amazed at it even today. Originally from Wielkopolska, he is a graduate of Adam Mickiewicz University in Poznań, majoring in geography and German studies, and a passionate devotee of history. His speech is energetic, he gestures a lot, and from time to time he pets his dog.

"Right after my studies I received the opportunity to work in the Ministry of Foreign Affairs, to travel to a diplomatic post outside of Poland. It all fell apart, however, when they discovered that Ewa's father had died in the Katyn Forest massacre, that one of her uncles, Franciszek Madejski, was in the RAF, and that another uncle, Kazimierz Hanus, his mother's brother, had been exiled to Siberia. I was accused of falsifying documents, hiding relevant facts; I was threatened with imprisonment. And so it was my dreams of diplomatic work remained and would remain forever only dreams."

They moved here to Brodno three years ago from Wilcza Street. Their apartment is not large but arranged with taste. A small living room with an adjoining glassed-in terrace is furnished with old furniture: an antique commode, wardrobe, credence, table, bent-wood table and chairs. On the walls are an old clock and a lot of paintings in heavy frames, some of them painted by Ewa's mother. There are also many family photographs. A period piece chandelier diffuses a gold-tinted light. A second room, the bedroom, serves also as a library. The small entrance hallway is full of mementos and knick-knacks.

"There is less noise here than in downtown Warsaw," Ewa asserts as she comes in. It is already dark outside. She is loaded down with groceries and the like, as befits a working woman.

We sit at the ellipsoidal table, under the light of a lamp, next to a mountain of prepared documents. "All of this is precious to me. Some of them are simply relics," Ewa says as she points to the archives.

She is an elegant woman, warm and cheerful. She wears a pretty scarf around her neck, has strikingly original silver earrings in her ears, and her hair is combed smoothly to the back, tied in a knot with a ribbon.

"I have worn ribbons in my hair all my life," she says with a smile.

We begin by looking at collections of photographs, beginning with those from happy childhood years, when her parents were with her, continuing into the school years, later as an orphan, right up to the difficult time of adulthood. Ewa, called Niunia (from the diminutive Ewunia), always and everywhere—the sole exception being her first communion picture—has her hair combed smoothly back, with a big ribbon tied in it. It is the same during her last vacation with her parents, in August 1939...

Ewa Leśnik is originally from Podkarpacie. Her mother, Janina Madejska, maiden name Hanus, was born in 1910 in Dukla, the oldest of five children. Ewa's grandfather, Józef Hanus, was a forester in the Bieszczady Mountains. He was in charge of enormous expanses of forest near Łańcut. Ewa's grandmother, Maria Hanus, was an eminent lady and of strong principles. She was a good friend of the daughters of Count Skrzyński of Dukla. In their youth, they would travel together by coach, even as far as Moscow and Petersburg.

Janina Madejska, after completing her studies in 1929 at the teacher's college in Łańcut, took work in the Wołyń district. She taught children under quite difficult conditions. She lived in near poverty but was happy with her profession and her independence. Such a conclusion can be drawn from her letters to her mother. On March 27, 1930, she wrote to Maria Hanus: "My Dear Beloved Parents!... as far as the eye can reach—marshes, where the water is rose-colored from the setting sun. Copses, in which leafless birch and alder cluster... I tell you, Mom, a magnificent landscape, so very like the Polesie region."

Ewa Leśnik, her daughter, opens up a box full of letters. Not only of her mother's, but also of her father's. Written with a fountain pen, quite legible, somewhat damaged by the ravages of time.

"My grandmother gave them to me some time ago," she whispers as she strokes the box solemnly.

In one of the letters the young teacher confides to her mother that she has made the acquaintance of Stanisław Madejski, also a teacher. Young, handsome, from a nearby village in Wołyń. He's 27, of average height, dark-haired, devilishly good-looking. They call him "Abyss" or "Mephisto," she writes.

Janina and Stanisław's wedding took place in 1932, perhaps in August since on their wedding photograph the bride's large summer bouquet is made up of field flowers. And in the background, behind a long floor-length veil, there are blossoming bushes and a wild, twisting grapevine.

After their vacation the newly wed Madejski's returned to their teaching positions in Wołyń. They settled in Holubno. Their only daughter Ewa, now living in Warsaw, came into the world January 15, 1934 in Przemyśl.

"I didn't like my nannies, especially Marysia who used to hit me." Janina shows me one of just a few pictures of the nanny and dog, taken in 1934.

When Stanisław Madejski received his law diploma in Lvov, he took a position in the court at Tarnopol. In January, 1938, he became a judge in the municipal court at Mława, under the jurisdiction of the Appeals Court in Warsaw.

Ewa Leśnik remembers Mława quite well, the court building, sledding, and even boxing matches to which she accompanied her father.

"Our house was beautiful, splendidly laid out." Her most lasting memory is of columns at the entrance as well as pictures in thick, golden frames in the living room. "We occupied the entire bottom floor. We had four rooms, and I had my own," she adds.

It was in August 1939, as the war with Germany was approaching, that the judge Stanisław Modejski took his wife to a sanatorium in Zakopane. He never saw her again...

Having returned from Zakopane, he was shortly to say goodbye also to his daughter Ewa. He left her at the forester's lodge, at her grandparents'. He received a telegram, like other judges and court officials, saying that he had to cut short his vacation and present himself immediately in Mława. The evacuation of the court was already ongoing.

"I accompanied him from the forester's lodge by carriage to the train." Ewa remembers the chestnut horses and that the carriage driver was named Nikodem. She was seeing her father for the last time.

She had kept in her little box the last letter that her father wrote to her mother, on August 29, 1939: "Dear Żaba ... a telegram was waiting that I had to go back to Mława. That being the case I am leaving today this evening. The political situation is such that war hangs by a hair... If I get to Mława a bit early, I'll try to send the most valuable things to Łańcut. Linen, bedding, clothes, coats, kilims, quilts, the radio, but the rest I'll leave... In any case I am not going to Przemyśl, to my parents, and I don't know if I will see them again..."

In early December 1939, Janina Modejska wrote from Zakopane: " My Dearest Parents! I don't know yet how I am to thank Mother for such a long letter, for all the sweet things you sent for St. Nicholas Day. My Dearest Daughter, how come you're poking around so much in the yard and getting colds? You have to be healthy; it's enough that Mom is sick and weak. What did St. Nicholas bring you; he brought me a lot of candy and other things. It's too bad I can't share these things with you. Bye-bye, sweetie—I send you hugs and kisses. Mom."

At the end of December the Gestapo threw the last fifteen patients at the sanatorium out into the street. Janina Modejska was one of them. The Germans got rid of the Zakopane patients in such a cruel manner because they were already preparing the sanatorium to be the location of a German secondary school, Deutsche Oberschule fur Jungen. Some of those thrown out, seriously ill, died right away since the temperature was below freezing. Janina Madejska made an attempt to get to Kraków and then further, to her parents in Pogwizdów. She didn't survive the hardships of travel. Someone along the way took this woman, terribly emaciated and frozen to the bone, to the hospital in Kraków. She died there on December 30, 1939.

"Only her oldest uncle was present at the funeral," says daughter Ewa. "He was unable to notify anyone else because the telegraph was not working then. I went with my grandmother to the grave site only in 1940. Five years later my grandparents placed a stone over it, putting next to her name my father's name, then with the addition 'he died tragically in Katyn.' To this symbolic grave of my father I brought over in 1995 some earth from the Katyn Forest."

After the German army took control of Mława, the Gestapo searched out the lawyers and court officials. The lawyers of Mława had fled eastward before the Germans and then ... they fell into the hands of the Soviets. Even today, however, the details of Judge Stanisław Madejski's flight are not known. The first and only letter from him reached Pogwizdów on January 14, 1940, two weeks after his wife's death. His daughter shows it to me as if it were something holy.

It isn't a large piece of paper, torn unevenly from a tablet. Small letters, written with an indelible pencil. Stanisław Modejski wrote this letter on October 30, 1939 in Kozelsk. He notified them that he was alive, and healthy, "despite the whole odyssey that I have undergone since the war's outbreak." He hoped that "Żaba," his wife, was now in somewhat better health and was with her parents. He asked how his "Most beloved daughter," Ewa, was doing as also "Szusi" (his mother-in-law). The judge hoped that in the course of a month he would return from captivity. He wrote also that he often saw Czesław Łuński, president of the district of Płock, who sent greetings.

"They were both executed on the very same day, April 14, 1940. Łuński had the idenfication number 02079 and my father had 02058. The exhumation confirmed that they were in the same grave," Ewa explains.

The family members had learned already during the war that Stanisław Madejski was murdered in the Katyn Forest massacre. The newspaper "Gazeta Krakowska" in May 1943 wrote about the crime of the Soviet NKVD against Polish officers. Judge Stanisław Madejski was already listed as one of those shot in the back of the head. As one who was not in uniform, because the judge had never been in the army except for a time as a volunteer in the war with the bolsheviks in 1920.

"I was then eight years old and so the news about his death never reached me at all. I knew only that I had to be on my own," says his daughter.

Professor Ryszard Juszkiewicz: "Thanks to her concealment with her grandparents in the forests at Pogwizdów, the orphan Ewa avoided forced entry into an orphanage for the purpose of germanization."

Even though the forester's lodge where Ewa was staying was rural and far from the world, the Hanus family suffered deeply the tragedy of the war. First of all, during the September campaign, their youngest son Tadeusz died near Lublin, and then in December their oldest daughter Janina, and next in the Katyn Forest massacre her husband Stanisław Madejski was shot. Too, the forester's lodge was invaded several times by bands of pillagers.

"They would break the windows at night, and enter through them into the house and loot us of everything." Ewa remembers that the most cruel ones were the "red-haired ones."

For a few months in the years 1939–1940, her grandmother "Babunia" would write a very personal journal, in which she expressed the tragedy of those days and the pain of having lost two children. Her granddaughter Ewa sometimes reads it but always pays for that with sleepless nights. "Babunia" wrote about Ewa in this way: "Ewunia, poor child, comforts me and tells me not to cry for Mama. She tells me that Mama has gone to the Lord and that it is always better there. She still doesn't really feel the absence of her Mother; oh, let God permit that this poor child never feel it, ever..."

Ewa began her wandering as an orphan when she was eleven years old. In 1945, she went first to her aunt's, one of her mother's sisters, in Katowice. There she attended the sixth grade.

"But in general I had no time and no situation for studying!" she now says. "To balance school with doing the cleaning, laundry, shopping, and taking care of children was impossible."

Once again "Babunia" had to think what to do with her granddaughter.

Ewa Leśnik with husband Marian at the Memorial Wall in the Katyn Forest, near her father's tablet. The photograph was taken during the opening of the Polish military cemetery in Katyn Forest in Russia on July 28, 2000. Courtesy of Ewa and Marian Leśnik.

The grandfather was already on a modest retirement. After a family consultation they decided to turn for help to Ewa's father's family...

Up to then the Madejski family, even though Ewa bore their name and they knew that she was now an orphan, had not shown much interest in her. Only one of her father's brothers, Franciszek, who had served in England with the RAF and who emigrated to the Republic of South Africa where he became a bank clerk, sometimes sent packages to her: of vitamins, chocolate, coffee. It was only after many years that Ewa learned that he had wanted to have her sent to South Africa, but one of his brothers in Poland was quicker and sent two of his own children to him...

"Strangers helped me more than family. Even though there were two families, one my father's, the other my mother's, except for my "Babunia" not one offered to take me into their heart. And even one of the aunts was exceptionally unkind. She would take for herself even packages that had been sent to me sometimes from America by my Grandfather Józef Hanus's sisters," she recalls bitterly.

And adds in tears:

"My childhood was shoes full of holes, blows, and tears. I even had to eat off the plate that one of my aunt's children had already used. And I always got clothes to grow into."

Her husband laughs: "I even took for myself one of her pairs of shoes, reddish ones, moccasins that had been ordered for her, which were three sizes too large for Ewa!"

Having her diploma from Przemyśl in hand, Ewa once again traveled to her grandparents. Her family determined that they couldn't afford to send her to higher studies. "Ewa should get a job," was the family's verdict.

In September 1954, now a seventeen-year-old, Ewa once again made her way to the Poznań region. She moved in again with one of the kinder aunts. Again she took responsibility of the children, but undertook also work in the General Consumers' Co-operative. She would hand over her earnings to her aunt. God compensated her, however, for the wrongs done to her. She met one of the handsomest young people in Chodzież, five years older than her, a geography student, Marian Leśnik. Her future husband took in hand the orphan's plight.

"I suggested to my mother that she rent to her an empty room in our large house. And that's how it began," smiled Marian Leśnik.

Ewa and Marian were married in 1954. After receiving a master's degree in geography Marian Leśnik received an appointment in Warsaw. Though he had initially wanted to go by himself to get things set up, Ewa categorically refused. "I wouldn't sit and wait at my in-laws'. I had a husband," she said. She packed her suitcase and went to Warsaw.

The Leśnik's recall with amusement their life's beginnings in the capital that had been rebuilt from the war's ruins: "Four empty walls. First we bought a couch so we wouldn't have to sleep on the floor. It came together with some boards, so we made a bookshelf out them. We covered the bookshelf with paper and hung a sheet on the window.

They placed great hopes in Marian's work at the Ministry of Foreign Affairs. Unfortunately, the Katyn episode weighed heavily on Ewa's family's past.

"Because of it we've lived in poverty for almost thirty years, right up to the dissolution of the political system," says Marian Leśnik. He has been a modest clerk in the Head Offices of Tariffs. It was only in 1980 that he was promoted to vice-director of the department, from which he retired ten years later.

Ewa Leśnik began her professional life in the capital at the Enterprise for Processing Building Stone. Then she worked eight years in the center for the overseas business Animex and longer, for twenty-six years, as a senior advisor in the Head Offices of Tariffs. She never mentioned Katyn outside the home, to anyone.

"Nor did I ever belong to any political party," she emphasizes.

She and her husband raised two children, Iwona (born in 1955) and Andrzej (born in 1960).

Despite her fate as an orphan, she herself has a great deal of warmth. She is also an eternal optimist.

"That's probably due to the Podkarpacie forests... And to my mother who had such a great heart and artistic soul," she says.

Marian Leśnik gives his own version, but without any reproaches: "Ewa doesn't know how to save. She loves giving things away. She will feed all the homeless dogs in the area, comfort women abused by their husbands, help anyone in need."

Ewa Leśnik does not, however, keep any warm relations with her family, either from her father's side or her mother's. It is true that her father's family recently made some overtures to her but she doesn't have the heart for it. None of them ever went to Katyn. The brothers of Judge Stanisław Madejski continually concealed the truth about his death, even from their own children.

Whereas Ewa has been to Katyn three times already.

The first time was in June 1995 during the first official national pilgrimage, when, in a ceremony at which the highest government authorities participated, a corner-stone was placed at the site of the future military cemetery. President Lech Wałęsa was among the more than one thousand participants. It took the train a whole day to get there. Ewa Leśnik didn't sleep a wink. She was the only one who had to spend the entire night in the corridor. Standing.

"Do you know that I had been waiting for my father for half a century? I had never accepted that he had been murdered! I kept thinking that he was alive, hiding, that he was afraid to reveal himself. Maybe in America, or perhaps somewhere else... But I believed that in the end he would give some sign that he was alive. I kept dreaming about him! That he was arriving somewhere, leaving, how he was going along, all worn out..."

It was only in 1995 that she had to admit that her father had been shot. She knew he had passed through the train station Gniezdowo, ten miles from Smoleńsk, where as a POW of Kozelsk he had been taken from the monastery. Then he was imprisoned, or perhaps taken on foot, another mile to the Katyn Forest. The recreational center for the functionaries of the Smoleńsk district administration of the NKVD was located there, on a high bank of the Dnieper River. They shot him just like the other Poles, over an open grave, and buried him in his place of death. The Katyn Forest covers the remains of 4421 prisoners from the camp at Kozelsk.

"I walked along the path, among the pines planted by the executioners over the fresh graves, and I wondered what my father would have been thinking of," she begins to weep. "Did he suspect that he was going to his death? Was he then with us, his closest ones, with me and my mother? Was he able to bid us farewell? And to pray?"

Despite the fact that the graves in the Katyn Forest are common, name-less, Ewa Leśnik singled out for herself a patch of ground at one of the mounds. She feels that it is there that her father is at rest. She always places flowers and lights candles there.

The pilgrims were under surveillance during the first trip. Ewa Leśnik's camera preserved proof that in the Katyn Forest police and soldiers were swarming behind almost every pine.

"But even so I came to love that cemetery. It is simply beautiful! I could be among those pines on and on!" she says admiringly as she shows me the pictures.

She went a second time to Katyn Forest in September 1995, to the funeral of two generals, Smorawiński and Bohatyrowicz. And a third time to the official opening of the Katyn cemetery in 2000. Then she took her husband with her.

"We'll go there again in the spring," they both assure me.

Ewa Leśnik takes her Katyn treasures out of a small chest of drawers: a small box with pine cones, dried flowers, earth. Among these is her father's picture. She also collects poems, clippings from newspapers, magazines and books. She reads for me aloud her favorite stanza of some unknown poet:

> At a very distant place
> in a green forest near Smoleńsk
> the earth opens
> it gives heart
> to silenced lips
> listen, you heavens, seas and lands
> the hour is striking, judgment is coming
> history's last page will be renewed
> the part played by the dead will be made known [...].

Ewa Leśnik is convinced that had there been no war, no Soviet betrayal and their pact with the Hitlerites, and no Katyn, her life would have turned out far differently. She would have certainly finished higher studies. Certainly she would today be quite well-off, without the orphan's onus. Would she per-haps have never left Podkarpacie? Would the *kresy* still be Polish? For sure there is no other country in Europe whose borders were so radically altered after the Second World War as Poland's...

"I have made a great exception in your case by telling you all of this, even though it is only one thousandth of the hardships I suffered, the terri-ble misfortunes of my life," says Ewa Leśnik in closing.

The Katyn Forest massacre comes up again during supper. Rhetorical questions come up. Why did the Germans make public the massacre right away and in some minimal degree render compensation for the all wrongs they did? Why did the Soviets release the documents concerning the Katyn massacre only in 1990? Why has the crime not been investigated and condemned throughout the world even though the signatures are known of the perpetrators who decided on the extermination of the Polish nation? Why? Why? Why?

Marian Leśnik replied: "A lot of the fault lies with our government. They were incompetent in the negotiations. They were unsuccessful in pressing the case for redress. And besides, in my opinion, Poland is not able to act independently in the political arena. Once again Russia is necessary to the West in its battle with terrorism. And as a result Polish affairs once more have become secondary and unpopular. There won't be an investigation, there won't be any indemnity made, and eventually talk about Katyn will come to an end. We will once again have lost."

"That's why," sighs his wife, Ewa, "it is fortunate that three cemeteries have come into existence after sixty years. For me the necropoli in Katyn Forest, Kharkov and Miednoye are components in the re-attainment of Polish spiritual sovereignty.

In the words from the publication of the Council for the Preservation of the Memory of Struggle and Suffering entitled "Polish Military Cemeteries":

"Historical memory does not mean historical justice. It is, however, a condition for the normalization of social and national life. The collective cemeteries are 'our contact with an undying past.'"

7

FAITHFUL TO THE
BLUE UNIFORM

Łódź, Poland, January 2002

"You were both a POW's son and simultaneously a POW yourself at Ostashkov? How was that possible?" I asked in unbelief when he opened the door to his apartment in Łódź. Not wanting to begin his story in the middle, Stefan Nastarowicz said nothing but only nodded his head in affirmation.

Ailing and stooping, quite grey, he began by showing me his personal archives. Most of his parlor is filled with books, picture albums, other publications, folders and files bursting with documents and records. He has documented his entire life. He has arranged for himself a sleeping area in half of his kitchen but there too it is full of memorabilia connected primarily with the themes of independence and the Katyn massacre.

"I don't know what I'll ever do with all this. I certainly won't throw it into the basket! I'd like these documents to be of service to history, not to have been gathered in vain, but who to leave it to?" Stefan Nastarowicz is seventy-eight years old. He has been alone for a quarter of a century and so has some concerns about this.

He speaks clearly and expressively, with a lot of pride and stubbornness in his oval face. Despite many illnesses he has retained a great clarity and sharpness of mind.

"Every day for an hour I do crossword puzzles to exercise my almost eighty-year-old mind which has gone through so much," he jokes.

He wrote the poem entitled "I swear" for the fiftieth anniversary of the crime:

> I, the son of a blue uniformed police officer,
> was rescued by the Hand of Providence,

yet my father rests among the thousand murdered
in their blue uniforms in the valleys of death
at Miednoye
I swear
to you who have worthily
worn the blue uniforms
to you, who have worthily served the Fatherland
to you, whose blue uniform
was hated
by the executioners of the NKVD
to you, who together with my father
until the late fall of 1939
were in the POW camp of Ostashkov
that I will remember, not forget
that I will stand guard over the truth
 that I will shout out the truth of the crime of genocide
I, the son of the blue policeman
I bow my head before you
I render homage, remembrance to you
Our dearest ones, I, commanded by fidelity.

A significant portion of the publications gathered together by him is dedicated to the Nastarowicz family, to its patriotism, its participation in struggles for Polish independence, its links to Łódź for five generations. Stefan
Nastarowicz has himself written some of the articles. Often he was rectify-
ing facts about Katyn that appeared in national or local press; some were
interviews, other clarifications. His own works too have been published in
several books, including his memoirs which received first prize in the competition organized by the Central Museum of War POWs in Lambianowice-
Opole.

"I began to speak openly of these affairs only in 1989. Earlier even an
allusion to the fact that there had been a blue policeman in the family was
enough to arouse suspicion. There was even the threat of death," he says with
fervor, sometimes with sadness, even bitterness, gesticulating vigorously with
his gaunt arms. His hands call attention to themselves; they are thin, restless,
with exceptionally long fingers. "I was to have been, as my grandfather and
uncle, a musician. Before the war I studied the violin, but I always felt drawn
toward the army." Today he no longer has hearing in one ear. Only two violins, from his grandfather, remain to him from his family's musical traditions.
His father's brother, Uncle Stefan, conductor of the military orchestra of the
52nd Infantry Regiment in Złoczów, in the region of Lvov, used to play
them. Today he has passed the violins on to his only son but they remain
unused.

Łódź is his most beloved city. He knows every nook and corner of it. In
the course of our conversation he often digresses and speaks with admiration

about some particulars of the city today, its growing collective beauty, despite the high levels of its oppressive unemployment. "My grandson, Marcin, trained in European integration, is also without work." Marcin Nastarowicz frets over this, but can't imagine living anywhere else.

He spent his childhood in the very center of Łódź. He was born on January 10, 1924, at 38 Ogrodowa Street.

"In the tenement house where we rented there was a small garden and a water pump where we would go for water. Our landlady, a real virago, used to go for the water barefoot, even in wintertime," he recalls as he serves coffee.

The tenement stood near the oldest Roman Catholic cemetery, Święty Józef where the graves of all his family are located. In 1991, a section for policemen was prepared at the cemetery. He remembers that in the years between the wars a tall metal cross stood there. On national holidays and All Saints' Day the officers in blue uniforms would gather there to pay homage to those who had departed to their eternal posts.

"I was raised with proper manners, in a traditional Catholic family. Mom taught me my prayers and I often attended religious services whether I wanted to or not." He laughs as he shows me an album with pre-war photographs of his whole family. Besides pictures of his father and uncles from the legions, there are a number of wedding pictures from April 1921, of his parents, Helena Spychała and Michał Nastarowicz.

He continues his childhood remembrances:

"My Mom used to raise pigeons in the garden. I remember how one of the pigeons fell into a hot cauldron of wash water and it was dead when we took it out. We also had a white cat with a ribbon around its neck. We would take it for walks on a leash. There were also various dogs at the house, one of which Dad used to bring in his pocket. Dad also had canaries in the house and they would sing beautifully!"

His father, Michał Nastarowicz, was a policeman and earned over 160 zloties a month. Mom took care of the house and the raising of the children, Stefan and his sister Jadzia, who was two years older than him.

"Mom got sick quite often. Even though she was four years younger than my father, she was the first to die, in 1937, when she was forty-two years old. Afterward our grandmother Spychała helped in raising us."

Michał Nastarowicz was born in 1891. Łódź was then in the Russian partition. He was required therefore to do his military service in the years 1913–1917 in the czarist army, as far away as Vladivostok. He took part in the First World War, serving from May 1917 to November 1918 in the 1st Polish Corps. After Poland regained its independence, he enlisted in the national police force then forming.

"On November 11, 1918, my father took part in the disarming of the Germans who were quartered in the military governor's accommodations in

Łódź's Grand Hotel. In our house there hung a Prussian saber confiscated in that action."

Talk of war began in the Nastarowicz family already in March of 1939.

"I was a scout and used to go to demonstrations on Plac Wolności and further down in the neighborhood of the Łódź cathedral where the German consulate was located. In his child's imagination, he never believed that war might menace Poland. Near the end of August he participated in the digging of anti-aircraft ditches in the sports field nearby.

His father, Michał Nastarowicz, was working at the time in the Headquarters of the Infantry Reserve. He was a senior policeman. On Friday, September 1, he woke his children early in the morning and spoke the memorable word, War!

"Indeed, I had gotten myself ready for the war," he says, raising his hands upward. "I already had a backpack at hand and fully outfitted: extra clothes, socks, medicine, flashlight, thread, matches and candles. I had been raised on military and legionnaire songs. The uniform, especially the blue one, had been my dream from childhood."

During the first days of September 1939, when his father did not return from high alert, and crowds of those fleeing from the western territories poured through Łódź, he reached for his backpack. The schools were closed, and there were disturbing news reports from the radio about the bombing of the city. On Tuesday, September 6, during the German air raids, he found himself in a fleeing crowd of terrified, panicked and confused people. His grandmother had bid him farewell with the sign of the cross, his sister Jadzia with hugs, his neighbors had given him sandwiches. He can still see today the crowds of co-refugees with their belongings and bundles: on foot, in wagons, on bicycles, horses, all in disarray, tired, heading toward a Warsaw preparing its defenses.

"I turned off into Dowborczyków Street where my father had been working." Michał notes that he was then fifteen years old. "It turned out that the police headquarters had been evacuated earlier. I found, however, a group of policemen, army personnel and firefighters. When I made it clear that I was looking for my father, they let me stay. We then began to go in a group toward Warsaw. I remember that we boarded some kind of bus. On the road, amidst masses of continually bombarded refugees, there were enormous traffic jams and tie-ups."

Along the way, one of the policemen from his group noticed Michał's father in a passing car. Father and son met up with each other at a stop in a small town near Warsaw.

"My father couldn't understand how I got there! He was surprised and uneasy that I had left my house, sister and grandmother." Stefan Nastarowicz remembers that despite his father's reprimands, he himself was exceedingly glad for the unexpected encounter. Finally he had some guidance.

Together they moved in the direction of the Vistula River. The weather was beautiful, warm and sunny. Then a change of orders arrived. They were to head eastward, in the direction of Lublin. The bridge had been put out of use as a result of the bombardment, so they got across the river in small boats and set off in the direction of Garwolin.

"On account of the constant air-attacks we traveled only during the night and early morning hours." Though he has an excellent memory, he sometimes assists it with some of his earlier articles. "We would often seek shelter in nearby villages; the women there would often prepare meals for us. We experienced the heaviest air raids of the German squadrons in the vicinity of Maciejowice. As we lay in the potato furrows, it was only by a miracle that we escaped death."

He remembers Lublin being completely in flames and the march to Chełm Lubelski where the police were still active in the defense of administration buildings and banks. At Kowel ... the weariness of walking, his exhausted legs, and the scout backpack getting heavier, all caught up with him. He hadn't imagined war to be like this... On September 17, 1939, they learned of the attack on Poland by the Soviet army. They met Polish soldiers and civilian refugees drawing back from the east. A general disorientation and an anxiety as to what to do next reigned everywhere. The return road to Kowel became doubly dangerous: Ukrainians were now firing at the refugees from the forests and buildings along the road.

"One day, we found somewhere a kind of one-horse cart. In it we made our way up to Ratno, where the police were regrouping in a large forester's complex. It was Friday, September 22nd."

The following day they learned that Brześć was unoccupied, which in the language of the time meant that it had been abandoned by the Germans.

"How much smarter I am today! Now I understand what unoccupied meant. But at that time no one was aware that the Soviets and Germans had— on the basis of the secret codex in the Ribbentrop-Molotov pact—invaded Poland practically simultaneously, partitioning our country between them and breaking earlier understandings with Poland," he says, thinking back as he straightens the corset he wears for a spinal problem.

Several miles from Brześć, on September 23, armed civilians with red bands on their arms, wearing caps and hats, took the group's weapons away. They also grabbed his scout backpack and threw it onto a pile with other haversacks.

"Then I cried and asked one of the Ukrainians to have it given back."

The Ukrainians were shouting in abusive language to the military and police personnel that their government was already finished. Some of them were obviously drunk and wanted to shoot the policemen.

"Once again I was crying and begging them to stop it but one of them

Stefan Nastarowicz at the Memorial Wall by the memorial tablet of his father at the Miednoye cemetery, Miednoye, Russia, 2000. Courtesy of Kazimiera and Janusz Lange, Katyn Family Łódź, Poland.

hit me with the butt of his rifle," he remembered. "In the outskirts of Brześć one sympathetic woman had advised my father and his colleagues to change into civilian clothes."

In Brześć they were thrown into prison. The fifteen-year-old recalls how they were situated on the first floor, and how the Ukrainians seized from the Polish police, military people and civilians their personal belongings, watches, cigarette cases, fountain pens, money and other items. He was terror-stricken. It was a good thing for him that his father had the bunk next to his in the crowded cell.

It's impossible for him to forget how the prison was getting more and more crowded. New people kept coming in and hunger was beginning to beset them.

"My father, knowing Russian from the time of his service in the czarist army, in order to increase our food ration, proposed to a certain Red Army soldier to give him his pocket watch which he had concealed up to this time. The soldier, suspicious but honest, agreed, under the condition however that he would get a *'rozpisk'* (document) showing that he had gotten the watch without coercion. From that time on we would be given a little more bread, rice and grain from the common bucket. However, we didn't have the where-withal to eat it. We had been carrying our food in the flaps of our coats, and in our hats..."

They spent five days in the Brześć prison (September 23–28). Leaving under the heavy escort of Soviet soldiers with rifles aimed in the direction of their column, they departed from Brześć into an unknown direction in cattle cars waiting at the railroad station.

"I was lying on one of the shelves by a tiny window, " he says. "The doors of the car were closed from the outside. It was crowded and fear was in the air."

They entered Russia on September 28. The next day was his father's namesday and there were a lot of hugs, kisses but no presents. The military issue biscuits were becoming even more precious. The Polish national anthem could be heard in all the cars.

"At times at the stops we would get a few dried, salty herring, after which our thirst would be terrible," he says. "They also gave us a black bread that was unknown to me and some kind of slop to drink."

Stefan Narastowicz still has his pocket calendar from 1939. Small, dilap-idated, it has the format of a notebook with notes for each day. He had it with him during each of his 99 days in captivity. As he gazed out through the car's little window, he would note down in it the names of the towns they passed. In 1989 the contents of the notebook were copied, thanks to which they were preserved since the pages written in with an ordinary pencil had begun to fade.

After five days the train stopped in Babynin and soldiers on horses surrounded the "green-blue column" made up of POWs. The fifteen-year-old looked them over closely. "Grey-dun, frayed coats. Rifles on sackcloth belts. Some kind of packs hanging on their backs," he later noted. Snow was falling. Following orders, the POWs set off down a muddy field road.

"In order not to lose our shoes in the morass we tied them to our feet." He says that this memory is associated in his mind with scenes known from pictures of exiles, those who participated in the national uprisings, being driven into Siberia.

After several hours of tortuous walking, they were rushed into a structure enclosed with a high wall and set amidst trees. In the midst of some sixteen or seventeen stone buildings, there looming before their eyes was a large bust of Stalin. This was Pavlishchev-Bor in the Soviet Union.

"The hardships of the road, the hunger, the lice and squalor were a sign to everyone. However, before we went to bed on the bunks made of hard planks, we said a quiet, common prayer."

The stay in this former sanatorium for those from Łódź consisted in an endless counting and listing of POWs, the hostile attitude of the Soviets, the uncertainty of the next day. Also the battle with lice and the paltry rations. His father was sometimes assigned to the group which carried water from outside the walls to the kitchen. While outside, in exchange for Polish coins and buttons with the eagle on them, he would procure apples from ragged Russian children...

"In Pavlishchev-Bor we celebrated the namesday of my sister, Jadzia, about whom my father was greatly concerned. And October 17 too, the anniversary of my mother's death. It was two years earlier that I had been in the hospital when she was dying."

His father and he talked a lot about home, their family, their beloved Łódź. His father also taught him Russian. He has the Russian alphabet written down in his pocket calendar. Sometimes his father exchanged tobacco shag for bread...

"Then I would move about less hungry." Stefan Nastarowicz, today still quite thin, notes that he was always skinny and on the small side. At home they used to nickname him "Shorty."

They were taken from this camp on October 26, after twenty-three days. Once again the same clammy road to Babynin, and at the station the same cattle cars. He noted in his small calendar with trembling hand the towns they passed. He remembers that on the following day the transport stopped at a side train station in Moscow. They were led to single-story buildings. It was a cafeteria with huge, propaganda posters and portraits of Stalin. There they received soup and black bread. They had to answer their bodily needs beneath the cars.

After five days, they reached the station of Ostashkov. In the dark night they were loaded on a boat and transported to an island. Again the buildings were located amidst trees and behind high walls. This time it was the cloister with its two 18th century and one 19th century Orthodox churches. At one time these buildings had served God but with the coming of the Soviets—crime. In all the rooms, even in the side navels of the sanctuaries, there were bunks four or six levels high.

"My father and I laid on a top bunk so as to get more warmth. The cold was already quite marked."

Stefan is a living witness to Ostashkov, called by the POWs *Miłaja Krystań* (devil's cloister). From his telling there emerges a picture of life in the camp on Stołbnyj Island, in Lake Seliger.

He remembered that most of those in Ostashkov were policemen in blue uniforms, from which he concluded that the policemen were perceived by the Soviet authorities as exceptionally dangerous enemies of the Communist system. Army personnel of various ranks as well as civilians and members of the clergy had also been put on the island.

Everyone would get up early in the morning. They would receive a chunk of black bread heavy as clay and boiled water which bore some resemblance to tea. Then there were always the assemblies, the noting down of personal information, and the taking count—during their transference from one place to another they were always assigned group leaders. In the course of a day the prisoners would talk about their uncertain situation, their families in Poland, and those who had already been killed. They would hunt down the lice which drank their blood mercilessly as well as the ever present bed-bugs which could not be exterminated in any manner at all.

No work was required of the prisoners but Stefan Nastarowicz noted down in his calendar that on November 12 he and his father and some others prisoners went outside the cloister grounds. They had been ordered to save from the rising water the logs that had been placed on the shore of the lake. They carried them further into the cloister which was being threatened by flood.

"It was at that time that one of the military men from among the Soviet guard took an interest in me," Stefan says with earnestness. "He asked me in quite correct Polish how it was that I found myself in the camp. Later I learned that he was the commander of the camp, Major Malinowski, a Pole who had left his country after the war of 1920.

They were usually given a loathsome, greasy fish soup for dinner, now and then some potatoes.

"If somehow there was a small piece of meat, my father would give it to me." He often changes handkerchiefs during the interview. "A wooden post in front of our building served us as a table. My father and I would eat our soup out of the same bowl with wooden spoons." Stefan gets up from the table and looks in the credence for the only item he brought with him from Russia. It is a Russian wooden spoon with the engravings: Pawliszczew Bór (3–26.X.1939), Ostaszków (30.X.-21.XI.1939). He keeps it together with a linen sugar pouch in a small box, as a relic.

The clergy present in the POW camp often celebrated quiet Masses, which were always conducted in a dignified and sublime atmosphere and some were even joyous: on All Saints', on All Souls' Day, on November 11... At a crate covered with a blanket, substituting for the altar, prayers were offered in common not only for their own fates, and that of their families and country, but also for those who died and were killed during the war. In the evenings, the POWs took part in common prayer, for "all our daily needs." "Their guards looked on in silence at these prayers in the former cloister of Niłowa Pustyń," Stefan remembers.

Nastarowicz especially remembers November 6th. On that anniversary day of the Soviet Revolution they received shag tobacco and larger food rations.

"It was a pleasant day. I cut the black bread into little squares and I dipped them in sugar. That was a candy substitute which I still like even now," he says smiling.

He recalled well the camp store with its small odds and ends, candy, tablets, pencils, thread, shoe polish. He would go there to look greedily at the candy. Mice would be running along the shelves...

He was in the bathhouse for the first time with his father on November 8. He felt very much ill at ease among the fully naked adults. Similar feelings could be read on his father's face as well. After the bath their clothes were given over for disinfecting. "But the lice didn't die, they came again onto our clothes," he complains.

The POWs were politically indoctrinated in the camp. Besides the interrogations by the NKVD, they had to participate in talks and to watch propaganda films on the superiority of communism.

"On part of the main altar a movie screen had been put up. We were forced to go to the showings. I still remember a few: about Lenin, about the accomplishments of the Soviet Union."

New transports of prisoners were being brought to the island all the time. Among the arrivals were police and border guards, prison, diplomatic and army personnel, and civilians. These would always seek out friends and acquaintances.

He thinks that he was the only one so young, and in addition the only son of a POW. He was however treated as an adult, even getting, like the other POWs, a tobacco allotment. "It seems that there had been another quite young boy. He had committed suicide by drowning himself in the lake," Stefan remembers.

A kind of market-exchange began to function among the POWs. His father acquired, probably for the tobacco, a blanket. From it he sewed for his son a scarf, mittens and foot-wrappings. It had been getting colder and colder at Ostashkov.

On November 18th, police officer Michał Nastarowicz learned in the camp headquarters that they were going to release rank and file soldiers, civilians and the very young. He saw his son's name on the list. "He told me that at first the commander of the camp had proposed to send me to school in Moscow, but my father had not agreed to it."

The teenager didn't want to leave his father. Michał Nastarowicz convinced him, however, that he should leave. Winter was coming close and his father feared that his son wouldn't make it through.

Stefan Nastarowicz relates his story:

"I left the island on November 21, 1939, biding farewell to my father with tears, hugs, and his blessing for the road. The boarding of the boat back was marked with fear and horror. The Soviet officers returned some of us back to the camp. Among those returned was Father Józef Kacprzak. They had recognized him probably due to his characteristic coat with its velvet collar and hat with a large brim. I remember my last glance toward the island where my father remained. I had never thought that I might not see him again."

Once more the cattle cars and a trip in an unknown direction. In his calendar he noted down the same towns which he had passed through before traveling with his father. General excitement reigned in the cars. They were going in the direction of Poland!

Fifteen-year-old Stefan carried in his clothes a disposition entitling him to the amount of 220 zloties from his father's savings account (unfortunately he could no longer make use of it), and in the visor of his student cap as well as in the binding of his shoe he had sewn the 90 addresses of the families of the police in Łódź who remained on the island.

"For six days our train stood in Brześć," he says. "I remember that the local townspeople kept inquiring nervously after their relatives and friends. The railroad people gave us enough to eat. On December 1, under the auspices of a prisoner exchange with the Soviets, we were given over to the Germans."

After a march of several miles, the exchanged POWs were taken into another camp fenced in with barbed wire and located on land that had belonged to the Polish Aircraft Enterprises. Ever anxious about their future, they lay down on the straw spread over the concrete floor of the abandoned hangars. Fifteen-year-old Stefan held close to the guardians to whose care he had been commended by his father. Even so he was greatly afraid. Without his father he felt himself in danger.

"On the next day during roll-call, the German officers asked him how it was he had been taken to a Russian camp. They joked that I wanted to fight with them," he recalls.

Four days later, with the help of his guardians, the teenager managed to escape from the camp. A pass had been made for him and he was made out to be a visitor.

"After the direction to Terespol had been established, I was thrown on my own wits. I distanced myself from there as fast as I could," he says.

Railroad people he met helped him out. When he told them the situation that he was in, they gave him food and helped him travel to Biała Podlaska. There another railroad worker, Andrzej Siedlanowski, took him under his wing.

"He took me to his own house, where for the first time in fourteen weeks I took a bath. His warm-hearted wife and children fed me generously. I was given clean bedding and a safe bed. The lady of the house washed, mended and disinfected my lice-contaminated clothes."

This family's neighbor who could speak German undertook attempts to get me an official pass which would permit me to go to Łódź. He got it in the regional offices on December 7. He has since kept the pass in quite good condition. Supplied with foodstuffs for the road, the boy could now travel calmly home.

"Passing through Warsaw, I arrived in Łódź the next day, namely December 8, 1939," he says with emotion. "It was precisely on the feast of the Immaculate Conception. Had not the hand of Providence been watching over me through those 99 days?"

Dressed in the torn clothes he had by now outgrown, he was greeted at home with joy and tears by his sister Jadzia. His grandmother who was living across the street from their tenement ran up to meet him. Their neighbors were amazed that he was still alive. On the feast of All Saints, votive candles for them had been lit at the grave of his mother because of the news that he and his father had been killed by a bomb during an air raid. Now their only concern need be for Michał Nastarowicz.

"I relayed to everyone my father's message that they wait for him. Then I began to make visits to the families of the Łódź police officers following the addresses given to me in Ostashkov. I was for them the first messenger of good news."

He still has the list of the 90 families. He informed the Episcopal Curia in Łódź as well concerning the fate of the canon Father Józef Kacprzak. "Each visit in their homes was for me a memorable encounter," he says again with emotion. "My greetings to them from their fathers and sons brought hope. The conviction was born in them that the stay in the Soviet camp in Ostashkov was only a passing one, temporary. The families of the POWs did not imagine that officers of the National Police Force would become victims of Stalin's bloody system."

However, Stefan Nastarowicz and his sister Jadzia never again received any letter or news from their father in Ostashkov. They made many inquiries through the Red Cross and Polish embassies in Tunisia and other countries. He still has those inquiries in his thick folders. They would always get the same response: "According to information from the Soviet Red Cross, inquiries within the USSR obtained a negative result. He was not found."

Only from documents transferred on April 13, 1990 by Mikhail Gorbachev to President Wojciech Jaruzelski, among which were lists of POWs imprisoned by the NKVD in Kozelsk, Ostashkov and Starobelsk, Stefan, himself a former POW, learned that his father Michał Nastarowicz had been taken from the Stołbnyj Island on Lake Seliger in Ostashkov on April 13, 1940 in transport number 4457. He had been shot in Kalinin, like all of the 6311 POWs from Ostashkov.

From other sources I gather the following:

The liquidation of the POW camp in Ostashkov was begun on April 4, 1940. The Polish police were driven to the train station Soroga and from there they were transported to Kalinin (presently Tver). From the station they were taken by prison wagons, "*cziornymi woronami,*" the "black ravens," to the district headquarters of the NKVD on Sowiecka Street and there taken to the lower levels of the building. In the so-called "red corner," after checking though the personal files, they shackled the POWs and dragged them to the felt-lined muffled death cell. The sentence was carried out with a bullet to the back of the head. Then the corpses were taken outside and placed in waiting trucks. At dawn the bodies were transported to the town of Miednoye, some eighteen or nineteen miles away. There, at the recreational site of the NKVD, the corpses were buried in pits four meters deep that had been prepared earlier. Each pit contained the "harvest" of one night: 250–300 murdered. There are twenty-five such pits in Miednoye.

The operation was completed on May 19, 1940. Almost thirty people filled the role of executioners. In general, in the *kresy* the number of Polish police interned was over twelve thousand.

Stefan Nastarowicz has visited the place of execution a number of times. In May of 1990 he paid homage together with a delegation from the central police headquarters to those murdered—at Katyn Forest, since the other places of loss were still not known. He went to Miednoye a year later, at the time of the first exhumations. He was also present in 1995 during the dedication of the cornerstone for the creation of the cemetery, as well as on September 2, 2000, precisely on his namesday, at the official opening of the military necropolis.

In 1991, he wrote in his poem "To Father":

> ... Walking through the forest at Miednoye
> in which thousands of murdered
> rest in the pits of death

> from despair I cling to the trees
> in pain I have lived through
> your innocent death
> I have asked for eternal peace
> in my fervent prayer to God
> for you, father, and the thousands of others
> I have not forgiven the executioners
> Forgive me, Lord.

The strongest impression made on him was by the muffled, underground death cell in Kalinin (Tver).

"The chief executioner, commander of the prison in Tver, NKVD agent Blochin would dress himself as a butcher: apron, rubber boots and gloves. He would liquidate in one night from 200 to 300 human beings." Stefan has tried over the years to avoid emotion and hatred. It isn't easy for him because he knows that he too could have had his life ended in this basement. "I was saved only thanks to Divine Providence," he repeats.

He has brought some earth from Miednoye to his mother's grave in Łódź, and placed a handful of earth from the Łódź cemetery in Miednoye. His life continues to be immersed in this massive massacre, which remains uncondemned by the world. He has done much for the Katyn Family which was started in Łódź in 1989. Thanks to his ceaseless efforts the graves in the police section of St. Joseph's cemetery have been put in order and a cross now stands there (the pre-war one had disappeared after the end of the war). In large measure he was instrumental in the erection in Łódź of a Katyn Monument, built from communal collections.

"I merely fulfilled my duties to my father and the thousands murdered in Ostashkov. I accomplished my motto: 'The memory of our fathers is a command of faithfulness,'" he says as he raises his blue eyes upward.

His 99-day participation in the war and his stay in the POW camps made him completely averse to uniforms. During the occupation he worked first of all as a bricklayer's helper and later at a dairy, where "though I got slapped in the face by the boss, I was able to drink as much milk and cream as I wanted." Weak, sickly and emaciated from his stay in the camps, he had periods when he was full of ulcers. His grandmother Spychała died in 1940. His sister Jadzia worked in a knitting factory but before he returned from captivity she had to sell parts of the family stamp collection to live.

They waited for their father. They realized that he might have been executed by the NKVD when later in 1943 the Germans discovered the graves at Katyn Forest and announced in the Łódź press the results of their exhumations. It was difficult to believe entirely since Michał Nastarowicz was not included on the lists. His son Stefan, a Soviet POW as well, did not describe to anyone his own experience in Russia but did write it down during the years 1956–57.

After the war, Stefan Nastarowicz had to serve his military duty in Kraków. He was already in love with Barbara Słowik, herself the daughter of a policeman. They were married in 1947.

"So it happened that the weddings in our family always take place in April," he jokes. "The weddings of my parents, of Barbara and me, and of my son Włodzimierz with Krystyna all took place in April.

"I worked my entire life as a clerk in a leather factory, most recently at Central Leather Factory, as assistant manager of the enterprise," he says, as he offers me some fruit candies. "I graduated from secondary school in Zgierz so that no one would know about my background. I wasn't accepted to the university since children of the pre-war police, if they acknowledged that connection, were excluded. And I would always write down the truth. I was and remain faithful to my father's blue uniform," he reaffirms.

He very much regrets one thing: that in 1995 he didn't go with the members of the Katyn Family to a special meeting with the Holy Father in Rome. "I was afraid that my heart would burst, that I couldn't take the emotion," he explains with tears in his eyes.

As Stefan Nastarowicz says good-bye—in an excellent mood even though tired and somewhat worn out by the difficult remembrances—he mentions to me that he had acquired the uniform of a pre-war policeman. He brings it out. It is an envelope with two ragged scraps of blue material. Under glass. They had been dug up during the exhumations at the former recreational grounds of the NKVD in Miednoye...

8

IN LOVE WITH THE
LAND OF HIS BIRTH

Ciechanów, Poland, January 2002

As the oldest son of Aleksander Korzybski, the last pre-war commander of the Opinogóra police station, amid the poetic landscapes of Zygmunt Krasiński six miles from Ciechanów, Jan had experienced with his father the most wonderful moments of his life. At the beginning of that September of 1939, however, they had to go their separate ways.

"As a boy, still for many years, I gathered German cigarette butts for him. I believed that my father would return. He had been the greatest influence in my life," says Jan, his father's first born, these many years later.

A large, colorful portrait of Aleksander Korzybski, a handsome, smoothly combed company sergeant in a navy blue uniform, occupies a prominent place today in the Ciechanów apartment of his son. Not only handsomely framed, it boasts four of his father's most important decorations. His small living room in the tenement building is luxuriant with flowers and artistically furnished with holy figures, a root sculpture and tapestries created by Jan himself.

This firstborn child, today seventy-six years old, Jan continues to look upon his father with great esteem.

"He was an ardent patriot," he sighs. "He fought in Piłsudki's Legions, disarmed the Germans, and then with the 32nd Infantry Regiment took part in the 1920 war. He did not hold anything back and was twice wounded. He raised us to have great affection and dedication to our country."

In September 1939, his five beloved children ranged from four to thirteen years old. The senior warrant officer Aleksander Korzybski was unable to complete the work of raising his children. As the commander of the post of the Government Police Force in Opinogóra he received six months' wages and instructions to evacuate his family. By September 3, he had already sent his wife with the children and the most essential items to his uncle, a forester in Gołoty, twelve miles outside of town, "for a few necessary days." He himself, according to his orders, was to remain at his post as long as it was possible.

His son, Jan Korzybski, today grey-haired, frail, of average height, remembers that final moment:

"It was the first time in my life that I saw tears in his eyes when he said good-bye to us as we sat in the farm wagon. I too was crying. As if I had the premonition that I would never see him again. And he directed his last words to me, then a thirteen-year-old boy, entrusting to me as the oldest the duties of head of the family. I remembered this solemn duty later throughout my whole life. But at the time I could not even imagine life without him. I felt completely helpless..."

Three days later the thirteen-year-old saw Germans for the first time. They awakened in him terror and fear as they entered on motorcycles, in leather jackets and helmets, into the village near the forest where the family was now living. They demanded that all the inhabitants surrender their weapons under penalty of death.

"We had with us father's double-barreled shotgun. I remember that it was in the basement behind a barrel. We would have handed it over but we were afraid of the Germans' reaction at its disclosure. Fortunately, they didn't look very hard!"

Those difficult and dangerous days, as well as an enormous longing for father and home, engendered in the thirteen-year-old boy a heretofore unknown feeling of sadness and fear. This was deepened by the proximate thundering of heavy weapons, the German air raids, the obvious September defeat. He would hide himself daily in the barn, in a stack of hay, or in some inaccessible corner of the grounds and would sob. Despair tore his heart apart.

A month later Maria Korzybska decided to return with her five children to Opinogóra. They took the wagon together with a cousin, Wodzyński. She had to change what money she still possessed into marks.

The estate of the family of Count Krasiński had been taken over by the Germans. Its new administrator, Fritz Skiel, was an irascible person who hated Poles. The townspeople called him "snot-nose," since his nose dripped into the ever-present cigar smouldering in his teeth...

The last legal heir of the Krasiński estate, Count Edward Krasiński, had been taken to a small room in the administration building. He didn't have a family, had dedicated his entire life and the income from the estate to the patronage of the arts, and especially to gathering items for the collection of the Krasiński Library at Okólnik in Warsaw. He himself had never needed much of anything. He hadn't even had rebuilt the neo-gothic castellated manor destroyed in 1915, the marriage dowry of his great ancestor, the poet Zygmust Krasiński. Count Edward did not live to see the work of his whole life go up in flames. The Germans burned down the library at Okólnik in September 1944. He himself was taken to several camps and eventually to Dachau where he was murdered in 1940.

The Opinogóra apartment of the Korzybski's was located in a building that was part of the Krasiński estate. The red-brick building was across the street from the frame office building that housed the police station. Their home waited for them empty, fatherless.

"We learned that he had left for Warsaw when the front line separated him from his assigned position." The pain in Jan's voice is palpable.

He knows too that in Warsaw his father had gone again to his cousin's sister, Rutkowska, to clean up and regain strength. She advised him to stay, to put on her husband's civilian clothes and not to leave for anywhere else. She tried to convince him that all was lost... He rejected the proposition. Aware of his patriotic duty he presented himself to a re-grouping area from which the police were evacuated eastward before the attack of the Germans. And as with the others, he too fell into the hands of the NKVD. All the policemen, border patrolmen, officials in the justice department, titled people who owned large estates and priests were separated out as "the most dangerous elements." They were placed in monastery cells on an island in Lake Seliger, near Ostashkov.

"We received some indications that he had been seen there in the camp." His son Jan says, however, that they never received any letters from him. "We knew then that the POWs were living in terrible conditions, eight of them to a two-person cell. Also that they were being underfed, harassed by constant interrogations, and that they were being forced to carry in the flaps of their coats dirt and rubble to build a link between the island and the shore. But we believed that our father would survive that hell. We were always on the lookout for his arrival."

Company sergeant Korzybski did not return however. Yet his son kept on crumbling up for him the tobacco from unsmoked German cigarette butts, drying it out, and putting it into a small box...

"It had always been one of my duties to roll cigarettes for my father," he says apologetically.

The Germans too were waiting for the last police chief. Even German settlers who had been brought to Opinogóra asked about him. They blustered that if he ever showed up he would be arrested and imprisoned, this time in one of Hitler's camps.

Without Aleksander Korzybski, his family found itself in a hopeless situation on their return to Opinogóra. The mother, Maria whose maiden name was Okoniewska, was unable to manage without her husband. Supplies of food and money quickly dwindled. Mr. Sokolnicki, owner of the town grocery, didn't want to give any more "on credit." In order to earn something for bread, the children of Opinogóra, under the eye of the school director but under the control of the Germans, had to gather into their school pinafores stones from the estate fields. They also helped every day in the field work for some few pfennigs. The German occupiers closed the school, introduced food coupons, curfew and stringent regulations. The worst, however, was yet to come...

One November evening in 1940 there was a clatter at the Korzybski door. The Gestapo gave them twenty minutes to pack up their essentials. The oldest son retells it years later as if it were only yesterday:

"We tore ourselves out of our beds. Mom was crying, everything was slipping from her hands. She didn't know what was most needed, what to take, and what to leave. She was completely unprepared even though information about the uprooting had floated around earlier. For each of the five children she made a bundle from their bed sheets."

Hurried along by the Germans, with aching hearts and casting a last glance at the modest home and hearth of their parents, they had to go out into a cold, friendless night. The boy asked in his thoughts the questions: What wrong had they done to them? Where are they taking us? What lies ahead for us? How will we manage? He can still feel the warmth of the bed covers he had so suddenly to leave, can see the burning kerosene lamp on the table...

It was raining; everywhere there was heavy, typical Opinogóra mud. Loud upraised voices, dogs' barking, reverberated in the village; flashlights were shining. That night the Germans had driven many neighboring families to the estate's stone barn. At dawn they loaded all of them into cars and took them to the camp, sixty miles away, in former East Prussia.

Northern Mazowsze had already been incorporated into Eastern Prussia. Ciechanów had been made the capital of the region with Erich Koch in charge. From the regional office at 33 Sienkiewicz Street in Ciechanów (renamed Zichenau) to almost ten neighboring districts, there went out criminal instructions for the liquidation of the Polish and Jewish peoples. Today in Ciechanów monuments and plaques commemorating the Gestapo murders, the mass executions, and torture and raids number almost twenty.

The camp at Działdowo was located in Prussian barracks. It was the provisionary camp for war prisoners. In the years 1940–1941, about 200,000 people passed through it, and of these about 10,000 suffered a martyr's death.

"At the gate we were ordered to lay down all valuables," Jan Korzybski tells me, today almost without emotion. "We received a small portion of something to eat and spent the night in a stall for military horses, family next to family."

After two days in the camp, we were loaded onto cattle cars with windows covered in barbed wire. The wagons were sealed and sent in the direction of Kielce, in the General Government section of occupied Poland. At the destination point of Końskie, people from the Polish Red Cross were waiting for them. With sympathetic faces, they separated the exiles into groups, sent them off in wagons to their "quarters" in assigned localities.

"We ended up in Radoszyce, a large, but poor village surrounded by woods," says the head of the six-member family of Korzybski's.

Their designated host gave them a log shed, with open spaces showing between the logs. No stove, beds, bedding, not even a pot. He brought only a teapot with hot tea. Nestled close to each other, worn out, they fell asleep on the straw that had been thrown in the corner of the open room. The next day a second family, of four members, was added to their number.

"There was an adult man in that family," says Jan. "I helped him build along the wall a flat surface to sleep on to which we brought in straw. Then ten people, always hungry, cold, slept there next to each other."

They received a miserly ration of bread, flour, sugar and soap. A small stove acquired by some miracle served them as a heater and range for preparing meals. The money ran out. The oldest Korzybski boy had to get a job. He carried the measuring rod used in surveying fields.

"Every day before dawn my mother would send me out. I would walk all day long with the rod in my hand, often up to my knees in snow, during wintry snow-storms and in the icy cold. I would come back already after dark. My earnings barely sufficed to purchase paltry portions."

He would rest only on Sundays. On those days a terrible yearning swept over him, for his father, his house, his friends, for beloved Opinogóra.

They endured the cold and hunger in this exile for two months. His father's half-brother, Michał Skóra from Ciechanów, had pity on their fate, wheedled a pass to the General Government, and came for them. From this trip Jan remembers best of all the illegal crossing of the border between the General Government and Eastern Prussia. They got across the border on foot, during a windy blizzard. They came out at the last station occupied by the Russians and made their way across the frozen Narew River. Nonetheless the Germans stopped them. They interrogated them but then ... let them go, even though Mrs. Korzybska with her five children did not have passes. On the other side of the river the head of the village put them up for the night, and later they went by train to Ciechanów.

"In Opinogóra it turned out that our apartment was occupied by a German settler, the translator Schlage. And we couldn't reveal our return; we would have been sent out again or taken to a concentration camp. Our family then had to be scattered all around the area."

His mother and each of the children went to a different family, friends or acquaintances. Maria Korzybska took a small corner with acquaintances in Ciechanów. She made a living as a domestic servant to the Germans; what she earned sufficed for her modest needs.

"I ended up with the best situation," smiles Jan Korzybski, cheerful and direct in his contact with people. "Uncle Michał took me to the forester's lodge at Kamionka. His friends, the Dembiński's, lived there. Even though I was a stranger to them, they welcomed me warmly and with all their hearts. They treated me as a son."

Because of its location, the forester's lodge became a sanctuary of Polishness, a refuge for patriotism and resistance. Far distant from the main roads, from visits by German police and foresters, it was initially a contact point for the Home Army, and then one of its outposts.

There was always some stranger at the forester's lodge, sometimes for as long as a few weeks. There were secret meetings, conversations behind closed doors, and partisans would drop in for something to eat. Jaś remembered also a Jewish couple hiding in the barn with their four-year-old son Hersz, refugees from the nearby ghetto in Strzegowo.

"And so it happened, not without pride, but also fear as well, we became members of the opposition movement. Even though we were young, we carried out our entrusted duties with seriousness, responsibility and dedication," Jan says.

The not quite fifteen-year-old Jaś and the thirteen-year-old Janulek carried conspiratorial materials to areas in the Mława district. When they would go by wagon to shop in Ciechanów, they would deliver various packaged materials. They didn't know the value of the materials entrusted to them. They only once looked into the large cardboard tube. In it were scrolls of maps. Among their duties was also the storage of the radio receiver which was necessary for listening to news from the world, and also of partisan bicycles and winter clothing.

Until one day, precisely February 25, 1943, because of a provocation instigated by the German police, they were arrested. The Gestapo seized many neighboring inhabitants, among them the entire Dembiński family, with Jaś included. He remembers the cruel and degrading treatment of the forester, uncertainty about his own fate, the mind-numbing fear.

At dusk they were taken to prison in the basement of the firehouse in Strzegowo. Janulek and Jaś, as juveniles, were put in a cell with the women. Laura Dembińska was also placed there. There were twelve people squeezed into a cell 12 yards square. The only thing on the concrete floor was a bucket for physical needs. They had to lie down side by side, and it was winter. Jan Korzybski will never forget the image of women kneeling on the concrete, begging God to save them.

"It wasn't an ordinary prayer, but sobs united into one murmuring, one whispering of a shared and ardent prayer. I had never seen before or since such a complete fusion with God, such trust in the justice and care of Providence as then."

But ironically all that the prisoners heard for several days were the key's clink, the lock's grating sound and the brutal shout: *Alle raus!* Shoved, kicked, tied on the right hand with a rope tied to another long rope, they were taken every evening—between torturers with dogs and rifles—to interrogations at the local school. There, as they waited motionless for their turn, with their faces glued to the wall, they heard terrifying groans and slaps. As against a dead object, as a flail into a sheaf of grain. There was no longer any weeping...

They would get back always after midnight. Not all. Many were buried then and there in the local cemetery...

"Despondency at the hopeless situation, terrible fear and apathy caused them to become passive, obedient objects. Without hope for rescue," sighs Jan Korzybski. And concerning his own interrogation he adds: "They asked me as they hit me with the butt of a rifle across my naked toes, whose bikes, radio and sheepskin coats were those found in the forester's lodge... My answers were frank, but they incriminated no one."

His youthful age saved him. Janulek, Jaś and their friend Jadzia Milewska were suddenly released a few days later, or more exactly kicked down the stairs. It was an icy, moonlit evening.

"Falling from the first floor to the yard, I fell on my face and injured my knee. Then, the three of us, we sobbed like little helpless kids. We didn't know what to do, how to begin."

They decided to go to the forester's lodge over field roads. It was on these that they used to travel by wagon. They knew then that the distance was more than eight miles. At night and during winter, however, the road was different, more frightful. Going across drift-covered fields, in the stark half-light of the moon, stopping periodically to check landmarks, they made their way to their goal just before morning. Jadzia had left them earlier, going to her parents.

The forester's lodge was completely lit up. It happened that peasants from a neighboring village were in it. They had been ordered to watch over it by the Germans. They attended to the boys and gave them something to eat. Inside the forester's lodge everything was in a complete mess after the search. The tables and chests were broken apart; everything else was piled in the middle of the room. Even so sleeping on the wooden, and not the concrete floor, felt like luxury to the boys.

They had no idea that this was their last night in Kamionka. In the morning the commissar from Ościsłów took Jaś and Janulek into custody. Shortly thereafter the forester's lodge was leveled to the ground and trees put in its place.

"Today only a hole where the well was, lilac bushes and fruit trees gone wild attest to the fact that once there was a lively, friendly, human habitation there," says Jan whose nostalgia leads him back sometimes...

Members of the Home Army kept tabs on the boys while they were in custody. Janulek experienced a nervous breakdown as this was the first time in his life that he had found himself without his parents. He cried continuously, such that Jaś feared for him. Fortunately for them people in town kept track of what was happening to them. They secretly made sure the boys had enough to eat, and a few days later snatched them out of German hands. Jaś and Janulek found work in different locations at horticultural sites some forty miles apart. They didn't meet each other again until the end of the war

Laura and Adam Dembiński, Janulek's parents, survived until liberation. But they had passed through gehenna, at the Gestapo in Ciechanów, then in other places of imprisonment and finally in Auschwitz. Despite barbaric methods of interrogation, they were never made to admit participation in the resistance movement.

The SS at Auschwitz tattooed on my adoptive mother's left forearm the number 47491, and on her husband's 126886," Jaś remembers. "After liberation they found themselves in the West. First in Italy, then they settled in London. The forester Dembiński died before long from tuberculosis, and his wife became a seamstress."

Eventually, Jan was taken again to dig trenches in Eastern Prussia, at the Mazurian Lakes. It was more difficult for him there than at Ostrołęka. Longer obligatory sections to dig, hunger rations, sleeping in barracks, unprovoked beatings.

"Washing ourselves and clothes in lakes without soap resulted in pediculosis; each of us had on our backs one great bloated scab. The disinfecting ever so often of our clothing in a great cauldron brought by the Germans gave only a reprieve of a few days from the insects."

He doesn't remember any longer the German names of the localities in which he dug trenches. They were always being moved around. Sometimes they would cut down enormous pines in the forests and then they would drag water-soaked logs to build German bunkers. There was no lack of tragedies. Once all of the diggers had to be witnesses of an execution by the Gestapo of two unfortunate wretches who had left off digging trenches to gouge out some potatoes from the ground. They were treated as fugitives.

"The executioners shot them ostentatiously, in front of our eyes. One from a traditional rifle, another from a machine gun. They ordered us to undress them, dig a hole and bury them naked. Even those filthy rags of theirs had to be saved for the Third Reich," he says shaking his head sadly.

It was now the winter of 1944. Jan was already eighteen. The group of forced workers was transported to the Augustowskie Lakes. They cut out blocks of ice from them and made two-yard ice pyramids, sprinkling them with water to make them fuse. The patchwork of these pyramids on the great lakes were to impede the Soviet landing operations. The front advanced anyway; nothing could help any more. Starting in early 1945, the Germans began to withdraw.

"In the course of two weeks we covered on foot tens of miles, both during the day and at night. Without any supplies. We were starving, begging, and stealing whatever we could to eat, sleeping along the way in whatever farm buildings we came across. Along the way we met terrified people from Prussia escaping with their things. The look of them reminded us of our own September 1939, except then the direction of the exodus was different."

Coming up against the Baltic, they continued on to Słupsk. There too, daily at dawn, amidst the snow and cold, they were hurried into digging anti-tank trenches. With pickaxes and spades, frozen and hungry, they chipped at the frozen ground until dusk.

In mid–February they were to be evacuated further, by boat, across the Łeba River, westward. Jan Korzybski and two companions, sensing the uselessness of such a trip and the end of their torment, broke off from the group near the Łeba. From a pile of hay at one of the seaside German farms, they saw the first Soviet tank, heralding liberation. Using German bicycles, many of which were lying in the trenches, they made their way to Słupsk amidst corpses, liberating armies going west, and the noise of automatic pistols. There the Soviet army put all those returning from forced labor to the work of gathering and bringing in the livestock.

Jan ended up in a Potęgowo estate where there was a manor house, a mill and a distillery which the Russians put into operation right away. "Our work was to drive the cattle and horses to the manor's barn. We had also to maintain the livestock until they could take them from us and send them to the east."

Once they went for straw to one of the German farms. The proprietress stubbornly barred entrance to the barn. Despite that, they took their wagon into the barn. Behind one of the haystacks they saw a German soldier. Then another one, then a third... At the sight of the pitchforks directed toward them they meekly raised their hands. The Poles delivered them over to the Soviet soldiers.

He did this work until mid–June 1945, until there were no more livestock in the area. Then he went by train, on a freight train loaded down with rails which were being taken to the east, ten days travel to Ciechanów.

His mother greeted him with tears of joy. She had lost hope already for his return. Jan, mindful of his father's injunction, took up the function of head of the family given over to him in September 1939.

"I began to bring together the scattered members of the family and reestablish our home. Everything had to be started again from zero," he sighs.

The entire family returned again to Opinogóra. Their home was now occupied by others, this time Poles. For four years they managed to stay together in one rented room. Jan got work at the local administrative center in Opinogóra and with the modest salary of a tax official he was able for a short time to support six people. The miserly wages did not suffice for long and his siblings had to disperse.

After work in the administrative center, Jan, a tax-official, would travel every day by bike to evening school in Ciechanów. Somehow he finished secondary school studies. It was only after many more years that he completed, also part-time, studies in law and administration at Warsaw University.

The negative atmosphere forced upon those who had lost relatives in the Katyn massacre had its impact on him. He couldn't tell anyone that his father died at the hands of the Soviets even though everyone knew about it since he was living in the same place. But it was a public secret. The Communist Party apparatus which decided everything and the local authorities were quite ill-disposed toward Jan.

"At every occasion they bought up against me that I was the son of a navy-blue police officer, an enemy of the people. I couldn't get promoted, especially as I didn't want to join the Communist Party. I couldn't join the party which was suppressing Katyn and was servile to the Soviet Union where my father had been murdered."

He remained condemned to the life of a lower administrative official. After moving to Ciechanów he exhausted himself for forty years in the Finance Department of the Ciechanów administration. The longest time, thirty years, was spent as director of the finance department in the Presidium of the People's District Council. But then anonymous letters reached the secretary of the district branch of the party. Jan was able to hang on to one of them as a souvenir. It said that "Jan Korzybski is the son of a pre-war policeman who informed on communists."

"Later in some way I extricated myself from this predicament and my situation improved a bit. But in comparison to others it was always more difficult for me to attain higher professional positions," he complains.

He and his teacher wife Aurelia hoped their children could, along with having a better childhood, finish their higher studies. And they succeeded in doing so. Their son Adam became a mechanical engineer and lives in Piastów near Warsaw. Their daughter Ewa works in Warsaw as an advertising specialist. Things have gone well for both of them and they often visit, with three grandchildren, their parents in the home town of Ciechanów.

"And guess who became Ewa's husband? Jacek, Janulek's son. They met each other during some of our times together and fell in love. We, my friend and I, have grandchildren in common."

Janulek Dembiński had finished Warsaw's Institute of Technology and become an architectural engineer. He now lives in Warsaw.

Jan Korzybski searched endlessly for his father, through different embassies and the Red Cross. The pile of negative responses fills one whole folder. Jan remembered the gesture of one clerk of the Polish Red Cross in Warsaw.

"At the mention that my father had been a POW in Ostashkov, he merely waved his hand. That gesture said it all, even though he himself said not a word," says Jan.

When in 1990, he learned where his father had been done away with, he very much wanted to see the final path. He realized his dream five years later, during the official ceremony of the stone laying at the military cemetery in Miednoye. He has been too at the cloister in Ostashkov, today in ruins, where he saw at the entrance gate a memorial plaque.

"It was a terribly sad experience. Especially in Tver, in the death cell. They shot the POWs there in the back of the head as they were shoving them into the basement... Whereas in June Ostashkov, Lake Seliger and the island of Stołbnyj looked simply marvelous. How painful it is to identify that tragedy with the beauty of that place..."

He knows today that his father was transported out of the island on April 22, 1940. He is listed as number 5664. He has no separate grave but is buried as the others in a common grave. Kneeling at one of them, Jan lighted a votive candle he brought from Ciechanów and pounded a red and white pennon into the blood-soaked soil.

Ciechanów honors today the memory of company sergeant Aleksander Korzybski. His name, together with others, has been engraved on the granite slab at the Z. Krasiński Liceum. In 1990, at Jan's initiative, a Katyn slab of white marble was unveiled at the church of St. Tekla in Ciechanów. On it are the names of the 29 citizens of Ciechanów who died in the three Soviet camps. There also are three symbolic urns holding earth from the cemeteries of Katyn Forest, Kharkov and Miednoye.

The first born son of the last, pre-war commander at Ciechanów is now active in social affairs. He was one of the chief founders of the Friends of Ciechanów Association. Registered in 1957, it belongs today to the group of the oldest regional associations in Mazowsze. This association today renders great services to the town and region. The most important places in Ciechanów have been memorialized in plaques and obelisks. At the association's initiative two important museums have arisen in Ciechanów, the Romanticism Museum and the Positivism Museum.

"Today the castle is in dire need of money because it is falling apart more and more," Jan frets. And so he continues to work with the association.

He has also been an active member of the Polish Tourist Association and of the World Alliance of Home Army Soldiers. He has written many published articles about the region. For many years he has also been interested in photography, has won prizes in contexts and had an exhibition of his work. He has today a rich collection of black and white photographs. Some of them are entirely unique inasmuch as they preserve places and objects which no longer exist. Too he loves to go fishing and was even the head of a fishing group. He has been active also in other social and cultural initiatives, among which feature other monuments erected in Ciechanów and Opinogóra: for Zygmunt Krasiński, for Struggle, Martyrdom and Victory, for Maria Konopnicka, and for the town's patron St. Peter...

In the town people say of him, that "he's everywhere where something is happening. Most often as treasurer or secretary, always reliable and hardworking."

The people of Ciechanów appreciate Jan Korzybski's work on behalf of the region. They have honored him with the most important decorations. In 1992, he was named the Ciechanów Man of the Year. Even so this son of the pre-war commander has remained a very modest man.

"The most beautiful period of my life was my experience in Opinogóra, at the side of my father," he sighs with a tear in his eye. "And even though time goes on, I will never forget his depth of heart, his care for us and his love for Poland. I have to go again, if only one more time, to the cemetery in Miednoye."

9

"WHEN TAPE SEALS OUR LIPS"

Warsaw, Poland, February 2002

Already as a small girl, I composed my first short poems. I used to tell fairy tales too to my younger brother. The beautiful world of fairy tales, full of good sorceresses, helped us children orphaned of a father to survive the menace of World War II and the German occupation.

As I got older I wrote more. I remember a poem about the forest which I composed in fourth grade. My teacher noticed my literary inclinations and would assign me more difficult work, on more interesting themes, completely different from the rest of the class, thanks to which I was all the more able to develop.

I had my official debut in 1961 in the *Young Writers Almanac* (*Almanach młodych*), when Artur Międzyrzecki took notice of my poems. My first small book of poems, *From the circle* (*Z kręgu*) came out eight years later by which time I had already received my diploma in Polish philology from Warsaw University. I have so far published ten collections of poems. Many of my poems have been translated into various other languages: English, German, French, Italian, Greek, Spanish, Japanese, Albanian, Russian, Bulgarian, and even Serbocroatian.

Only one of my poems has been published anonymously and was circulated around the country without attribution. I wrote it in 1968 and it is entitled "To the memory of my father."

> He whose name is not mentioned
> dies twice
> He whose memory is soiled with oblivion
> dies shamed

when the source is quenched and does not replenish the river
the riverbed goes dry
how to kiss away blood from the thorn
and recast suffering into a monument
engrave in conscience hands tied by a wire
how, father, to re-call you
when tape seals our lips
One can count only on the kindness of history and
Time which goes round and round

That poem found its place ultimately in the anthology of poems about Katyn, *Cry at Dawn* (*Krzyk o świcie*). I prepared the volume together with Stefan Melak and it appeared in 1992 as a publication of Queen of Apostles Publishers. The anthology includes almost sixty works, of different styles and artistic merit. The authors, numbering forty-eight, are all very different. They include Polish officers, prisoners of Kozelsk, Starobelsk and Ostashkov, as well as children orphaned by the Katyn massacre. All the poems in the anthology give expression to an acute pain and agony, grievance at the violation of human and divine laws, and, bearing witness to the truth, expose the lies of the Russian crime. It is poetry which best of all responds to the terror that occurred in the Katyn Forest. The cry of those who were murdered is given in these poems a voice which will not be silenced even after many years. A cry always resounds with an echo.

It was our intention to speak to this but, above all, to render homage to those who died a martyr's death. It was the first and only such collection of poems in Poland. The poems from it were later included in the anthology *Katyn in Literature* (*Katyn w literaturze*), which was prepared in the United States by Professor Jerzy Krzyżanowski. A second poem of mine, "They rose up again," was included in both publications:

Complaints striking the chord-strings of the trees
with the echo of a drill tearing roots
the whispers of children's and widows' prayers
pleas
for forgiveness
thoughts of vengeance
and complaints in chorus pierced heaven
until pity raised its hand
they stood in ranks rose up again
from the earth as if from a book
Word had become flesh.

This poem was written in 1991. I was then at last able to sign my name beneath it without fear, to speak openly of Katyn, without tape over my lips. That tape has pained me throughout my whole life. When I would write a biographical note, I always tried to include the place of my father's death, but I would always hear: Cross it out! Arbitrarily cross it out! That's what happened when I was applying to the university, that's what happened when I wanted to publish my first book...

I don't even remember my father's face... I couldn't because when he went off to the war, I was not quite two years old. And my brother, Wojtek, was even younger.

But Mom told us a lot about Dad, always using only superlatives. It was from Mom that I know that when he would set out each morning for work, he would always leave a piece of candy in my small cape. He was a psychologist and a pedagogue and worked at Warsaw's Institute for the Deaf and Blind. As a student of Górski Liceum in Warsaw, and then in college, he used to write poems and so had the sensibilities of a poet... Tall, handsome, dark-haired with beautiful eyes and a black moustache, he was for us a legend, something like an idol.

He left for the war from Stara Wieś near Warsaw. Our parents used to go there during summer holidays. The pine by the train station in Stara Wieś beneath which they said good-bye still stands. It seems that the leave-taking lasted a long time. Dad would move away, say good-bye and then come back again...

"Don't come again, Kaziu, it's not good...." my Mom said.

But he came back home and looked a long time at his sleeping children... It was difficult for him to part from us.

After the war Mom didn't go any more to Stara Wieś. Once, but only once, she took me with her and showed me the pine...

My dad, Kazimierz Roman Grabowski, was thirty-eight when the war broke out in 1939. Mom, Stanisława, was beautiful, also well-educated, a math teacher by profession. Much younger than he, she was then twenty-nine. A great love united my parents, but they had managed to be with each other hardly six years...

My father was called up as a second lieutenant to Colonel Sosabowski's 21st Infantry Regiment. During the September campaign, he fought in defense of Warsaw and Siedlce, and then ended up in the monastery made into a POW camp at Kozelsk in the Soviet Union...

Mom with her two tiny children, her own mother and father remained in Warsaw. Later they took lodgings in a four-room apartment in the Old Town.

I don't remember much from the years of occupation in Warsaw. I do remember better the Warsaw Uprising which found us in the Old Town. The air raids and the bombing seared themselves into my memory and since then I experience a terrible reaction to loud claps of noise. The headquarters of the Home Army and the People's Army were not far from where we lived, and so the air raids were constant and the bombs would fall every half-hour.

I can still see people huddling up against the walls... And how the partisans fashioned underground passageways among the buildings for communication. Food supplies were lacking, and water, and all we had to eat was cooked grains. Sure, we did have a pump in the courtyard but it was hard to get out to it for water. The time of the uprising was for me loud noises, fire, hiding in the basement...

Of the four rooms occupied by my family, three of them were in ruins. I remember how my brother got sick one day from scarlet fever (my grandfather was no longer living, he had died in 1943). The doctor ordered Wojtek not to go to the basement and so during one of the bombardments Mom stayed with him and my grandmother in one of the still habitable rooms. My brother was lying on the couch. Suddenly it got dark in the basement where I was with other people from the tenement. The acetylene lamps went out and pieces of rubble fell in. And then at that moment something simply incredible happened! After a bomb had struck, a part of the ceiling collapsed, yet that part precisely above the couch where my grandmother, mother and brother lay remained intact. The people had already begun to cry out that Mrs. Grabowska and my mother and her son had died... But I huddled against the wall and prayed to my dad... We didn't know then that he was no longer alive. He had always been with us, in our hearts, conversation, expectations...

A neighbor put her arms around me then and said:

"Don't be afraid, I'll take care of you..."

"But my Mom is alive. She's alive!" I insisted to her.

"Don't be afraid, you will be like my own daughter..." she said, trying to comfort me and stroking my hair.

After a short time, all three of them fell on their knees. Nothing had happened to them, they were only in terrible shock. We, all of us in the basement, were saved by a miracle! Because the bomb had exploded over the basement without penetrating the beamed ceiling. Was it perhaps thanks to that prayer of a child?

One day I couldn't stand the constant sitting in the basement any more and when it fell quiet I ran out. For a moment, as a child would do. At that instant a projectile fell into the courtyard. A five-year-old child was running with me at the time and it took off her hand right before my eyes. I was only slightly wounded by a fragment to the head.

I remember too, how they hurried us along, just before the end of the uprising, to Warsaw's West Station. Everything around us was on fire. At Starówka there was nothing left but smoldering ruins and flames. I won't forget the Zygmunt Monument, how the toppled king lay with his beard pointed up...

It was a miracle that they didn't take us then to Auschwitz. A German nurse perhaps had pity on us small children and directed us to a different transport.

The train into which they had packed us stopped somewhere around Radomsko. Farmers gathered us up from there into their wagons and transported us to various villages. There wasn't anything to eat. My grandmother knew her mushrooms and since it was September she went to the woods to gather some. At that time too I would compose small jingles and make up fairy tales for the village children. They would come to our village to listen to me. And they would bring eggs, sometimes a lump of butter, or some local cheese...

Later Mom began to teach in the villages. After two years we returned but no longer to Warsaw, only somewhere near Pruszków. Before 1939, Mom had taught mathematics in those little towns outside of Warsaw and then had conducted some clandestine classes there during the occupation. At first we had nowhere to go but were taken from one place to another. I remember that for one year we lived in a classroom.

We received only one letter from my father. It was written on November 26, 1939 in Kozelsk and reached us a few weeks later. Mom read it to us several times over. Dad wrote that he was alive and well, that he was thinking a lot about us, fearful for us and homesick. He told us that he loved us and that he kissed mother's feet... He begged us not to worry about him because the time would come when we would be together again...

That letter kept us company in the most difficult times. It filled us with the belief that our father was alive. Even in the spring of 1943, when the Germans printed lists after the exhumation of Polish officers murdered in the Katyn Forest massacre by the NKVD, we didn't completely believe in his death. There were three Grabowskis on their lists, and two of them with the first name Kazimierz, but we counted on there being still some mistake... That letter stayed in Mom's pocket through the Warsaw Uprising and the subsequent expulsion.

I look with indescribable emotion at that already badly yellowed card which my father's hand had touched. A great longing and concern breaks through from the words of his father for the loving young wife and two tiny children he had left behind. Even so for half a century I was not allowed to have this card with his final words in my possession. There is a whole history connected with it, another miracle...

In 1948 my Mom began to request her husband's pension benefits. She had been told that of course she was entitled to them but that she had to present documentation. In the municipal court in Leszno she submitted then what she was able to, among which were for her treasured remembrances: her husband's Katyn letter saved in the uprising and his picture. They promised to return them to her in a week. A week later they told her to return for them in two weeks, then in a month, and finally advised her that she "should shut her mouth up tight." Dunning letters didn't help, nor other correspondence, nor the intervention of a lawyer. And so the only remaining relics of her husband disappeared...

She never received benefits from her husband's pension. Instead she was sent a document saying that her husband had died a natural death on May 9, 1946, that there was a five year break in his work record and thus no benefits were due. I remember my mother's anger and resentment when she found out. I can still see her anger when she saw the mendacious document.

Those experiences and repressions were the cause of Mom's constant fear. She ceased speaking out loud about her husband's Katyn past. She understood that the word Katyn was a stigma, that it awakened panic, and that it meant the cancellation of opportunity in the lives of her children. My brother and I had to swear to her that we too would keep our silence and not ever bring up any mention of Katyn. Mom placed tape not only over her mouth but over the mouths of my brother and me as well. From that time forward we lived not only in sorrow for our murdered father but also with the consciousness of a lie, with the feeling of being wronged, with shame and humiliation. And with the questions: For what? Why?

Mom didn't live to see the time when it was possible to speak openly and loudly about Katyn, without any tape over the mouth. She worked long and hard, and she taught my son as well. She never remarried and she loved my father her entire life. She died in 1983. Could she perhaps not have met her husband again then, forty-three years later, beneath that pine in Stara Wieś?

In April 1989, when people in Poland began to speak openly of the Katyn massacre, I went to the archives in the municipal court. With tears in my eyes, I began to beg the workers there to try to find the documents taken from my mother forty years earlier. I wanted to retrieve the Katyn letter and my father's picture; I yearned to know at least how he looked, what his handwriting was like... All the more so since Mom often told me that I was a lot like him, not only in physical characteristics but also in temperament.

The archivists pointed out to me three large shelves with file folders... They said that if I found my father's case number somewhere in the folders, then perhaps they would be successful in locating his records in the basement. I looked for a long time, and several people helped me. Until finally I found it. Kazimierz Roman Grabowski appeared on the final page of one of the folders and there too the number of his case. The women promised me that they would look for the records. On the second day the phone rang: "Please come, we have found the file..."

When, out of breath, with pounding heart and tears in my eyes, I had shortly taken in my trembling hands the file, partially molding, with the words "Criminal Case," which meant "destined to be burned," I could not call it anything other than another miracle in my life. Among other documents in the file,

I found my father's letter from Kozelsk and his now partially yellowed photograph... I saw it for the very first time and I had the impression that my father had suddenly returned to life, that he was next to me... I was now permitted to keep them as well as the message calling him to the army. I could even copy other documents.

The next miracle took place a year later when General Jaruzelski received from Gorbachev the lists of officers murdered in the Katyn massacre. It was written in Russian. The group of Katyn children from Warsaw who knew the language divided the records among them to translate. Then the lists were printed in "Rzeczpospolita."

I too got part of this list to translate. And what a strange twist of circumstances it was that my father's name appeared on my pages. It turned out that he had gone to his death in the first transport, April 2, which means he was shot on April 3. It affected me terribly...

But then one more miracle happened... I was fortunate to go with Andrzej Wajda's film crew for a few days to Kozelsk and Katyn Forest. Among us was a witness to the crime, Officer Cadet Wojtecki, who had escaped from the bolsheviks' hands. I learned then that my father had been imprisoned in one of the three, the largest, of the Orthodox churches of the Kozelsk monastery. I don't know on which tier his bunk was, but each individual there experienced his own kind of misery. Hosts of bedbugs falling from the black ceiling attacked those who were lying on the upper bunks of the fifth or sixth tiers, and lice mercilessly devoured those on the lower bunks. The outside latrine too was a torture. Three meters deep, it was fenced off from the users by only a flimsy pole. The pole would break often and drownings would occur. But those who were rescued by their friends had to stand in a long line to the only water pump in the camp... The trip had an enormous impact on me."

From Kozelsk we went to Katyn Forest. And there, during Holy Mass, I leaned against a pine tree on which there were bullet holes. I pondered whether my father too had leaned against it... Could he have stood beneath it and longed for us? It was in this way that my "Katyn Impressions" came to be dedicated to my father:

> What kind of thought
> as you knelt
> passed through your skull
> What image
> before your eyes
> when the cold barrel
> pressed on your neck
> And feelings?
> Anger
> powerlessness

sorrow
despair
in one second's flash
Were there no witnesses?
What of heaven?
keen and menacing
The trees rustled for a long time
to shout out the crime
A wounded sun
sets
in memory of
our DEPARTED

I visited Katyn Forest later once more, together with Polish government delegates, during the cemetery's inauguration in 2000.

I have felt all the time my father's guidance and protection as well as God's providence. As one who works with the pen, I have had a rich and creative life. Besides the Katyn anthology, I put out two anthologies of Polish Women Poets. Among other things, I received in 1996 in Italy the title of Professor of the Academy of Literature and Art "La Crisalide" and was granted the title of Great Lady of Literature. I am the author also of two theatrical pieces, *Wall (Mur)* and *Commandments (Przykazania)*. Both of them were given awards, but because of their anticommunist themes, they never emerged beyond Warsaw's House of Literature.

It's not easy being a poet. Poets are extremely sensitive and it's difficult for them to live when all around them there is so much vulgarity, coarseness and degradation. Maybe that's why I so willingly spend time creating things for children. I have published for the very young many things in poetry and prose, among others *Lullaby (Kołysanka)*, *The Adventure of a Droplet (Przygoda kropelki)*, *Before Sleep (Przed snem)*, *Christmas Eve (Wigilijny wieczór)*, *The Adventures of Doll Babi and Spider Koko (Przygody lalki Babi i pającyka Koko)*, *Seasons of the Year (Pory roku)*.

Writer sessions with little children give me a lot of joy. Surely it is something I have from my father who adored children, understood them and knew how to work together with even those whom fate had so terribly afflicted.

The first reader of my works for children was my son Mariusz. Today, though a physicist, he loves poetry and drama, even wrote the introduction and also did the selection of the poems for my latest collection, *Poems (Wiersze)*. The poem "Give me your hand" ("Podaj rękę") is, among others, one of the poems in the book. It contains biographical elements. I wrote it while thinking about my uncle, my father's half-brother, who was killed at the hands of SS in Auschwitz. To write that poem I deliberately went there in 1973. I felt very deeply the drama of those murdered and I lived myself their tragedy. I don't think that a visit in Auschwitz can leave anyone indifferent.

In the poem I included my own observations of two young people. They had come to Auschwitz on a school trip, and one of the girls was even singing carefreely at the beginning. However, when they realized what place this was, as they looked at each subsequent pavilion, the place of execution, I saw how the girl changed, became sad, felt a deeper and deeper fear as she began to hold her partner's hand convulsively...

> The gaping maws of shoes exhale feet
> in each shoe a coagulated warmth,
> mandibles bare their teeth, scream
> the corpse of a doll with one foot
> a small shoe she squeals wants milk
> an enormous wailing
> so great the walls shake burst
> their shaved heads lean down over us
> O give me your hand
> it's still warm Our hands still live
> That's good
> Let's go down to the very bottom of this hell...

I am perhaps the only Polish woman poet who lost her father in the Katyn massacre while continuing to write, appearing in the press, publishing books, and also advancing the work of her father. All that time I've had a swath of tape over my mouth and lived in perpetual fear, especially for my son. I always have had a child's feeling of being wronged by the murder of its father and unable to speak of the crime or the perpetrators... I have had to live with a wound in my memory, as is expressed in the poem "Wound of the Earth" ("Rana ziemi"):

> Wound of the earth
> wound of memory
> The sun rises
> it sets
> You have to live...

10

CUSTODIAN OF THE HOUSE
WITH THE TURRET

Vilno, Lithuania, February 2002

Halina Kalwajt is still afraid of talking about the Katyn Forest massacre
even though it is sixty-two years after the deed and we are sitting and talking together in her family home in Vilno, in the sovereign Republic of Lithuania.

The house is large and broad and it has a turret which causes it to stand
out from the rest of the neighborhood. It is located in the eastern section of
Vilno, an area known as the Vilno Colony (in Lithuanian Pavilnys), on a large
one-acre lot, among oaks and pines. The Wilejka River murmurs nearby and
all around are hills and forests. Before the war the Vilno elite built their villas here.

The house is almost one hundred years old. When Halina Kalwajt's
father purchased it in 1934, it was in a state of ruin. He succeeded, with care
and precision, in repairing the 13-foot-high interiors and also restoring the
turret. He moved in a year later with his whole family yet didn't enjoy this
home of his for very long since he was called up to the army in the spring of
1939. He would never again see his house with the turret.

It wasn't many years ago that Halina Kalwajt didn't even know the date
of her father's birth. She remembered from her childhood that he had celebrated his namesday in September, but in the *kresy* birthdays were not celebrated. She knew that Bronisław Hołub was a career officer in the Polish
Army, that he was a major nominated to the rank of lieutenant-colonel, that
he had fought with the bolsheviks in 1920, and that he never returned from
the war of 1939. All her life she wrote in documents: "My father died before
the war."

"No documents or any decorations survived him. Vilno changed hands many times. There were, successively, the Soviets, the Lithuanians, the Germans, and again the Soviets. As a result my mother, fearing for our safety, hid them somewhere or destroyed them. Then right afterward she died. So the documents about him, as well as the date of his birth disappeared forever," Halina Kalwajt explains in her soft *kresy* accent.

She moves about quite elegantly. She has kept also a beautiful shape and that strength of character one identifies with the *kresy* regions. Despite her seventy-two years of age, there's no trace of grey in her dark hair.

On her bookshelves she locates a volume entitled *Katyn: The Cemetery Book* (*Katyń. Księga cmentarna*) published in Warsaw in 2000, by the Council for the Preservation of the Memory of Struggle and Suffering. It was then, thanks to this publisher, that she learned the exact date of her father's birth. Among thousands of others, she found his short biography:

"Bronisław Hołub, son of Józef and Alina née Reutów, born November 23, 1890, in Lithuanian Mińsk. Soldier in the 1st Polish Corps in Russia. In 1920 he fought in the ranks of the 31st Infantry Regiment; wounded twice. Next in the 27th and 33rd Infantry Regiments. In the years 1931–1936 commander of the PKU in Włodzimierz Wołyński. In 1936 transferred to the retired list. Then the commander of the 11th Battalion in the Youth Work Corps. Awarded the order Virtuti Militari and other distinguished medals. Married, with two daughters, Jadwiga and Halina."

"Thanks to this book I learned also that my daughter Mira was born on the very same day and month as my father, only seventy years later. The recurrence of birthdates is a characteristic trait of our family." Despite the *kresy* accent, Halina Kalwajt speaks beautiful, classical Polish.

Her daughter, Mira, joins our conversation. Thin, tall, pretty, her Polish is even more lilting. Before she discovered the concurrence of dates, she felt she had been wronged.

"Because I was the only one like that in the family! And now I think how glad my grandfather would have been had I been born on his date of birth! I would have known him. Seventy years difference isn't so much... But it wasn't given to me...." Born exactly on November 23, 1960, Mira's eyes fill up with tears.

Halina Kalwajt knows very little about the ancestors on her father's side. Only that the family of the Hołub's was of the nobility, had large estates in an area that is now part of Belarus. All those estates are gone, as are her father's six brothers who died during the time of Soviet rule. Her father's only sister, Zofia Hołub Stankiewicz, had settled in Vilno. And following her, in 1934, Bronisław Hołub came to the Vilno area with his wife Maria and two daughters, Jadzia and Halinka.

"Dad, because of his officer status, often changed his place of residence."

Halina Kalwajt explains that that is the reason she was born in Warsaw in 1930.

Bronisław Hołub met his future wife during his military service, in the course of a stay in Żuromin. Maria Gródek was a teacher there and her father had a mill. The marriage took place in the church in Żuromin in 1925.

"Our family on our mother's side still lives in that Mazovian town. The musician and vocalist Ryszard Rynkowski comes from Żuromin and belongs to that family," smiles Halina.

Then Bronisław Hołub, due to a recurring leg contusion which he had contracted during his service in the Legion, had to terminate his active service early. In 1934 he decided to settle in his beloved Vilno and see to his family and garden.

"He was a good, cheerful person and he loved to raise flowers," remembers his youngest daughter Halina. "Even though there was an orderly and servant in the house, Dad loved to keep busy and did much of the work himself."

He loved his uniform. Even when retired he would often put it on, especially when he went out. In the few photographs preserved by his daughter, he looks quite distinguished, wearing his decorations with pride.

"Zosia Stankiewicz later lived with her husband in our house. They bought for themselves a piece of property not far away and had plans to build their own villa. But the war interrupted everything," Halina Kalwajt explains during our "picture session."

She doesn't remember whether her father bid farewell to them in any special way. No one imagined that Major Hołub, called once again to active service, would not ever return. There was no war in the spring of 1939 though some had already been mentioning its possibility.

"In December 1939 we received from Dad his only letter," Halina Kalwajt remembers. "He wrote from Kozelsk. The letter was optimistic. Dad assured us that we would see each other shortly."

While waiting for the major, the family supported itself by selling or bartering family reserves or valuables for food. Jadwiga and Halina studied at clandestine classes. A lot of acquaintances from Vilno came to the house with the turret where there was some protection from the bombing and the frequent changing of military occupiers. "Somehow we lived through it all, though it is hard to believe today," sighs Halina Kalwajt.

In April 1943, the Germans began to print lists of Polish officers, prisoners in Kozelsk, murdered in Katyn Forest. The Germans announced to the world that the NKVD was responsible for the murders. Though Major Bronisław Hołub was not on the lists, his wife Maria had a breakdown. She died on April 28, 1943.

"Mom went into hiding, often in terrible circumstances. She feared that because she was the wife of a Polish officer she and we would be sent to Siberia. She got a cold, then pneumonia. She didn't have any requisite medicine..."

Maria Hołub is at rest in the Rossi cemetery in Vilno. It is one of the largest and most beautiful of Polish cemeteries. Maria Hołub is buried without her husband, but not far from Marshal Piłsudski's heart.

The time of occupation in Vilno became even more tragic and incomprehensible for the inhabitants. The teenage Halina Kalwajt did not leave her house with the turret. Within it she experienced all the drama of family, city, and region.

The Vilno section of the Home Army under the leadership of General "Wilk" (Aleksander Krzyżanowski) was one of the most energetic in the Polish Republic. From the end of 1943 on, Poles effectively destroyed the German terror apparatus. The Germans, in answer to the Polish resistance movement, formed a special corps under the leadership of General Povilas Plechavicius, made up of Lithuanian volunteers (the so-called LVR). This led to many skirmishes between the Home Army and the LVR. The Lithuanians also murdered people suspected of cooperation with the Polish underground. The final blow to Plechavicius' corps was given by the partisans on May 13, 1944 near Murowana Oszmianka.

The Home Army had by no means a minor role in the liberation of Vilno on July 10, 1944. The Poles took Góra Zamkowa. Three days later the red and white flag flew for the last time on the Giedymin Tower as it was quickly taken down by the Soviets. After the joint victory over the Germans, the Russians didn't permit any kinds of manifestation of the Polishness of the city. The situation was exceptionally complex inasmuch as the Soviets were on the one hand allies in the fight with the Hitlerites, and on the other enemies who had several times occupied Polish Vilno. Despite a lack of trust, General "Wilk," together with the leadership of the Home Army, decided to form an independent detachment of the Polish Army alongside the Red Army. The Soviets initially accepted this idea with enthusiasm. But on July 17, they deceitfully arrested General "Wilk," the majority of the officer cadre, and a large part of the Home Army soldiers.

"We were terribly disoriented by these events," remembers Halina Kalwajt.

The arrests made the Poles realize however that Vilno was now under Soviet occupation. Massive round-ups of Poles, especially those connected to the Home Army and their families, had already begun in July 1944.

"They imprisoned and sent to Siberia a great many boys from Vilno Colony together with their families," remembers Halina Kalwajt.

It all became clear in February 1945 after the conference at Yalta. The Western powers had given the *kresy* to the Soviet Union.

The Yalta agreement and the repression by the NKVD produced in the Vilno area a massive yearning to leave for Poland. The "repatriation," actually "deportation," began in the spring of 1945 and ended in 1947. It was repeated again in the years 1955–57. However, not all of those 380,000 Poles seeking to leave did leave. 170,000 left the areas around Vilno, with about 100,000 leaving the city itself. Out of fear of repression almost the entire Polish educated class departed. Lithuanians and Russians poured into those places left vacant by the deported Poles and the Jews murdered by the SS (in 1939, in Vilno, out of a population of 200,000, there were 55,000 Jews, and less than two percent Lithuanians and three percent other nationalities).

Jadwiga Hołub was among the first repatriated. She left for Żuromin, to her mother's family.

"But I remained here under the care of Aunt Zosia Stankiewicz." Halina notes that she was four years younger than Jadwiga. "Aunt Zosia had been taking care of me and I would have felt bad in leaving her. Had my aunt decided on leaving, I would surely have left this house, and even traveled to her husband's in England. But my aunt believed, almost like everyone else here, that a new war would break out. We held on for a long time in hopes that the Allies wouldn't leave us this way, with strange borders, under Soviet occupation. We miscalculated."

Zofia Stankiewicz was staying to wait for her brother. She would say: "When Bronek returns, would he find no one here in the house?" For this, she sacrificed the opportunity of being reunited with her husband, one of Gen. Anders' soldiers. He didn't want to return from the West because he had experienced so much torture in Soviet camps that he feared even going to Poland. He is buried in London whereas his wife, beautiful Aunt Zosia, is buried in the Vilno Colony, in the very same cemetery where Home Army soldiers have been buried.

But nothing was ever heard of Major Bronisław Hołub.

In 1946 the house with the turret in Vilno Colony was nationalized. It became entirely peopled with compulsory tenants. A different family was housed in each room. Halina Kalwajt and her aunt were put in the smallest one, without water, kitchen or bath.

Halina attended school under conditions of intimidation, overcrowding and want... She had hoped that she might reach the same level of education as her parents. She didn't attain the level of her mother, who before the war had completed the teacher's program, or that of her father, a graduate of the School of Technology in Odessa. She had to content herself with a diploma of the Polish *gimnazjum* in Vilno.

In 1958 she married Ryszard Kajwalt, a friend from the *gimnazjum*. He advocated leaving in the second wave of "repatriation," because he too had his whole family in Poland.

"But we continued to wait with Aunt Stankiewicz for my father's return. It was clear that a departure to Poland was not an option for me," she repeats, at peace with her fate.

Two daughters were born of this marriage, Jadwiga and Mirosława. Ryszard Kalwajt took a job in a factory and was a guild leader. She worked her entire life as an accountant.

She got her house back in the sixties, thanks to Jadwiga. Her sister had come during that time to Vilno for the first time, from Warsaw, where she lived with her lawyer husband. It was he who suggested that the house had been nationalized illegally. He calculated that the house and surroundings occupied less than 220 square meters and that the Soviet authorities had a legal right to nationalize only homes larger than that. He hired a lawyer and proved in the Vilno courts that the size had been reckoned inaccurately.

"The court gave us our house back," sighs Halina Kalwajt. "But for many years we were unable to get rid of the occupants! The last one left us only in 1988."

It was hard for the Kalwajts then to believe that no one was eavesdropping anymore on them through the wall, that no one was making a mess anymore around the house. It was a great joy!

Thanks to her sister from Poland Halina Kalwajt learned that her father had been killed in the Katyn Forest massacre. Returning from a visit to her Uncle Stankiewicz in England, Jadwiga had smuggled across the border a book with lists of those lost. This was in the sixties, a quarter of a century after the crime.

"My aunt was no longer living then and I had to work through the sorrow by myself." It is still hard for Halina Kalwajt to speak about it. For sixty years in Soviet Lithuania, the simple mention of the word Katyn was cause enough to disappear from the face of the earth. Even today the crime is treated as a social secret. After years of silence, Katyn means nothing to the majority of Lithuanians; there is no knowledge at all about it.

The Kalwajt's went to Katyn Forest in 1981 during Brezhnev's regime. A professor from Warsaw whose acquaintance she had made encouraged her to do so. During a visit in the Vilno Colony he said that he himself had been there and he explained how to go.

The entire family went to Katyn Forest: Halina and Ryszard Kalwajt, their two daughters Mira and Jadwiga as well as the sister from Warsaw. They traveled together in the same car. Halina Kalwajt remembers how, at the road sign indicating "Katyn," she felt herself become weak. She thought that she couldn't go on, that she had to take get some medicine. Along the way they passed numerous monuments in praise of Soviet soldiers...

After traversing 375 miles and sleeping along the road near Smoleńsk, they reached the site of the crime. A vast area was encircled by a high, impenetrable, wooden fence, painted green. There was thick mud and puddles all around. Only one small door was open.

"We entered through it," she said with difficulty as she simultaneously referred to a hand-drawn map of the area. She had made it during that visit because the Russian signs indicated that it was an animal sanctuary. It was also forbidden to take pictures and to go off the marked path. They followed the path to a Soviet monument with a plaque, which said in Russian that in the autumn of 1941 Polish officers had died here at the hands of fascists. "At that moment a mushroom picker appeared. He continued to follow us around with his basket though it was not the season for mushrooms." She tries to relate everything calmly but it is hard for her to hide her emotions.

Her daughter Mira, the one who had been born on the same day and in the same month as her grandfather but seventy years later, decided to go back on her own into the area. She helps fill out, with her own difficult story, that of her mother:

"I felt the need to be for a moment alone with my grandfather, I and he, and to leave something personal with him. When we were already by the car I turned and ran back. And the mushroom picker followed after! I reached the monument first, took a silver ring from my finger and buried it in the earth. I was alone only for a short moment. The mushroom picker once again came close by and didn't take his eye off of me. I am sure that he later checked for what I had buried."

They went to Katyn Forest a few years later, during the time of Yuri Andropov. At the time Jadwiga's husband and her daughter had come to Vilno from Warsaw. They too wished to pay their respects to those who had been murdered, but in Katyn they found all the gates closed. They were able to take only a few black and white photos. Halina Kalwajt noted down on a small card the gist of the plaque at the gate. She still had the card. She wrote the gist of it in Polish, keeping its mistakes: "Here are buried captives, officers of the Polish Army, murdered in terrible circumstances by the German fascist occupiers in the fall of 1941."

Halina Kalwajt has been to Katyn Forest six times. Later with pilgrimages, and attending Mass at the site. After her last stay, the area had been cleaned up and put in order. It was possible to visit it though always under strict observation, without any chance of going off to the side. She saw the opening of the new cemetery in 2000 only on Polish television.

"Now we don't go there any more," she says hanging her head. "We are from a different country and now visas are needed to go to Russia. What would happen if she requested a visa to go to Katyn Forest? Certainly I wouldn't get it! And maybe I would be killed along the way... Officially no one from here goes to Katyn yet."

Seeing my surprise, the Kalwajt women add:

"It is possible to speak about Katyn today in Lithuania. But no one does. What for?"

There has never been place in the Vilno area for members of the Katyn Families. Everyone left after the war under the sanctions of "repatriation," or they were sent off into the depths of Russia. The only ones who remained were isolated individuals who had to hide assiduously the very fact of the existence of this tragedy. Even today there has not arisen even one Katyn Family Association in Lithuania, and no monument or plaque in Vilno commemorating that monstrous Soviet crime.

"We join ourselves to our grandfather by lighting votive candles in our church Christ the King. There is also soil there from different places where Poles suffered. We placed a handful of soil from Katyn Forest also at Rossi cemetery, at the grave of Grandmother Maria Hołub," says Jadwiga Szlachtowicz, the second daughter of Halina Kalwajt.

Both sisters, Jadwiga and Mira, are teachers. They work at the local Vilno Pavilnys Elementary School. Jadwiga's training is in Polish and music. Mira is a mathematician. Though they teach in Polish classes, they are bilingual. They had to pass the state exams for Lithuanian.

Jadwiga also leads a children's school song and dance group, "Strumyk." It has been in existence since 1989 and includes about one hundred children ranging in age from eight to sixteen.

"Our group has already given more than one hundred concerts in Vilno, in the Polish community in Lithuania, and in Poland," Jadwiga Szlachtowicz says with ardor as she shows me her colorful binder on "Strumyk." "The parents are the ones who help us the most. They are the ones who sew the beautiful regional costumes."

Both daughters have Polish husbands. Their children study in classes that use Polish and both sing and dance in "Strumyk." They also know the facts about Katyn. All belong to the Center for Polish Culture in Lithuania and are active in the Polish Schools.

"It is a bit easier now for Poles in Vilno, especially in the area of culture and politics, though as regards material things it isn't easy for anyone." They give as an example that at the last festival in the Center for Polish Culture in Lithuania 57 Polish groups from Lithuania participated. The majority of them came into being in the last ten years. "Now 'Mazowsze' and 'Śląsk' don't come to us anymore because we have our own groups," the Kalwajt women say gladly.

Besides, the Kalwajt family often travels to Poland.

"Neither official documents inviting us nor visas are needed now; we can just get up and go to Poland to any city. From Vilno to Warsaw it's 300 miles and to the Polish border not quite 125 miles," they say.

Today Halina Kalwajt lives in the house with the turret with her two daughters and their families. She is happy that the house now is of benefit to the family as her father had hoped.

The house is holding up, though it is now a bit crowded and the high interiors again need renovation. The oak trees around the building have grown tall, and every year there are more and more acorns. The garden looks much like it used to. Halina Kalwajt, now older, loves to take care of it. She especially loves the flowers, much the way her father, Major Hołub, did. And the air from the forests, hills and valleys around Vilno is always pure and healthy.

Despite the change of borders and countries, the house with the turret has preserved its Polish character. There are still many family pieces of furniture in it as well as other pre-war objects. A self-portrait of one of Major Hołub's brothers who was lost to the Soviets even hangs on the wall.

Halina Kalwajt's husband died ten years ago. Her sister Jadwiga from Poland is no longer living either.

"This is where the graves of my family are, these are my roots," she repeats. "And here stands the house in which I have lived through so many tragedies and so much joy."

She alone has survived it all. She watches over the family hearth with its turret like its custodian.

The house in the Vilno Colony has become a center of Polishness. Halina Kalwajt has been retired for seventeen years, looking after not only her own family but friends as well. She draws here colleagues from school, organizes gatherings of graduates of the Polish *gimnazjum* in Vilno. Not long ago they celebrated their fiftieth reunion.

"My contemporaries now live in many different countries, but for all of them the easiest place to gather together is in Vilno," Halina Kalwajt says, both in joy and wonder.

Every July she also welcomes participants walking in pilgrimages from Suwałki to the shrine at the Narrow Gate. Vilno Colony is their last stop on the way. "Usually twenty or more pilgrims stop over in our home. We even have regular repeat guests!" she smiles.

"They are drawn here in their later years. They want to see, to remember the places where their youth, or that of their relatives, was spent."

Occasionally Poles from Poland visit Vilno and Lithuania. Vilno needs more and more guides to show the arrivals from Poland the common, six-hundred-year history of Poland and Lithuania, to show them the historical buildings and the culture of the Polish *kresy*. Mira and Jadwiga work likewise as guides in the rich cultural heritage of Vilno. They are in love with their city and the surrounding areas.

"There are many like us here," argue Halina Kulwajt's daughters. "We could live and work in Poland but we have chosen Vilno."

Halina Kalwajt, their mother, custodian of the house with the turret, explains further calmly and with her own distinctive refinement:

"Here each of us has a duty to perform. The Polish intelligentsia is slowly being reborn. Here Polishness will not die."

Opposite top: Entrance to the Kharkov cemetery, Kharkov, Ukraine (previously USSR), 2002. Courtesy of Kazimiera and Janusz Lange, Katyn Family Łódź, Poland. *Opposite bottom:* General view of the Kharkov cemetery, 2002. Courtesy of Kazimiera and Janusz Lange, Katyn Family Łódź, Poland.

11

WITNESS TO MORE THAN ONE CRIME

Vilno, Lithuania, March 2002

I met with Józef Wasilewski first at his sister-in-law's, in one of Vilno's tenement buildings through which the Soviet era still makes its presence felt. Ugly buildings, huge grey masses. The staircases have foul odors, the plaster and tiles are falling, the dilapidated banisters are terrifying. We go upstairs on the muddy, cramped elevator to the top floor. Józef Wasilewski and his wife Freda, are bringing his sister-in-law some goat meat as well as some "harvestings" from their small garden plot. They've come to Vilno from the village of Rakańce (in Lithuanian Rakonis), fifteen miles from the city.

"I'm living now in a small village though I am city-born from Vilno," is how he begins his narrative. In Polish, but in the manner of one born in the *kresy* around Vilno, mixing in Russicisms and with a strong, eastern lilt to his words. His wife Freda and her sister have withdrawn to another room. He shuts the door completely after them and we converse alone. The apartment is a typical one, with shiny furniture, papered walls, on this tenth floor.

Józef Wasilewski amazes me not only by his upbeat mood but also by his intelligence and superb memory. He is still relatively young, being sixty years old. Yet the "baggage" of wartime experiences dating from his childhood years, being orphaned early on, and his difficult life in the East have all left their stamp on him. Despite it all he is sturdily built and strong. At times he is coarse and rough-languaged, which resonates well with his quite expressive face, high forehead and already thinning grey curls.

"My grandfather's name was Józef, my father's was Józef and so is mine. It's a family tradition of sorts. I didn't want to depart from it and so I gave the same name to my son," he laughs loudly and whole heartedly, with shining gold crowns on his teeth.

Born in Vilno on August 19, 1938, he doesn't really remember his father who went off to war a year later. Józef Wasilewski senior never had the chance to enjoy Józef Wasilewski junior.

The son often reaches for the only surviving letter from his father which he brought with him here to his sister-in-law's. Second Lieutenant Józef Wasilewski wrote the letter on November 28, 1939, in Starobelsk. I read the quite legible words, written with an indelible pencil:

"My dearest Lilenka! I am sending you and our son the most heartfelt greetings. I am healthy and in general feeling fine. Write to me, my dearest, how you are both getting by, and any news from our relatives. Write to me only of family matters. How is my dearest son growing up? How many teeth does he have? Is he healthy? Watch over him, my dearest. Teach him to speak and you yourself be full of hope. How is Dad's health? Send me your picture, the one from the Benedictine church, in the white dress. Take care of your health, my love. Give a kiss to all and wait for me. Kiss my dearest little one. I kiss you. Ziutek."

"When other letters did not come, Mom began to look for my father through the Red Cross," he says. "I know that on March 18, 1940, she received an answer from Geneva that said: 'The addressee has departed the camp.'"

To the very end Helena Wasilewska refused to believe that her Ziutek had died. She searched for him to the day of her death. She always held on to the hope that he was alive. She would ask everywhere, read every newspaper announcement, even though the disappearance of the Polish officers was hush-hush in Soviet Lithuania, "a dangerous and deadly secret."

In fact, though he lives now in an independent Lithuania, Józef Wasilewski doesn't know that in 2000 a Polish military cemetery was opened in Kharkov. Nor is this son of a POW aware that prisoners from Starobelsk were buried there.

From family stories and documents Józef Wasilewski knows that his father came from the village of Wisztoka, in what is now Belarus. He has kept his father's certificate of birth on April 10, 1908, as well as his certificate of baptism.

"The Wasilewski family had been brought there in the 16th century from Poland to guard the eastern boundaries of the Republic. Today a whole swath of Wasilewski's live there." He laughs at how they have multiplied.

His father's family was not particularly wealthy. They had a farm. Only Józef, one of three brothers, wanted further education and so, after finishing secondary school and then military school in Kraków, he was sent to Vilno. He studied law at the University of Stefan Batory, and at the same time was a shooting instructor in the military group "Strzelec." He had to work to earn his own upkeep and then later that of his family.

He married Helena Rebkowska, called Lila, when he was twenty-five years old. Their first born son takes from his file the next document: the certificates of marriage at the church of Ss. James and Philip, from November 27, 1933. Helena was from the same village as her husband and was exactly three weeks older. She lived in Vilno in the house of Count Jeleński. She had two sisters, Mania and Lola. Their stepfather, Andrzej Śliżewski, was a mechanic at the Count's and was in charge of the private power plant. Because of this, he was entitled to living quarters on the property.

Helena completed the Czartoryski Gimnazjum for girls in Vilno, and then taught Polish language in a private French school. Her husband entered his final year of law studies in 1939. A son was born to them and their prospects for the future looked bright.

Second Lieutenant Józef Wasilewski did not return from the war. A reign of terror and persecution began in Lithuania, and the forced departure of the Vilno intelligentsia and landed gentry to Siberia. Particular repression was directed against the families of Polish officers.

"Mom, in order to escape people's notice, left Vilno in the spring of 1940 to her sister Lola's in Ponary, a beautiful, forested town, six miles northeast of Vilno."

Aunt Lola Sajewicz lived there with her husband, a retired officer, Jan Sajewicz. She was a teacher and he a musician in the military, first in the Czar's and then in the Polish Army. He played also in the opera. After his military service, he settled with his wife in Ponary. In 1933 they bought themselves a parcel of land and began to build a house.

"The Ponary hills and forests were my childhood!" Józef Wasilewski speaks with emotion, descriptively and with a lot of gestures. He stands up: " Imagine tall, slender, elegant pines growing freely on a wide sandy expanse and how they had created a dry, luminous forest. With short undergrowth. In the spring the forest was violet from the pasqueflower which grew so thick that there was nowhere to step. In the fall, it was also violet from the heather. There was a narrow-gauge railroad that made its way from Vilno to Ponary. Before the war there had been some work toward a swimming pool. Traces of the excavation remain in Ponary yet the inhabitants are still waiting for the pool." Still standing, he laughs boisterously as he finishes his description.

Ponary's beautiful hills have been both blessed and cursed.

"When we sought refuge in Ponary, it never entered my Mom's mind that we would be witness to one of the largest extermination sites in Lithuania and to such wrongs," Józef Wasilewski says seriously.

After the annexation of Lithuania, the Soviets began to build in the Ponary hills a fuel base for a planned airfield. They dug enormous holes and paved them with stone. The "caverns" were from forty-five to sixty feet in diameter and up to twenty-five feet deep. The entire area was enclosed with barbed wire.

"Aunt Lola's house, where we were living, stood barely two hundred yards from the nine-foot tall fence which was topped with crisscrossing barbed wire," he says. "There was also a train station not far away as well as one of three entrance gates."

A good access road to the "base" was needed. So the Soviets rounded up the inhabitants of Ponary for the road's construction. Mother and Janka, my aunt's sister, also worked there. They would haul stones for the pavers laying down the cobbles. The Soviets paid for the work with food coupons.

"It enabled us to survive. But the sandy, forest paths were changed into a road that led to the holes. Żukow himself was in charge of the work." Some images of those years have imbedded themselves in the boy's memory: noisy Soviet tanks, columns of marching soldiers with a red star on caps with their characteristic peak.

The Soviets didn't succeed in finishing the construction of the fuel depot. The Germans were already in Vilno on June 25, 1941. A number of German rifle companies had quickly overrun the "base." The bodies of the murdered Soviets and locals remain today in the Ponary forest.

The SS took advantage of the bolsheviks' work. They selected the "base" for the place of mass executions. In the course of three years, from 1941 to 1944, one hundred thousand people were murdered there, among whom were seventy thousand Jews transported from all over Lithuania, and even from France. Also soldiers from the Home Army, the intelligentsia from Vilno, Gypsies, Lithuanian communists.

"The Germans were cunning; they didn't do the killing themselves!" Józef stands up again. "A section of the Gestapo especially created for this purpose, the 'Ypatingas Burys,' were responsible for the transportation of victims to the place of execution, for the execution itself and too for the burial in the holes made by the Soviets. They called it the Ponary rifle detachment and it was made up of Lithuanian volunteers."

Many other incidents from that time remain fixed in his memory. He relates them now with grim humor.

"One day as they were hurrying their victims from the train station, the prisoners began to run off. They ran in all directions through the Ponary forest. Our neighbor was at that time gathering armfuls of wood in front of her house when shots rang out from those in pursuit and she fell dead. We in our house dropped right to the floor at my uncle's orders."

He still hears the cawing of black birds from that time. There were whole swarms of crows, ravens. They used to hover over the "base."

He recalled also that one day a "handsome officer in a black uniform" came up to Aunt Lola's house. Had a riding-whip by his leg. He gave them twenty-four hours to leave "so that not a living soul would remain there." The German officers supervising the executions wanted to take over the house.

"We changed our clothes into those of railway employees and moved to Mr. Ciesiul's house. His house was on the other side of the tracks, a half-mile or so from our house but still in Ponary." It was crowded there in our generous guest's house. Among the others hiding there were the journalist Kazimierz Sakowicz and his wife. He would write down a lot about the happenings in Ponary, then put the manuscripts into bottles, cork them and bury them in the forest in front of the house. Later his accounts from those days became priceless, and were used in books. Not all of his texts were found. He himself died nearby in murky circumstances just after liberation.

"Sakowicz liked to play with me. He made paper pigeons and other toys for me," recalls Wasilewski.

There wasn't the wherewithal to live. So Helena Wasilewska went to work for the Germans, to a military canteen. She received food coupons and as a result her son didn't experience excessive hunger. They moved out of Mr. Ciesiul's, got a small corner in the house where the food was prepared.

"The Germans there liked me a lot, gave me sugar-plums, chatted with me. I quickly learned German." Józef puts on his plastic glasses again and shows me a photograph of a small boy from that time: a pretty face, hair white as linen in bangs and dark eyebrows. They thought that I had painted them," he comments in a loud laugh.

In 1944 they returned with Aunt Lola's family to her house. They, like other inhabitants of Ponary, thought that they could at last breathe easily, but they became, like those Ponary pines, witnesses to subsequent tragedies.

First of all they lived though the criminal investigations of international commissions. Many witnesses were interrogated or questioned, proceedings were written down and documentary evidence of the massacres was prepared.

Later, in the years 1945–47, due to the repressive measures of the NKVD and the determinations at Yalta, thousands of inhabitants of the Vilno area left for Poland, most often to those territories taken from the Germans. They would board the trains at the railroad station near their house.

"On the way the 'repatriated people' would draw water from our well," recalls Wasilewski. They would form long lines, up to fifty yards, because the water tasted very good, was clear like spring water! They would take in so much, so very much that they would drain the well. It turned out that the pre-war divining rod was right; it had correctly indicated the place for the well! Today there's an artesian well there, providing all of Vilno with water."

In subsequent years (1948–1952) Ponary was declared a military town. They closed down the area; only long-standing inhabitants could stay. The "base" was closed off; pilots were stationed there. They flew fighter planes, often at night, and a lot of them got killed in crashes.

"The landing-lights for the fighter planes were used by the NKVD also for the deportations to Siberia," recalls Józef. "They would light up our railroad station when they loaded up people at night into the cattle cars. Once again we and the Ponary forest had to gaze upon a great wrong, hear the cries of despair. That was real tragedy! Who did they send into the depths of Russia? Everyone! Whoever was among the wiser, richer, larger farmers, or whoever was in the Home Army, whoever had held public office. The central authorities of the Soviet Union even sent down leaflets dictating how many more still had to be sent to Siberia. Those were the times. The horror of it!"

His vividly expressive face grows even more somber as he talks about this. He wipes his face with a strong, large hand. After pausing a moment, and breathing deeply he adds:

"My Mom and I lived though it all only because people in Ponary didn't know us. And no one informed on Mom that she was the wife of a Polish officer, a POW of the Soviets."

Aunt Mania, his mother's second sister, left for Poland as part of the repatriation. Her husband, Kazimierz Boguszewski, a chauffeur in the pre-war Polish police, had been deported. He returned in 1947, "a mindless lump, rife with lice."

"Mom and I too had planned to leave and even had our suitcases packed. But at the last minute Mom broke into sobbing. And we stayed. She loved her Vilno and Ponary too much."

Then Józef asks me openheartedly, in his lilting accent: "Do you have any desire to see Ponary? I can take you. Today the area is now part of Vilno..."

The next day we're off. He drives up to the Dom Polski where I am staying, punctually at nine in the morning, together with his seventy-year-old wife Freda. We go in their old, dilapidated car.

"This Soviet machine is already twenty-four years old. I really used to look after it, and worried over every scratch. Now I leave it alone and it keeps on going strong." Józef Wasilewski tells me to put on the seatbelt. He likes history and as he drives his Niwa tells interesting things about Ponary's past.

Ponary Mountain was the place of many battles, meetings, executions. It was in the forest that the Vilno philomats and philarets, including Mickiewicz, Zan, Czeczot and others would meet. The insurgents battled the Russians there, Piłsudski was there with his partisans, and Dzierżyński with his.

We leave our car on the hill. Three roads spread out from there: to Kowno, Grodno and Troki. A chilly, February wind is blowing but there isn't much snow.

On the hill there is still a former inn, today redone into peasants' apartments. On the other side there is a historic but neglected Polish church from the XVII century.

"In July 1944 a bomb fell on the church," he says. "It fell right on the gothic tower but that was all that collapsed. The bomb came to rest on the canopy and didn't explode. It stayed there, whole, until a Polish soldier from

Vilno disarmed it. The people proclaimed it a miracle. However the bolsheviks later closed the church, as they did most of the sanctuaries and cloisters in Vilno, for decades. Only recently has it been restored and partially opened for use."

A small cemetery adjoins the church; the names on the tombstones are almost all Polish. "Mostly Poles lived in Ponary," explains Wasilewski.

We continue on around, going to the other side of the Ponary hills. The Niwa works hard. His wife Freda sits in back, quiet, hardly ever joins in. We drive over the tracks, past the freight station and a few factories.

Summer villas used to stand here among the slender pines. Of wood, they were covered primarily with thatch. Today these villas have aged, fallen apart, or had their thatched roofs replaced with asbestic tile. Among the trees there are a few modern homes, not especially attractive. Many ugly, tin garages disfigure the forest.

"I haven't been here for some time," murmurs Wasilewski. "And here the forest is 'trashed,' overgrown with shrubs. There are only a few pines because they have been pulled down helter-skelter. Everything has changed."

Melancholy takes hold of him: "There's less and less to bring a person here for. All the houses are strange, the people unknown."

But Aunt Lola's yellow house, where he grew up, hasn't changed in shape. Only a veranda has been added on the southern side.

"The two pines in which I used to do exercises are still standing. Oh, even some tree scars are still there on the trunks." He points out too one of the windows where his room was.

Aunt Lola's house no longer belongs to anyone in the family. Not long ago the son of her deceased daughter Janka sold it. And Aunt Lola had died in 1978, two years after her husband Jan, the military musician.

"And over there, on the other side of the railroad, where the pines are, was Mr. Ciesiul's house. That's where we hid. And that's where the SS man shot our neighbor during the flight of prisoners!" he says as he tries to show as much as possible in his Ponary.

We go on to the mausoleum. Wasilewski points out where the barbed wire was, the railroad station, the gate, along which the prisoners would be hurried from the station and how they scattered trying to escape.

A number of monuments commemorate the place of execution. On the main one, from the Soviet years, the writing in Lithuanian and Russian informs that from July 1941 to July 1944 the Germans shot here more than 100,000 Soviet citizens. In order to conceal traces of the crime, in December 1943 they began to incinerate earlier buried bodies. Of these 70,000 were Jews.

New monuments have been added to the old one. These have been placed by Jews, Poles, Lithuanians... Lists of names... How many Poles were killed? It's hard to know, but somewhere in the neighborhood of 20,000 of the intelligentsia, *gimnazjum* graduates, priests, Home Army soldiers, hostages...

Józef Wasilewski now offers some precise details of one of the greatest crimes committed in Lithuania.

"Lithuanians, under the direction of the Germans, would kill two, three thousand people every day. One person had to execute about one hundred. With a shot from the rifle, in the back of the head. They would lay the bodies in the holes and sprinkle earth over them. Starting in 1943, because they wanted to obliterate traces of the crime, the Germans forced eighty-two young Jews to dig up the buried bodies and incinerate them. Some of them managed to escape and to expose the truth."

They didn't succeed in burning up all the victims. Many lie under the beautiful pines, among the gulleys and ridges "in the holes dug out earlier by the Soviets for the fuel tanks. Or they are all scattered, throughout the forest, leveled by bulldozers..."

The pine forest gives off a soft hush, a pleasant odor, and one can hear the first birds of the coming spring as the sun trickles through the branches.

"Who would have foreseen that in such a beautiful place a fuel base would be put? And then here to murder people?" Wasilewski constantly poses this same question. Though it was so long ago as a child that he had imbibed the atmosphere of this crime, he has never been able to become accustomed to it.

He adds: "They would kill only in the daytime and not every day. There would be quiet for a number of days. They would bring the victims at night."

He recalls: "After the war I would often return this way from school, from Vilno, on foot to Ponary, sometimes at night. More than once with my heart in my throat. But I would ask myself: "what can the dead do to me? It's rather the living who are the most dangerous..."

And he thinks out loud, with his *kresy* accent:

"You know, I would often ask myself why after the war an international commission did not investigate, as they did here, where the several thousand Polish officers disappeared to. Did I have to find out about it only in the last few years?"

Since the war Ponary is no longer a summer settlement. It still awakens fear. The people from Vilno ceased coming here for Sunday walks. The pines are less slender, the underbrush is overgrown, not many violet pasqueflowers or heather remain.

"One day Mom and I went mushroom picking. I saw a nice boletus and I was just about to put it into my basket when I saw the bones of someone dead. We ran out of there shouting!" Ponary—the beautiful place of his exceptionally terrifying childhood—is now a large cemetery. A place of crime and human wrong.

After the liberation, Helena Wasilewska took a position at the Ponary

school. In the beginning of Soviet Lithuania there were no Russian books
and so they studied from Polish texts.

"We still sang songs in honor of Piłsudski." Józef quotes a few from
memory. He started going to school in September 1944, in the second grade.
"I finished four classes in Polish, then the Polish schools were closed."

He then had to continue his further schooling in Russian. It was difficult
for him and the one class that he did better in was mathematics. He got sick
a lot, lost a year, but eventually he had to master Russian. He completed the
Russian language secondary school in Vilno but then got lucky: in 1955 a
Polish Teacher's Institute was launched in Nowa Wilejka. Later he was
accepted into the Lithuanian Pedagogical Institute.

"You see," he jokes again, "I am an internationalist. I began my education in Polish, completed elementary and secondary school in Russian, and
then received a diploma in pedagogy in Lithuanian." He mentions how he
has forgotten only his German "because of lack of contact with it."

For a long time after, his mother Helena dreaded being deported to
Siberia. She gave up her work in the Ponary school and decided to leave alone
for a distant province. She became the director of a school in a village twenty
miles from Vilno.

"Her departure was our permanent leave-taking." Józef says that he was
then twelve years old. "I stayed at Aunt Lola's in Ponary and would travel to
Mom's in the summertime. I would help her in caring for her garden. It was
there that I developed a taste for hunting, having shot my first field pigeon."

Helena Wasilewska would come to Ponary only at Christmas, and sometimes at Easter too. Only in 1956 did she return to her beloved Vilno. She
taught and lived at the schools.

She searched for her husband all the time. She found a Józef Wasilewski
once in Gdynia. She went there but it turned out that it wasn't him...

"She returned from Gdynia terribly upset, felt quite sick, and almost got
an infarct," Józef remembers. "But, up to her death, even though she already
knew otherwise from Radio Free Europe, she counted on finding her husband alive. It had been drummed into us that the Polish officers had been
killed at the hands of the Germans, or that they had escaped to Manchuria,
perhaps to the West..."

Helena Wasilewska, nicknamed Lila, remained alone to the end of her
life. She lived to see grandchildren but not the public disclosure of the crime.
She died in 1982, being seventy-four years old. She was laid to rest in Vilno.

Her son learned only in 1990—when an exposition about the Katyn
massacre was brought to Vilno—that Second Lieutenant Józef Wasilewski
had been a prisoner at Starobelsk.

"I too had hoped to the end... Hope is always the last to die..." Józef
Wasilewski turns his eyes away, crosses his legs.

He began his own professional work in a school in Żodziszki where he taught mathematics and physics for three years. There too he married, very early, being hardly twenty years old. His wife Freda Siemierikowa, a Russian by birth but a Catholic, was a Polish language teacher in that same school. In 1959 a son was born to them, Józef.

A year later the position of director of an elementary school in Rakańce was offered to him, fifteen miles from Vilno.

"It was a place of exile," he decidedly asserts. "The school lay a mile and a half from a road, through hellish mud where I left several pairs of new shoes. There was no electricity and many problems. I spent thirty-nine years there."

There were quite a lot of students. From the neighboring settlements about 180 persons came daily to school, and over 100 studied in the evenings. All of them were Poles. Their second child, Jola, was born one year later in their apartment by the old, wooden school. Besides his work as director, Józef Wasilewski taught both mathematics and physics.

When he would be asked about his father, he would answer: "He went to war and didn't return." He was taken into the Communist Party. In the course of his work he received several letters of praise from the Ministry of Education, and the decoration of a leader of education. But one day the past made itself felt. He had been nominated in Vilno for the medal of Lenin because of his good work in education but the letter had been sent to Moscow for confirmation.

"And there my name was crossed off. Evidently in Moscow, it came to them that my father had been a Polish officer and a POW at Starobelsk," he figures.

On the occasion of the fiftieth anniversary of the October Revolution, the Soviet authorities built in Rakańce a new school, brick instead of wood, closer to the road. They put asphalt on the road and brought in electricity. Today the school is still Polish, with ten classes.

"And I bought the old school!" Józef Wasilewski is genuinely ebullient at the thought. "I used it in building my own house in Rakańce."

The Wasilewski house stands out from the others in Rakańce. Large, yellow like gold, with an expansive garden. They have raised two children in it: Józef and Jolanta. The Wasilewski's still live there with their daughter, the present director of the school in Rakańce. Jola married during her studies in Moscow, to Wolodia, a Cossack from the Caucasian region, also a teacher.

The new, brick school, a present on the fiftieth anniversary of the October Revolution, stands across the street from the Wasilewski's house built as it was of "timber from the old school." It is next to the village store, where the Poles stop in for a glass of vodka.

"The kholkozes have now been replaced with farm cooperatives. They have let go of most of the people and those who are still working are not getting paid.

Nor do they want to give back the nationalized land, especially to Poles. And so there is growing poverty, unemployment, crime," the Wasilewski's tell me.

Here and there we see the ruins of palaces and manor houses, fallen into ruin not because of the war, but primarily because they belong to no one after the owners' flight, dismantled piece by piece by people in the neighborhood. Not many of the former magnates or the *kresy* families remain here today. Only the jokes, with which my guide entertains me.

We are passing the Waka River, a river that is torrential, deep, gathering in victims every year.

We drive up to a large church in Biała Waka. The coat of arms of the Tyszkiewicz family, two white swords and three green crowns, still hangs on the fronton. When the Soviets closed the sanctuary at Ponary, Józef Wasilewski turned to this church for his first communion; here too he was confirmed. He turns off the motor of the car, leans on the steering wheel. He gazes at the church.

"Nothing has changed here since my childhood." He admits that he now goes rarely to church. "I am not a practicing Catholic. Of course, I assist at funerals, I go on all the special feasts, we sit down together at the traditional Christmas Eve meal, we color our eggs for Easter. On the feast of the Three Wise Men, my wife even marks with blest chalk over the door the three names. But that is rather tradition than deep faith. I am unable to imagine to myself God and the saints."

And for his wife Freda? "Well I go to the Catholic church. And the priest is always asking me when we plan to have a church wedding. Maybe in our fiftieth year of marriage?"

Her husband starts up the Niwa and we're off again.

"The church was forbidden in the Soviet school. And so that's how we have lived with only a civil marriage ceremony. It's not worth changing things in one's old age," he asserts.

Józef Wasilewski is now in his third year of retirement. But he still has eight classes weekly at the school in Rakańce.

In order to meet expenses one way or another, they raise rabbits and goats. Last winter they killed two young kids and one old goat; they have just one nanny-goat left. And one hundred and fifty rabbits.

"We made it through thanks to that. I sold some of the kid-meat in the market place. Formerly, when I worked as director of the school, it wasn't dignified to sell anything. But a retiree can't be embarrassed." He wipes his face with his worn-out hands, one of which is missing four fingers.

They also have a garden, "Oh, just to nibble on some chives and lettuce at home." He sowed his five acres with annual grasses and some alfalfa and clover. He has feed then for both his rabbits and his goats.

The Vilno area is for him the most beautiful place in the world. Here we have everything! Healthy, pine-filled woods, gentle knolls, valleys, rivers and lakes. And everywhere there are beautiful views. And the people are open and honest, though too a bit rascally at times, just as in every country..." at which he laughs in his own unique way, loudly and heartily.

12

STALWART FROM THE PODKARPACIE REGION

Rzeszów, Poland, May 2002

The worst was the silence, the prohibition against speaking openly of their death, of a dignified burial, for half a century. It was forbidden even to visit the places of execution. My youngest sister, Zosia, always envied those friends of hers whose parents had died in Auschwitz. They at least could go to the grave sites, and didn't have to hide the truth...

I, unlike Zosia, remember perfectly our father, Ignacy Dec. When the war broke out I was already sixteen years old; our father had had the opportunity to raise and form me and impart many things to me. I have drawn from his wisdom throughout my life. He was for me a beloved figure, an ideal and model in every way. He was a handsome, wise, spirited and innovative pedagogue, educator, social worker. He was one of those "steadfast" people for whom honor, fatherland, family and faith in God were their highest values.

As a newly graduated student from the Teacher's College in Rzeszów, barely eighteen years old in 1914, he joined Piłsudski's Legions and marched along with the 2nd Carpathian Brigade through the entire military campaign. Then he was attached to the Austrian army where he served on the Albanian front, and then, during the Polish-Bolshevik War, he served in the Polish Army. After being put on reserve in June 1921, he returned to his native Sokołów. I have managed to preserve many precious mementos of him, even a small military notebook from 1914 with thirty-four battle sites and encounters in the Carpathian Mountains mentioned as well as an annotation about the battles near Stochód. I have also many of his letters, writings, even his speeches to young people. I have myself made use of them many times.

I wrote many things about my father in my youthful diaries. I kept writing in them until 1932. The notations I made depict a happy childhood, a young girl's maturation, the hard times of living through war...

I was born in the Podkarpacie region, in my father's home town, in Sokołów Małopolski. Both parents were teachers. My Dad was a Polish teacher as well as the director of the school. He also taught me. I still have my notebook from Polish class with my sixth grade compositions. In it there are the grades and comments of my father, as, for example, "Continue to work hard and Almighty God and your parents will help you so that your life will be bright and cheerful." Or "In your sentences I see much care, good will and effort. Be aware moreover that without this a person accomplishes nothing in life. Therefore break and conquer difficulties from childhood on, and you will have fewer of them because of this in later life." I have also kept a book, one of my school's awards, with a beautiful dedication by my father: "Read, dear Józia, a lot in life. Know that books are the best friends of man, because they bear witness to so much good and demand very little in return."

My Mom, Julia Dec, of the Głodzik family, a native of Sieniawa, was also a teacher, in all areas. Our Mom was also marvelous! Modest, tolerant, diplomatic, religious, very family-oriented. She was the kind of Mom whose advice one simply had to heed. Our life in small Sokołów went along in an exceptionally happy way. My parents loved each other and enjoyed the respect of the townspeople. Dad had often received awards and decorations; he especially valued two of them: the Cross of Independence for his participation in the Legions and the Golden Service Cross for his achievements in his social work and professional life. I remember how proud Mom and the rest of us were when Dad was honored at the monument for the Sokołów Legionnaires to the sounds of "The Legion..." (From the first line of the military anthem of Piłsudski's Legions, 1914–1917)

I, Stanisława Dec, now Sojowa after my marriage, was the oldest of the children. I came into the world in April 1922, a year after my parents' wedding. My sister Wisia was three years younger than me and Zosia was ten years younger.

In 1934, we moved to Rzeszów. My father had been transferred there to be the director of the Stanisław Jachowicz Elementary School. It is now General High School No. III, but it has a memorial plaque dedicated to my father...

Mom was then already on a disability pension, having fallen ill with kidney trouble. She never returned to her work. But those years too were happy ones. We settled in Rzeszów in a large, government apartment, next to the new school building. Mom took care of the house, and together with Dad looked after our upbringing and formation. We grew up healthy, and were good students. We were the hopes of our parents...

"Let us give to our children while they are young everything which is necessary to them for health and development so that our consciences might not someday accuse us of refusing them this or that. Neither of us had a bright, happy and pleasant youth—may our children have the kind that we can afford them..." is what my Dad wrote to his beloved Julia.

That whole world of happiness and hope came crashing down in 1939. It was exactly in that year that I had graduated with very good results from a private girls' *gimnazjum*. There were two funerals that year as well: first, that of Grandma Rozalia, and then of Aunt Marysia, my Mom's beloved sister.

During vacation I was able to go to the last of my scout camps. I have to add that already in Sokołów I was an avid scout, and had received the scouting cross at age eleven from my Dad's hand. He had always attached great importance to the growth of school organizations for young people, especially of the scouts, and gave special attention to them, advised them, and himself visited their camp-sites.

I wrote down my experiences in the summer of 1939 almost daily as I lie on the camp bunkbed. The camp in Zełemianka prepared the older girls for the level of "rover" and the function of leader. The Central Office of the Lvov Command had organized it. The participants came not only from southern Poland but also from abroad; I still remember well Hela Zawistanowicz from Chicago. Our instructors were students of the Lvov universities. I will never forget my chats with them, our intense discussions, the gathering around the fire, excursions, patrols and alerts. As for alerts, the last of them was not just a drill since we had to pack up and go back home because war was hanging by a thread...

German bombs fell on Rzeszów only a few days after my return home...

Dad, though he was already forty-three, was impatiently awaiting the call-up to the army. When he finally received it, I remember that he immediately went and took down from a shelf his uniform which had been made ready, of a second lieutenant in the 17th Reserve Unit of the Polish Police, as well as his officer boots. He put them on, pinned on two of his most important decorations and went to a photographer to have his picture taken. Could anyone have guessed then that this would be his last picture? After his return home he said good-bye to us and hurried to the place designated—the police headquarters in Rzeszów. He moved out with a detachment of the Rzeszów police toward the East. He was in such a hurry to join battle with the Germans that he forgot his light overcoat. Mom told me then to catch up with him and hand him the coat. Thanks to this I was the last person that he kissed...

Later we learned that he visited also the presbytery in Brzeżany and Father Adam Łańcucki, my Mom's uncle. It was there he spent his last night before being apprehended by the bolsheviks.

Father Adam Łańcucki managed, unlike my Dad, to survive the war, even though he was a chaplain in the Home Army and often hid those in need, including Jews, in the presbytery. After the war his name was placed in the "Book of the Just" at Yad Vashem in Jerusalem. During the occupation he was made to stand before an execution squad, and after the liberation he was imprisoned and sentenced for his activities in the organization Freedom and Independence. He was a displaced person, and died in Chojnów in Lower Silesia.

Mom hadn't intended to leave Rzeszów. She couldn't imagine that the Germans who had crossed into the city on September 9, 1939, would change the school and our residence into military barracks. They gave us two hours to collect our things, everything that fit in hand-held bags. We were forced to find some corner with neighbors and acquaintances and as a result we each of us lived in separate houses. Mom began to entreat the German commander of the city to let us return to at least one part of our home. And so we did. We found it severely plundered and we were allowed to stay only in one room. Our luck at returning turned into a nightmare...

A small guardhouse and a German soldier with a rifle stood at the entrance gate to the school property. He would check the passes and would search us each time. He led us in and out of the house. An enormous Alsatian hound would sniff even under the bed. Too the Gestapo were always visiting us in search of our father. But we, though concerned as to his fate and without any news of him, continued to hope that he would return...

I remember Christmas Eve of 1939, our first without him. One of the Germans living under the same roof with us brought us a Christmas tree, a small spruce. We decorated it with meager, paper ornaments and in tears we broke together the Christmas wafer. When from behind the wall the sounds of "*Stille Nacht, heilige Nacht*" came to us, we sang softly with trembling voices "*Cicha noc, święta noc,*" ("Silent night, holy night") as we struggled to hold back our tears. I don't remember now the modest meal of that Christmas Eve, only our crying... Zosia, the youngest of us, was then seven years old...

It was only two weeks later, precisely on January 13, 1940, that we received from Dad his one and only letter. He had sent it on November 30 from the camp in Kozelsk. My God, for how long and in vain did we search on a map of the Soviet Union for that small town! How many tens of times did we look at and read the small sheet of paper torn from a notebook, on which Dad had jotted down with an indelible pencil words of love and yearning! In each sentence we found some kind of subtext, some hidden meaning... But he didn't write much about himself: "My health is of a kind that is usual at home during the winter season. My stomach bothered me some during October. I'm coughing a bit but in general I am healthy. That's enough about me though I know you would like more..." The rest of the letter contains questions full of concern about our fate, relatives, acquaintances, colleagues, about the state of the school, about everything which made up the stream of his life before he went off to war. This sheet of paper, this treasure, remains today a family relic...

Mom immediately wrote back to him but her letter never received an answer. Which is why during the next lonely Christmas Vigil, in 1940, we kissed this single sheet from Dad... We couldn't have guessed that he was by this time no longer among the living... That second Christmas Vigil also we spent in Rzeszów but in a small, damp house on a slope of the Wisłok River. Mom had been successful somehow in finding it and we moved our things there "out of the nightmare."

In this house in 1943 we celebrated also the darkest Christmas Vigil of my life... From a list of Polish officers in a German newspaper sheet published July 24, things became clearer: at number 3341 was the name Ignacy Dec, reserve lieutenant... During the exhumation the letter from Julia Dec of Rzeszów was found on him... It is difficult for me to express in words the pain and despair we experienced on that holy, Nativity evening of 1943... What good was it that our neighbors, shaken by our fate, gave us help in organizing a vigil meal, even if without delicacies, but still a renewal of tradition? Our father wasn't there, nor was there a Christmas tree, nor joyous caroling... I remember only the crying around the vigil table. I read then the unabashed letter-poem I had only just finished to my father:

> The war took you from us and a fateful sentence surely
> Drove you, Father, on a far-flung road, to foreign places
> You yearned for us, you suffered terribly—the one letter
> You sent from the northern, Russian land tells us this
> And we have longed for you, and dreamt of you
> But it never occurred to us that you might lay in your grave
> Your grave so far away, is there a simple cross on it?
> Does anyone kneel there at times, or dress it with flowers?
> Foreign trees murmur above you, foreign birds sing
> A foreign earth covers you, dearest, only father,
> But your bright, luminous spirit is near us and will lead
> Us always through life's dark, arduous, and slippery roads.

We didn't have anything to live on. Mom had exchanged for food everything that could be negotiated. She was ailing but they took away her pension. People from the school and friends helped out. It would happen that I had to carry a loaf of rationed black bread over twenty miles in my backpack. It had to do for an entire week so it had to be very sparingly divided among us four. Perhaps that is why lack of respect for bread offends me even today... Instead of tea or milk we would drink an infusion made from herbs, and we would be thrilled if at home there was some sweetener or margarine. Sometimes

Mom would buy a quarter-liter of goat's milk... However even these meager supplies of ours would become the booty of the German soldiers during an inspection. I remember that Mom would then cry, pointing to us, thin and emaciated; she would beg the Germans to leave the children at least a bit of the food...

Since I was the oldest daughter, I became the only person able to work. I was directed by the German work administration (*Arbeitsamt*) to the Austrian firm Rittman which was in charge of construction work at the airport in the town of Jasionek. Only three Poles were working there: I and two men. I did everything; I typed, prepared the pay-rolls, took goods to Jasionek. I was able to do this thanks to the very good knowledge of German that I had from school, having always had a talent for languages. I had graduated from high school with exceptional achievement in German and even today I still am able to make good use of it in speaking and writing. When Rittman ceased its activity after the defeat at Stalingrad, I found work in an insurance company. I would do translations. Besides this, I would give German lessons. Later my sister Wisia who was three years younger than me also began to work. Fifteen years old, she was hired at the Polish Airplane Plant in Rzeszów which the Germans had converted into the Flugmotorenwerk. In addition she would knit sweaters. For children to find work locally during the occupation was very much a prize; it would save them from being sent to forced labor in Germany. We were lucky then in Wisia's situation...

Our desperate situation, the collapse of my world after the loss of our father, the struggle with poverty and the exhausting work caused me to have a nervous breakdown. I wanted to die. I looked for death... In the end half-unconscious I managed to get to a hospital in Kraków. Mom was unable to visit me because a typhus epidemic limited train travel. When after several months she came to take me back home, I could hardly recognize her. Emaciated, with pain in her face and with hair, formerly black, now white as milk, she stood at the entrance to the hospital ward... I thought that it was her ghost... That woeful smile accompanied her from then on to her last day.

After the end of the war our material situation did not change at all for the better. We continued to live in the little house by the Wisłok River. It is true that Mom did receive her pension but it was a very meager one. When she sought redress from the authorities in Rzeszów explaining that her husband, a civil servant of Rzeszów, had been killed in the war, she heard: "It's good that he was killed because he would be jumping up today against us..."

Little by little the schools began to get organized and we absolutely wanted to continue the studies that the war had interrupted. I very much wanted to finish the *liceum* but I didn't have the registration fee. We worked at making up the difference by tutoring and manual labor but it wasn't enough. I remember how I used to walk around the city wondering how to earn money. Until one day I ran into my former directress at the school. She told me the address of a *liceum* and said that if I gave her name I wouldn't have to pay the registration fee. I know full well that it was thanks to her I was able to finish two levels in one year and graduate in July of 1945!

I began to look for work in a school; perhaps I inherited from my parents a fondness for teaching. And it turned out that one day I received two offers for work. The first was as a teacher in Rzeszów, the second came in a letter from my uncle, a teacher. My uncle encouraged me to move to that region because, he explained, teachers were needed there and the school system in the regained territories was starting from the very beginning...

I didn't spend a lot of time thinking about it. I made up my mind to leave for the West. The sense of adventure drew me. I also greatly desired to finish higher studies and to shut myself off from my father's suppressed past. I said good-bye to Mom and my sisters. Then, together with some displaced people, I boarded the train going toward the area that had been shifted to Poland after the war, long ago Polish but for the last few centuries German. To the "wild west"...

That was on October 2, 1945... I was twenty-two. Dressed in a dilapidated jacket made over from my father's pre-war smoking-jacket with its collar gnawed at by moles, and in old fur boots made of Russian leather, I set off into the unknown. The trip took three days. I left Rzeszów at night, in a freight car coupled to a repatriate train: a crowd of people, foul air, small children crying, dantean scenes during stops in Kraków and Katowice. For the whole trip I stood in the passageway between cars, with the wooden trunk of all my possessions under my legs. I remember the huge, ruined station in Wrocław; we waited there a half-day for the next engine. The massively ruined city still smelled of the front, here and there one could still hear shots being fired...

Then Legnica. I rested a bit there with the Ptak family who had accompanied me on the trip. They had been given an apartment here in Lower Silesia and employment. This was the first time that I had seen the appropriation of a German apartment, fully furnished, with couches, piano, and even fresh supplies in the larder... I also saw a large number of Russian soldiers. I remember their broad, smiling faces and the songs they sang to the musical accompaniment of a concertina.

In a small town by the name of Chojnów I stopped in at the presbytery of my Mom's uncle, Father Adam Łańcucki. Three days later a farmer's wagon with one of the farmers came for me. He took me to "their school" in Nowa Wieś (formerly Neudorf Groditzberg). There on the porch of a tall, storeyed building, instead of children a bony woman greeted me with a warm "*Guten Abend.*" I felt angry at it, but... I couldn't, however, be discourteous, so I leapt from the wagon and politely extended my hand. Frau Heiland attended to me very solicitously. The room where I put my things was clean and warm and supper had been placed on the table. She told me that she had been a teacher there before the war and that her husband had been the school's director. She had lost her husband and three sons in the war and a fourth son was in an American POW camp.

Besides the apartments for the teachers there were two classrooms in the building. Unfortunately, they were almost empty, without any teaching materials. The father of one of the students told me later that the newly arrived people had plundered them. They had taken away the maps, instruments, chemicals, even the skeleton for the biology lessons. They had put them all in a pile and set them on fire in an act of revenge. With their pitchforks they had also rained havoc on all the "German honeybees," and now the beehives around the school stood empty. These events perfectly illustrate the mood of the newly arrived displaced Poles from the East.

On the next day the school's director, Roman Głodzik, a displaced person from around Brzeżany, called. I remember my excitement and fear just as I clasped the doorlatch and entered into the classroom. Forty pairs of eyes turned warily in my direction. Of various ages, some of them were taller than me. We began by telling something about ourselves. I learned from them that they had come from the village of Polan in the Lower Ustrzyki district, that it was really nice there because they could go skiing, but that there were no hills here and the skis they had brought would be of no use... They had been transported with their entire families to these new lands because Ukrainian bands were roaming where they used to live. Almost all the chickens they were bringing died on the way and the cows and horses they brought were useless. They were amazed too that they had to share their homes with Germans (the original inhabitants were expelled later).

I managed in that first lesson to divide them into classes and to judge their levels. And then normal classes began in this mixed collection of students. Polish, mathematics, geography...

I got to know my surroundings bit by bit. I enjoyed wandering around and riding my bicycle, though sometimes it was dangerous. The militia was liquidating young SS members, the so-called "little wolves," and one time, at the edge of a forest, rifle shots began to whistle around my head so much so that I was already saying good-bye to my life. Hugging the bicycle that had fallen to the ground I felt myself a weak, defenseless Stasia, and not the pioneer and hero that I had been praised as...

That wasn't the only dangerous episode I happened to experience in Nowa Wieś in Lower Silesia. Bullets often whistled around my ears when soldiers would travel parallel to me on the same road and laughingly fire at wild game. I thought I would die once also when I was returning from the train station in Chojnów. A slant-eyed "liberator" laid hold of me but fortunately for me he was so drunk I was able to break free from his grasp.

One day I set off with some children to Grodzisko which also had been settled by displaced people. In a terribly devastated medieval castle standing on a hill, there were heaps of books pilled high amidst smashed elegant mirrors, candelabra and marble bath-tubs. It seems that the neighboring people were burning them in their stoves... There were among them valuable copies, many with the seal of the Berlin University Library.

I also discovered with the children a large number of books in a former manor house in our Nowa Wieś. They were beautiful and priceless! Most of them had leather jackets, with golden spines, published in previous centuries in German, French, English, Italian, Latin. One of the oldest, in wooden binding coated with white, embossed leather, bore the title *M.T. Ciceronis De Officis Libri III*, published in Lipsk in 1603. I remember too other items: *La Rhétorique de Aristote en Français* published in Lyons in 1691 or *Oeuvres diverses de M. Rousseau* published in Amsterdam in 1729. We didn't know what to do with them. We carried them to our school in wagons and then I notified the educational authorities. Shortly thereafter trucks from the Ministry of Education came for them and left me a receipt for the transfer of the about 4000 volume collection. I kept for myself only a couple of volumes as the beginning of our future Polish school library.

After a while my pioneer adventure in the West ceased being fun. Loneliness, the lack of simple comforts, newspapers, the meager diet, all these wore heavily on me.

Despite the fact that I liked my students, anger and bitterness often took hold of me. I took my work very seriously but they would stammer out their lessons, murmur, scribble in their notebooks... My relationship with Frau Heiland also became chilly. One day we were both in the attic looking for canning jars. Suddenly Frau Heiland fell quiet, stood almost motionless. I saw how very carefully she dusted off and gazed with admiration on a portrait discovered among the attic odds and ends. I thought that it was a photograph of her husband or one of the sons killed in the war.... But it was a framed picture of Hitler! A canning jar almost fell out of my hands... All my warm feelings toward her vanished at that moment.

I requested a transfer from the education authorities. But they didn't want to give their approval inasmuch as in the whole district there were barely 21 teachers. My dreams of higher studies had been reborn and become an irresistible longing. I made up my mind to take the risk. I resigned from my teacher's position...

This new stage of my life, begun with tears, was not easy, but it was full of hope...

In Wrocław I found myself with neither a roof over my head nor the means to support myself. I had to rely exclusively on myself and so had to work and study at the same time.

Yet student life had its own charm. We helped out in clearing up the rubble in Wrocław and often helped collect money. And I am proud that I sat on the same bench with people whose names will enter forever onto the annals of Polish learning and culture, as my colleagues and later themselves professors of higher studies: Ziomek, Kaleta, Reczek...

During my studies I married Zenon Soja who was six years older than me and also from Rzeszów. He had come to Wrocław at the direction of the educational authorities in Rzeszów for studies in physical education. I had known him before because during the occupation he had worked with my sister, Wisia, in the Airplane Plant.

We were married in 1947, in our Rzeszów. We took an apartment in a half-wrecked tenement building in Wrocław. When it would rain, we had to arrange an umbrella over ourselves. When I was in my third year of studies, our first son, Marek, was born. We took turns taking care of him. My sister Wisia, who had also come to Wrocław to study, also helped out. It is hard today to believe how we balanced all this, how we were able to do it all...

I never received professional promotions as I was quite content being among young people. Nor did I seek such promotions because I realized that they would be hindered by my father's death in Katyn and the fact that neither my husband nor I belonged to any party. Yet I haven't been without rewards, both in my professional and social life. A number of distinctions have been very gratifying to me, such as the Medal of the Commission of National Education, given me by the Literary Association of Adam Mickiewicz, the Remembrance Medal for services in the domain of literature, or a special diploma from the Central Committee of the Literature and Language Olympics for my participation in its work and the achievement of my student-olympians. But the most significant of all I think is the Gold Medal for the Care of Places of National Memory, given me by the Council for the Preservation of the Memory of Struggle and Suffering. That distinction, for work in the dissemination of awareness concerning Katyn in the national consciousness, carries with it obligations for the rest of one's life.

These and other honors, my husband's as well, have given us great satisfaction. They rendered bearable that constant companion of our lives, the small teacher salary...

Our other joy was our children and grandchildren. After Marek, who was born in Wrocław, two daughters came into the world, Barbara (1952) and Małgorzata (1958). Today all three live in Rzeszów and have finished higher studies. Marek has followed in our footsteps and become a teacher. Barbara is a dentist and Małgorzata a specialist in German. All of them are very hardworking and held in esteem at their places of work. We have lived to see five grandchildren and have helped out a bit in their upbringing. Four of them are at university now. They visit us often and show their interest in our well-being. Our modest, two-room apartment near the school facilities is still a center of family life. Five years ago we celebrated here our golden wedding anniversary.

Do we consider our lives fulfilled? Most certainly. Above all we have remained faithful to the ideals and teachings taken from our homes. In that same spirit we have raised our own children. We are joined as well by our difficult jobs, our mutual respect, love of our country, and help to others.

I terribly regret that my Mom did not live to see the public disclosure of the Katyn crime, that she could not light candles on the grave of her husband, Lieutenant Ignacy Dec... Whenever we would place a votive light at the graves of unknown soldiers, Mom would weep bitterly. She died in terrible suffering, in 1956, of cancer. She lived to know only a measure of pride in her three daughters.

Our whole family knows the truth about Katyn. In People's Poland we didn't make much of my father's past. Only since 1990 have we actively taken part in the Katyn movement. I preside at the meetings of the circle of the Association of Katyn Families of Southern Poland and I write a lot in the press about the crime as well as take responsibility for the annals. My husband takes the pictures, the children help, and the grandchildren take an interest. One of our grandchildren, Gabriela Soja, was even a winner at the general competition "Golgota Wschodu" ("Golgotha of the East"), the prize being a trip to Katyn.

I am very pleased that Rzeszów has several winners of the "Golgota Wschodu" competition. Besides Gabriela, five other students in Rzeszów schools shared the prize of the pilgrimage to Katyn.

About thirty people belong to our Katyn circle. We have been instrumental in having a Katyn Cross built at the communal cemetery in Rzeszów and in dedicating a number of places and plaques memorializing Katyn. Three plaques dedicated to the Katyn POWs now hang among the others in Sokołów, on the wall of the church at the cemetery. We have organized many exhibitions, lectures, meetings and celebrations. We are trying to spread knowledge of Katyn, to correct the historical record, preserve both the memory and vestiges of those from our region who fell as victims of this horrible crime. In fact there is now a street in Rzeszów called Katyn Victims Street. But we have no particular office, just our teacher's apartment...

I have been in Katyn twice, in 1989 and at the official opening of the cemetery in 2000. Also, my husband, son, daughter, granddaughter, youngest sister Zosia, and sister-in-law have all been in Katyn. I passed with emotion through the same forest and road down which on April 16, 1940, a "black raven" took my father to the Katyn pit of death... When I placed on the Katyn mound an armful of red and white carnations that I had brought from Poland, I thought not only of my father, but of my mother as well. In the rustling of the Katyn Forest it seemed to me that I heard the whispering of them both. Those very same whispers that came to my ears as I lay sick in the children's hospital... And I begged God at the Katyn cemetery that I might yet be able to hear at least one word from those guilty of this exceptional and as yet unavowed for crime, "we are sorry"...

13

MAJA AND THE
CHERRIES

Toronto, Canada, June 2002

"It is thanks to the Katyn Family Association and the support of Father Antoni Medreli that 'Our Lady of Kozielsk' is here with us in Toronto," Maja Kaszuba whispers to me in the Polish church of St. Mary's Polish Roman Catholic Parish at 1996 Davenport Road. She points to the picture hanging on the left side of the sanctuary. "The idea for it was born in my mind already many years ago, but it was only on September 14, 1984, during the papal visit in Toronto, that John Paul II consecrated it."

The portrait of the Madonna and Child, in a gilded frame, is a copy of the well-known bas-relief which was made in 1940 in Kozelsk by Tadeusz Zieliński. The Polish POW sculpted it in wood secretly, under camp conditions, with a knife contrived from a nail. Later this POW Kozelsk Mother of God miraculously journeyed with the Polish Army along its road from Russia, through Iran, Iraq, Palestine, Egypt, Italy until it arrived in the British Isles. The original hangs today in St. Andrew Bobola's Church in London. An inhabitant of Toronto, Ryszard Wieczorkowski, a dentist by profession and a devoted painter, took on himself the obligation of making a copy of the famous bas-relief. On the basis of a picture Maja had brought from the celebration of the dedication of the chapel of "Our Lady of Kozielsk" in Orchard Lake (USA), he created an unforgettable picture: somewhat stylized, in sober colors, with the Madonna's expression one of extreme sadness and pain. It is surrounded by a large wooden rosary—a votive offering by Maja Kaszuba, which she brought from Rome. Flowers and a silver casket with earth from Katyn Forest always accompany "Our Lady of Kozielsk." Above the portrait, on a beautiful marble slab, the Katyn Family of Toronto had engraved in Polish and English the history of this picture.

"I still dream that one of the churches in Toronto, perhaps one of the six built here by Poles, might bear the name 'Our Lady of Kozielsk,'" Maja adds just at the beginning of Holy Mass.

Old Polish songs echo in a small church on Canadian soil, with the altars decorated by bouquets of red and white carnations, very much reminiscent of Poland. Entire families—children, parents, grandparents—are singing together, with clear voices, from thick Polish hymnals at the benches. Almost everyone present in the overflowing church goes to communion. This broad and active participation of Polish immigrants in the Mass, the whole-hearted attentiveness to the Word of God, the greater recollection, and too the joy of prayer always touch me when I am abroad, especially in another hemisphere. The Masses are usually an occasion for charitable collections for various purposes, primarily in Poland, for picking up the parish bulletin and conversations and social gatherings. They often conclude with tea and cake in the parish hall or in the church basement.

After Mass and after Maja had greeted all her acquaintances, we take public transportation to the largest Polish church in Toronto, St. Casimir's. It's located at 156 Roncevalles Avenue, in the largest Polish section of the city. Polish signs are everywhere, stores, restaurants, bookstores, various shops. Near the Polish bank Credit Union there stands a bronze statue of the Holy Father John Paul II with outstretched arms.

"Our Pope is reaching for Granowska's pastries," says Maja, repeating jokingly the line that the Poles here have coined. Indeed Mrs. Granowska's bakery, one of the best known in Toronto, is directly across the street.

St. Casimir's Church is larger but also crowded and full of song. A large sign hangs next door: The Polish Office of the Seventeenth World Youth Days. All of Canada is preparing for these celebrations which will take place from July 23rd to the 28th, when the Pope and hundreds of thousands of young people from 150 countries will come to Canada. Canadian Polonia would like at that time to fund for the Pope the largest statue in the world.

The most important Polish holidays are celebrated at St. Casimir's Church. It is from this church that the processions, all the parades and marches, begin with the accompanying banners and orchestra. Then, all traffic having been stopped, Canadian Polonia goes down Roncevalles Avenue and continues straight down the boulevards of Lake Ontario to Beata Parkett Square where the Katyn Monument is. It is the most important obelisk funded by the Polish Canadian Congress, its pride and joy. The creator of the monument is Tadeusz Janowski. The celebration of its unveiling—on a portion of land donated by the city—took place on September 14, 1980, in the presence of city officials as well as all of Canadian Polonia, with scouts in the front. This monument was the first in the world raised in a public location to give place and witness to the crime of Katyn. Among those unveiling the monument were Jadwiga Puchalik, the mother of Maja Kaszuba and a widow of the one of the Polish policemen lost in Katyn.

We followed the road from St. Casimir's Church to the monument on Lake Ontario, on foot, as members of a procession, though it is a mile away.

The monument is huge, heavy, square-edged. It recalls a shattered, heavy wall and bears beneath it the word KATYN. It is meant to symbolize the Republic torn and divided in 1939 by the Germans and the Soviets. Among the shrubs blossoming around the monument, there are fifteen separate and unattached stones in the shape of soldiers' hats. The monument is always decorated with red and white wreaths as well as two national flags, of Poland and of Canada. Both of them are red and white except that on the Canadian one, the bands are perpendicular and decorated with a maple leaf.

"The monument is the heart of our patriotism," Maja Kaszuba explains as she straightens out the ribbons on some of the wreaths. "It is here that ardent speeches are given during national holidays and celebrations and it is here that we lay our wreaths."

Today is Sunday, June 9. The lilacs and chestnut trees are blossoming in Toronto. Despite the hot and stifling day, many Canadians are spending an active day biking, roller-skating, running or simply walking along the boulevards of Lake Ontario. We stop for dinner at the Polonez restaurant. The service, clientele and the food are all Polish. The prices too are similar to those in Warsaw.

We return by bus, subway and trolley. The Kaszuba home, a large one-storied building of red brick with white windows, is located on Glenn Murray St., a small, villa-lined street near downtown. We settle in comfortably under an umbrella in the garden. The birds are singing. There are a number of sculptures, a small pond with a fountain, well-cared for lawn, bushes and trees. The most beautiful blossoms are the camomile and the viburnum ("white balls"). The loudest of the birds are the sparrows which have built some nests under the eaves of the house and are fluttering about in the air together with others having quite colorful wings; it feels almost like a rookery. The garden is Mirosław's passion. He is a history teacher by profession, one of the six adult sons of the Kaszuba's. Only a few years ago he even won a competition for the prettiest garden in Toronto.

It is quiet here, without any wind, idyllic. Maja has changed into a light, summer flower-print dress. She is thin, delicate, already slightly stooped, but meticulous in her appearance. In her brown, attractively combed hair there is not a trace of grey. She brings in a thick volume, *Cemetery Book. Katyn*, in which she has highlighted the short biography of her father:

"Cpt. Zygmunt Puchalik, born December 23, 1891 in Prusiek, Poland. A participant in the 1920 war. A graduate of the Training Center for Military Police in Grudziądz (1923). He served in the Police Unit in Tarnopol and the Border Defense Corps (1923). He was assigned to the 4th Military Police Battalion in Warsaw, and then in Łódź; he was the deputy commander of the Police Battalion. His wife was Jadwiga Pelczarska and together they had a daughter Maria."

She brings also to the garden family photographs and documents. And calmly, with concentration, she begins to unravel the narrative of her rich, difficult—given her fate—, but ultimately happy life. She speaks flawless Polish and reconstructs the events in detail, perfectly...

In point of fact she is from Lvov. She came into the world on December 10, 1928, as Maria Lidia, though she has always been called Maja. She still keeps a medallion of Our Lady of Częstochowa on which is engraved her birthdate.

As an eleven-year-old child she remembers him not only as a good father but also as a very disciplined individual. At the same time he was cheerful and friendly, a gentleman in every sense. He loved sports, went horseback riding and skiing, was a good swimmer. His daughter, now a seventy-four-year-old woman, brings his photograph in a glass frame: not very tall but handsome, dark-haired, with large eyes and thick eyebrows. He was thirteen years older than his wife.

Maja Kaszuba says with a sigh: "I spent my most joyous and beautiful years in pre-war Warsaw. On Sundays we would go to Mass in Wizytki and then to the confectioner's shop for cake. In the capital I attended pre-school and elementary school and in winter I would take figure-skating lessons on the ice-rink at the Swiss Valley. I was also a member of the ballet school and I performed a solo waltz at the National Theatre where I received a bouquet of violets from my cousin."

She remembers how she said goodbye to her father as he left for the war. Before the war had started, he had planned to retire. He had already been using his vacation to complete the formalities for retirement while Mom had gone with her sister on vacation. Maja had remained with her father, Grandmother Puchalik and the servant Józia.

"In the morning I alone escorted my father to the bus." She remembers that the summer of 1939 was beautiful and very warm. "My Mom and aunt were coming back only on the next day. A week later my father arrived at the house during the night, on a motorcycle, with another military person. He said goodbye to us, comforted us by saying that the war would soon end. It was the last time we saw him..."

She remembers perfectly the bombardment on September 1. One of the bombs exploded in their garden and in an instant the new villa lost all its window panes. Because their house was close to the airport and the Mokotowski Fort, her mother decided to move to the center of the city. She took Maja and fled in the car with the tenants from the second floor.

"We spent the siege of Warsaw hiding out in a basement. There wasn't anything to eat. During one of the air raids I was slightly wounded in the head. I kept praying to Our Lady of Perpetual Help," Maja remembers as she closes her eyes.

It was only after the cease-fire that they were able to work their way back to their house in Mokotów. It had survived though still without windows. They were able somehow to last out the first winter of the war crouched up against a small room stove in the basement, although they were almost asphyxiated one day. The Puchalik's succeeded in re-glazing the windows only in the spring of 1940 and in renting out three rooms upstairs as well as the basement, thanks to which they had the means to support themselves. Maja began to attend classes at the *gimnazjum*.

As there was no news from her father for a long time, her mother was very anxious. Her women friends, whose husbands had ended up in German POW camps, regularly received letters. It was only toward the end of 1939 that the first card came. Her father informed them that he was in Kozelsk, a Soviet camp. All together he sent three or four cards, always short, laconic. Then there was a long silence. One day a vase fell from the shelf, of itself, and shattered. Maja's mother said then that it was a bad sign... that surely her husband had been killed...

Then one spring day in 1943 she heard downtown through a public loudspeaker incredible news: the Germans had uncovered in Katyn the graves of Polish officers executed by the NKVD. Names were given, among which was mentioned Capt. Zygmunt Puchalik. Maja's mother bought a newspaper and saw it in black and white: Zygmunt Puchalik...

"We had to accustom ourselves to the tragedy gradually. My mother bore the bad news sturdily and did not express despair." Her daughter did not fully believe that her father had been killed.

Despite the war there existed in Warsaw regular social contact among the young. There were even dances and other kinds of amusement. Maja knew that her older friends belonged to secret opposition groups. With her mother's consent she joined the Home Army.

"On the day before the Warsaw Uprising I distributed the orders. I did not have a list of the addressees, so I had to have it memorized." She recalls that she was 15 then but looked younger. The Germans didn't even suspect her as a participant in this national upheaval.

Near the end of September, 1944, the Germans removed her family in the first transport to the interim camp in Pruszków. There she and her mother were loaded with others to cattle cars and transported into an unknown direction.

"During the trip I saw through a chink in the car that we were crossing Poland's border. I thought that I would not survive it, that my heart would break. We didn't know where they were taking us," she said as she folded her hands together.

They ended up in the Mauthausen camp in Austria. At the orders of the Germans they had first to undress and go to the baths. As they moved along in line, completely naked, the Germans wrote down the names of every person. They were lodged in enormous tents where there were only women and children. Maja still remembers that they were given some kind of awful soup. They spent an entire month there inactive. Then they were hustled again to cattle cars. At that time Maja and her mother found themselves in an international work camp.

"When the Germans would call mother out to work, she would pull me along by the hand. Thanks to that they took us both with a twelve person women's group to Gmunden, a spa on the Ebensee lake. First they locked us up in prison. Then we lived in barracks. I would sleep on a top bunk and mother on the lower. We worked in a thread factory, mother on the first floor and I on the second. We had to monitor large machines with spools of thread. Initially I didn't cope well but later things got better. The time in Gmunden was the most difficult. I was continually hungry, cried at night but in such a way that Mom wouldn't hear me. I remember that the Austrians sometimes had pity on us. The foreman made Mom some shoes and they often gave me, a small and thin sixteen-year-old, something extra to eat.

The liberation of the camp by the Americans took place on May 5, 1945. It was at the first dance party in the interim camp for Poles that Maja made the acquaintance of Janek Kaszuba, her future husband. It was on St. John's Day, 1945.

"We danced and danced until midnight!" She laughs as she remembers that she was then seventeen and very haggard and that Janek was seven years older. At midnight he told me that it was his namesday. He joked that he would like to have his own kingdom. So I wished for him to find a princess..."

It turned out that Janek was in charge of the camp. Better times were finally coming for the Puchalik women. Janek placed Maja and her mother together with a friend of hers in a separate hut. The camp cook even brought them some food. During the day Maja and Janek would go bike-riding, take walks. Janek taught her how to swim in a neighboring river. And in the evenings they would dance...

After an acquaintance that lasted several weeks, Maja and Janek became engaged. Extravagantly for the times, Maya even received a gold engagement ring with the initials JK. A dress was sewn for her from parachute material, and there was wine, some light delicacies to eat, the works. And her mother's joy.

"Shortly after our engagement, we crossed over through the green border to Italy." Maja says that they didn't want to return to a Poland occupied by the Soviets. "It was an extraordinarily difficult passing, because it took place at night, through the Alps, across ravines. I remember that we encountered a rainstorm. We took cover in some kind of shelter because it was then quite dangerous."

Her fiancé Janek was steered to the II Polish Corps and immediately after to the Cadet school in Matera, Italy. Janek explained: "I myself wanted to do this. As did the majority of soldiers, I thought that the Western powers would not so easily give over Central Europe to Stalin and that I would shortly be fighting for Poland in a new war." Today in his garden he admits that he was naïve.

The Puchalik women were once again alone, this time in southern Italy. It was extremely fortunate then that her mother found work with Catholic Action. In a camp for Polish refugees in Galatone she received a blue uniform and an officer's salary. Maja became her assistant. In the evenings they would prepare sandwiches for the soldiers and sell them, and also serve tea and distribute newspapers.

Maja's mother learned that at Porto San Giorgio there was a Polish military *gimnazjum*. In order to be accepted there, Maja had to enter the Women's Service Corps. Her Mom added one year to her age since she had to be eighteen to enter. She too received a uniform, but a green one.

After her first year of *gimnazjum*, in the process of the demobilization of the II Polish Corps, they were transported from Italy to the British Isles. Each went separately, Cadet Corporal Janek, his fiancée, her mother. They didn't know whether they would even find each other in England.

They all found each other in England thanks to Polish organizations. Maja met her mother in the camp at Foxley and resumed her studies there. After finishing high school she attended design school for women's fashions.

During this time her mother rented a room in London and began to do sewing work. Initially she didn't know how to do many things and would only do the simplest work, such as sewing on buttons. Gradually she did more and more of it until sewing became a way of supporting themselves. Janek for his part finished Cadet school and was assigned to the 2nd Warsaw Armored Division while at the same time being admitted to the School of Technology in London in chemistry. He and Maja saw each other often.

After knowing each other for two and a half years, they decided to get married. The young couple rented their own apartment in London. A year later their first son was born, Jan who is now a mathematician, a graduate of a university in Toronto. Then they changed their dwelling place for something larger. Her Mom settled in with them and then would travel from there to her sewing work. Maja had to give up her fashion designing school. She raised her sons and took care of the house. It was for her a sad time. The English climate didn't suit her and she suffered because of the lack of sunshine and social contact. They were no longer in such dire straits but they lived quite modestly. Janek was getting a decent stipend which increased with each child. Their second son, Zbigniew, who eventually completed studies in city-planning in Toronto, was born in 1950. A third son, Andrzej, was born in 1952. He was an aspiring actor but died at a youthful age in Toronto.

In November 1954, the Kaszuba's decided to leave England with their three sons. The children were still quite small.

Maja's mother, Jadwiga Puchalik, didn't want to leave. Her daughter lived through a period of great indecision and left London in tears.

"However, I had always agreed with my husband and became reconciled with my fate," she admits. "Today I think that to leave for a strange, unknown country, with three tiny children, one of them still nursing, was to a certain degree heroic." We continued our conversation on the following day.

They took ten days sailing to Canada. The ship put in at Quebec and they reached Toronto by train precisely on All Saints' Day. The engineer Jan Kaszuba quickly found work, being hired by the Dunlop Company the day after their arrival.

"Even so it was difficult for us with three children to find an apartment." Maja notes that Toronto in 1953 was a small, provincial town in comparison with London. It grew larger only during the last half century, before their very eyes.

After working seven years at Dunlop as a manager, Jan Kaszuba started his own chemical company. For thirty-five years, right up to retirement, he produced latex, meerschaum and pillows. Likewise he insulated containers and wiring. He employed almost twenty people including his wife as his assistant.

They purchased their first house in Rexdale and two years later a multi-storied residence with white columns at Baby Point Crescent where they lived for twenty-five years. The extra space was needed as the family increased with three additional sons: Zdzisław (in 1957), Mirosław (in 1960), and Marek (in 1964). Maja never had any domestic help and raised her children completely by herself. She insists, however, that even so she had it much better in Canada than in England; here there was central heat and warm water whereas in London she began each day by lighting a fire in the fire-places and had to do laundry in cold water. She only heated water when bathing the children.

She assures me that she has always been proud of giving birth only to sons.

"I loved all of them equally. I cared for and watched over them the same. Today all of them speak Polish well and four of them have completed the university. All six of them live in Toronto, and two live together in the house with us. And we have lived to see three grandchildren."

In their villa with the white columns, named Belvedere, at Baby Point

Crescent, the Kaszuba's have entertained a large number of special guests from Canada, Poland and the entire world. In 1980, Jan Kaszuba was elected president of the Polonia Congress of the Free World. He occupied this position for three terms, 1980–1986.

"It was a time rich in important events, especially so for Poland but also for Canada," they both emphasize. "We were close to decisive, historical changes and came to know a great many distinguished and interesting people. We still keep contact with some of them."

They traveled a lot during that time, not only across Canada, but Europe and all of America as well. Maja often accompanied her husband at sessions of the Council of World Polonia. She participated in the conventions of various organizations and celebrations. They went together to Rome many times and had audiences with John Paul II at least ten times, even in his private papal chapel.

"It often happened that I would see the Holy Father almost daily," for which reason he has so many photographs: greeting the Pope in Toronto, meeting with him in the Apostolic See. On others they are standing close to Cardinal Wyszyński in Rome, laughing with Lech Wałęsa during the celebrations surrounding the fiftieth anniversary of the Polish Canadian Congress in 1994, participating in the solemnity of the unveiling of the Katyn Monument in Toronto... Many well-known personalities, many thick, memorial albums...

The funeral of Cardinal Stefan Wyszyński in 1981 was a very moving experience for them. They were met at the airport in Warsaw by representatives of Solidarity and the Canadian ambassador. Jan Kaszuba was a member of the official Canadian delegation at this solemn occasion. He and his wife represented Canadian Polonia as well, forming part of the honor assembly, at the coffin of the Primate of Poland. After the funeral, together with representatives of the Polish American Congress, they visited the Gdańsk shipyards and met the leaders of Solidarity.

"Besides our sadness at the passing of the Primate we experienced as well moments of joy and pride in the Polish nation," they remember with emotion.

Canadian Polonia did a lot for Poland during this time. They publicized the Polish situation in the international sphere, opposed the transgressions against human rights, stepped forward in defense of the activists of Solidarity, often sent donations and money. For example during the time of martial law, the Polish Canadian Congress helped about 150 thousand Polish citizens flee the People's Republic and prompted the Canadian government to establish a fund for their temporary support and English instruction.

"The work in the organizations of Polonia was a continuation of our service to Poland," asserts Jan Kaszuba who considers himself a devoted nationalist.

Despite the difficulties in raising six sons and fulfilling the duties of wife and housekeeper, Maria Kaszuba was at the same time active in Polonia organizations. First there was the Circle of Friends of the Boy Scouts, the Women's Federation, Alliance of Polish Teachers, the Polish Combatants' Association, the Alliance of Former Prisoners of German Concentration Camps, the Home Army Association, and, in addition, since 1984 the Katyn Family of which she is a founder and the president. On her roster there appears 31 members, most of them advanced in years, inactive. Meetings are usually held at the Polish Combatants' Association and anniversary memorials at the Katyn Monument. Even though the organization supports itself exclusively by good-will offerings, it has supported financially the Stefan Cardinal Wyszyński Foundation in Warsaw, the cemetery in Katyn Forest, the construction of the Katyn Victims Gimnazjum in Piatnica. Some members of the Katyn Family in Toronto have already visited the Polish military cemeteries in Katyn Forest, Kharkov and Miednoye.

"I went to Katyn Forest in 1955 and took part in the official opening of the necropolis in 2000," says Maja. "I was happy to be able at last to place red poppies at the site where my father had been killed."

All the homes of the Kaszuba's have always had a Polish character. Each was full of Polish books, keepsakes and trinkets. Polish still resounds in their house, and moreover Maya doesn't know English well and doesn't write it. All their sons are interested in Poland, have visited it, some several times. Their oldest, Jan, spent a full year in Warsaw teaching English in one of the schools at Rembertów. It's Mirosław who has grown into the strongest devotee of Poland in the family. As a historian and teacher, he is very knowledgeable concerning the history and culture of Poland. He has often been in Warsaw, has returned with paintings to such an extent that the walls of their houses don't have enough space, especially as the houses have gotten smaller with the departure of their sons. However, none of them have left Toronto and often visit their parents.

"I always prepare a little extra for dinner, for one never knows who might drop in and when." Maja is very glad that her family is so close.

Maja had lost two homes in the former Polish Republic. The first was the three-storied house in Lvov. She had spent her first four years in it before she left with her family in 1932 for Warsaw. Her grandparents, Pelczarski, had built it and Maja's mother had been raised there.

"That house still stands and is even in pretty good shape," she says showing a photograph of it. Other members of her family who moved from Lvov to Kraków after the war had taken the pictures. No one had ever made attempts to reclaim the house, having resigned themselves to the fact that after the war the house was now in a different country.

Maja has only once visited Lvov, the place where members of her family are buried, among them her grandparents. This was during the German occupation, when she was thirteen. Even though it was wartime, she remembers the city as being colorful, happy, multi-national with a style of life similar to Vienna's.

Maja's second lost home is located in Warsaw. It too is still there, maintained in good condition, but it is controlled as investment property by a certain agency. Which is why she is trying to regain ownership of the building. However, her petitions and the high appanages for lawyers in Poland have come to nothing. The family building of the Puchaliks in Warsaw remains in the hands of outsiders.

"There's probably no other country in the world like this," she concludes with bitterness. "My father, a Polish officer, built this house and went off to war. He was killed for his country, for Poland. The state, instead of rewarding him, took his house away. And too it concealed the crime at Katyn. Even though Poland was on the side of the victors in that war..."

14

ÉMIGRÉ BECAUSE OF MARTIAL LAW

Mississauga, Canada, June 2002

She called me just after the broadcast of my being interviewed by Krystyna and Ryszard Piotrkowski on Radio Polonia in Toronto.

"You have to meet with me! I would have so much to tell you!"

We agreed on a time and she came for me in her car. She looked so young and energetic for someone who in 1940 had lost her father in Katyn. She scrutinized me intently with her brown eyes as she drove to her house in Mississauga, about thirty kilometers from Toronto.

"It's really my son's house," she said tersely in Polish, without any trace of an English accent.

Along the way she pointed out some features of the city. Mississauga is a metropolis that has sprung up only in the last twenty-five years, now with a half million people and expanding like lightning. It has at the moment probably the largest concentration of Poles in Canada. They have built a large church under the patronage of St. Maximilian Kolbe and, right next to the church, the Pope John Paul II Polish Center of Culture, well-known in the area for its many interesting activities.

"It's quieter and more pleasant here than in Toronto," she assures me as she parks her car in the garage. "Only the street names are difficult to pronounce. They originate from the language of the Indians who lived here earlier, much the same as the name of the city, Mississauga."

From the garden so beautifully adorned with flowers next to her house, I especially remember the numerous hanging bird-houses and feeders. "This year we had broods of baby birds in almost every bird-house," she says proudly with a beguiling smile.

Her house, spacious and opening out onto the garden, has many Polish touches. Pictures, photographs, books. Her laundry room is unique: many family photos brought from Poland, primarily black and white, hang on the walls.

"The people in my family were very beautiful! When I do the laundry here, I sit myself down, look and think. I ought to enlarge these photographs." Her lively, darkly framed eyes reveal her longing. Her tanned complexion harmonizes with her bright blouse and pants, with her general elegance. Though she supports herself with a cane, she moves sprightly without losing her dignity and good breeding.

"I have to use it because of an automobile accident that I had here in Canada. I had a shattered hip. They put me back together with all kinds of screws," she explains as she leads me around the house.

Her son, Jacek, has his office downstairs on the first floor of the house. He provides financial, legal and translation services. He happens to be in his office when we arrive. He greets us warmly. He is tall, wears glasses, is about forty years old. There is a framed photograph of his grandfather in military uniform and next to it a pre-war staff picture of generals of the Second Polish Republic. Jacek completed studies in economics at the university in Toronto and has also studied business administration and law. Because of such an educational background he had received many offers of work but decided on his own company.

"In my own company I am free and independent even though I would probably make more money working for a government institution," he explains in heavily accented Polish.

Halina Kozłowska has lived in Canada for barely twenty-one years. Her home town in Poland is Skierniewice. She was born there on July 19, 1937, went to elementary school and to Bolesław Prus Gimnazjum. As a pupil she had been proud of the fact that the name of her grandfather, her mother's father, Stanisław Wyrzutowicz, a successful businessman and activist, co-founder of other important initiatives in the city, was on the memorial plaque in the *gimnazjum* lobby among others of the school's founders.

After graduation and two years work in the Institute of Domology, she decided on agricultural studies in the Warsaw Agricultural University. After receiving a Master's degree in 1963 in microbiology she didn't return to her home town.

During her studies she married Tadeusz Kozłowski, who was a graduate of Warsaw Institute of Technology. She herself began working professionally at the Microbiology Institute of the Warsaw Agricultural University. Then she changed her place of studies to the Polish Academy of Sciences. When her son, Jacek, was eight years old, she left for two years to gain practical agronomical experience. After her return to Warsaw she specialized in the cultivation of mushrooms and was an instructor in this discipline at the Horticultural Cooperative. Later for many years she was an insurance consultant specializing in garden products.

It was in November 1981 that she went to Canada on her annual vacation.

"I wanted to visit Canada and earn some extra money. I was healthy, energetic and not afraid of any kind of work." She explains that she had no family across the ocean and that it was by chance that some Canadian acquaintances in Warsaw invited her.

That was some years already after her divorce but the technicalities of the divorce had lingered on and had been very taxing. When the divorce was finally approved, she still had to share the same apartment with her ex-husband. In addition she no longer had both of her parents. A year earlier she had buried her eighty-three-year-old mother, Stanisława Kismanowska, in the cemetery in Warsaw. The widow of an officer murdered in Katyn, she had spent the final six years of her life in Warsaw, among her closest family.

Leaving for Canada, Halina Kozłowska took two suitcases with her one of which was empty and inserted in the second. She had planned on returning in a few months with both of them packed full.

In Toronto she took various jobs, one of which was as a waitress in a restaurant. Just then martial law was declared in Poland. She wanted to wait it out and so after a few weeks she went to extend her visa.

"I was asked then whether in view of the situation existing in Poland I didn't want, as other Poles, to request permanent residence in Canada," she recalls as she serves tea and homemade cake. "It was a serious decision and I had to consult with my son. But I didn't know exactly where he was..."

Jacek had left for the West and was then in Austria. After graduation he hadn't been accepted for philosophy studies at Warsaw University so he took advantage of an invitation from a friend in Innsbruck and went there. His mother didn't even know his address, yet in the end she was able to inform him of the possibility of staying permanently in Canada. He gladly agreed. It was then, almost at the last moment, that she submitted the documents.

Canada was in a financial crisis during that earliest period of theirs. It was a time of recession, lack of movement in investments and high unemployment. Many people were looking for work just at the moment when the emigrants from Poland were arriving. They were often sponsored by the Polish church and old Polonia. They had to take difficult jobs, sometimes in wretched conditions. Many of them were unable to tolerate it, returned back to Poland, often with dramatic consequences. Halina and Jacek Kozłowski reacted to their situation differently. They began by perfecting their English and improving their qualifications.

"That was wonderful help on the part of the Canadian government!"

Halina Kozłowska says in admiration. "The money we received was sufficient at the time for modest foodstuffs and the paying of a rented room. One had only to have the will and endurance."

After finishing language school, she took her first important job in a law firm. She learned a lot there, getting to know life in Canada in the realm of its laws and regulations. Soon afterward her Polish Master's degree was officially acknowledged and she found work in the Ministry of Environmental Protection. In her laboratory, she would determine the levels of pesticides in drinking water at various water intakes from Lake Ontario. The work was interesting, but a few years later she experienced her own Canadian tragedy. She was involved in an automobile accident in Toronto. It was only after a long period of recovery that she could stand upright, yet because she could not walk very far she had to change her job. After completing many courses and successfully passing numerous examinations at the oldest Canadian insurance company, Sun Life of Canada, she received her license and became an insurance representative.

Years later it turned out that she had to have a hip operation. She underwent the operation and went on a disability pension. This is the reason for her cane which she says "she is beginning to like because it is so helpful."

She will never forget how, just after her arrival in Toronto, she came upon the Katyn Monument. She didn't know anyone in the city and so she first of all went for a walk through the Polish neighborhood, primarily Roncevalles Avenue. She had known that this street was famous as the Polish one, that most of her countrymen lived there. She went down this street, looking around, entering stores, gazing at window displays, reading Polish advertisements... She met Poles everywhere. She went as far as Lake Ontario and there suddenly, on the boulevard ... she saw a monument with the inscription KATYN. She couldn't believe her eyes!

"I had no idea that such a monument existed here, even though I knew that there was already a Katyn Monument in London and that the truth about Katyn had already been known and accurately publicized in the West," she says with a sparkle in her eyes.

Shortly after her arrival in Canada she saw the Katyn roster. She had never seen it in Poland. She had only heard that it existed. In the home of newly made Polish friends in Toronto, she was shown the book of Adam Moszyński with the names of officers murdered in Katyn.

"I found my father's name, Captain Jerzy Kismanowski! It was a shock! I was speechless. I burst into tears right then and there, among my friends... I relived the news about my father's death all over again. In an exceptional manner, because it was in another country. It's too bad that my Mom was never able to see the book."

Jacek, though born only in 1964, is very interested in the events concerning the life of his grandfather, Captain Jerzy Kismanowski. He read his first book about Katyn when he was a young boy, in the early 70's. It was published in the Stalinist era and declared that the massacre was perpetrated by the Germans.

"They tried to inculcate this false information whereas everyone in Poland already knew the truth about Katyn." Jacek is still amazed at that. He recalls that he was at a youth camp in 1979. One evening they were talking together about the war, camps, the concentration camps and the POW camps... Someone brought up Katyn. Jacek mentioned that his grandfather had been killed there...

"Everyone, even the very young, maintained that the Russians had murdered the Polish officers. Only one boy, who usually didn't say too much, asked us whether we were sure that the Germans didn't commit the crime..."

Jacek knew also that his grandfather held the office of president of the "Sokół" association. And then one day, while he was in the *liceum*, he read somewhere that the "Sokół" association was being reactivated in Poznań. So he wrote a letter with the question as to whether they might know something about his grandfather. In response he was invited to the first general meeting of the association. It turned out that the Secret Service (SB) intercepted his letter. He remembers that on August 7, 1981, precisely on his eighteenth birthday, he was very surprised to receive a call from the Secret Service. They invited him to one of the coffee shops in Warsaw's Starówka district "for a discussion."

He recalls: "I went and there were two of them. They said they were history graduates. They asked me a lot of questions. Among other things they asked why I wanted to gather up information about my grandfather. They wanted also to learn things about me, about my opinions. They showered me with praise, saying that I was intelligent, that others had a good opinion of me in school, that they trusted me and eagerly would help me even to the point of travel overseas. They probably wanted to draw me in to working with them. They didn't however know everything, especially the fact that I already had a passport in my pocket and had plans to travel on vacation to Austria."

Jacek had earlier read a special brochure with instructions on how to behave when going to an interrogation at the Security Service (SB).

"I behaved exactly as the brochure directed. I knew that I couldn't give them any signature or tell them what I was really thinking. And they were naïve, even comic...," he adds.

Halina Kozłowska knows her father, Jerzy Kismanowski, truth be told, only from pictures and stories. In 1939 she was barely two years old and remembers only a few moments spent with him. One of them was when he was playing in their living room with her and her sister, Zosia, who was two years older than her. "We were climbing on his back and laughing boisterously!"

Their living room in Skierniewice was exceptionally beautifully decorated. In the high-ceilinged room there was mahogany furniture and a piano. There was an authentic chandelier as well as large paintings in golden frames. She remembered best of all, however, a huge crystal mirror framed in inlayed mahogany, with a decorative superstructure on top; it had tall columns, a number of tiers and reached right up to the ceiling.

Another scene is deeply imbedded in her memory. It was autumn 1939 and her father had already been called to the military. The war had begun. She and her mother and sister, Zosia, were going along in a farm wagon packed with their things and their father was on a bicycle alongside them.

"He was taking us to his parents and family in Warsaw. He thought that it would be safer there in time of war," Halina Kozłowska remembers, enunciating each word carefully. "I remember how he held onto the wagon with one hand and the handlebars of the bicycle with the other. All of sudden for a moment he broke off from us and disappeared in the press of refugees, horse-drawn wagons, bicycles, and people on foot burdened with small bundles... And we kept going on... We didn't see him again... After two or three days we returned back to Skierniewice in the midst of a crowd fleeing Warsaw."

She has learned his biography perfectly.

Jerzy Kismanowski was born on August 20, 1894 in Warsaw but he was from a land-owning family from the Great Poland region. He was a graduate of Władysław Górski Gimnazjum in Warsaw and participated in the First World War. He first served in the Prussian army and was a prisoner-of-war as a Prussian subject in the Russian camps at Orenburg and Tashkent. Joining the Polish Army in 1919, he was an assistant commander in Vilno and a liaison officer in Lvov. In 1921 he took command of the 42nd Infantry Regiment, and later was with the 58th Infantry Regiment in Poznań. After entering the reserves as a captain in 1922, he began work in the Military Institute of Publications in Warsaw. In 1926 he completed studies at the School of Political Science in Warsaw. He was the author of many literary works in military magazines. Among his many distinctions was the Virtuti Militari medal.

His daughter in Toronto has kept the original biographical sketch he wrote, and numerous other documents. "My father was a great Polish patriot. He was active socially and politically, corresponded with many political persons. His superiors described in their reports about him the characteristics of sense of duty, excellence, conscientiousness, sharp mind, exceptional talent and skill for organization, responsibility."

In 1934 Jerzy Kismanowski married Stanisława Wyrzutowicz from Skierniewice, who was younger than him by three years. She was one of the most beautiful and elegant women in the city. After the wedding they settled in Skierniewice, in her apartment house near the central market place. He served as a military commanding officer while she worked in the family pharmacy.

When Captain Kismanowski left for the war, his wife Stanisława turned to running a store with items needed in the villages. She sold grain, farm and garden tools, even carbide. There was a lot of work involved in this for her but the income was sufficient for the modest support of the family. When she was busy in the store, a kindly old man, Mr. Aleksander, took care of the two girls, Zosia and Halinka. He wanted to support an officer's wife when she had been left alone.

"He helped us dress, went with us on walks, got our food, read children's books to us, told us stories." Halina speaks of him today with affection, calling him "our beloved nanny." "He was our guardian and a genuine friend. Zosia and I loved and respected him. To this day the name Aleksander stirs in me warm feelings."

The family waited impatiently for Captain Kismanowski's return. All of them yearned for him, but his wife Stanisława the most. She received from him one or two letters. She knew that he had been imprisoned in the Kozelsk monastery. She would often lock herself in his beautifully decorated room with its mahogany furniture and she would play on the piano works reminiscent of their five years together, the most beloved period of her life. More than once the girls heard her sobbing and crying out, "Jerzy, come home..."

"She so loved that refined, upright and handsome man! She believed that in some miraculous way he would live through the Soviet captivity and return. She would say to us that even without hands, without legs, but only that she could see him alive," Halina still remembers.

After a long, uneasy silence without any news about their father, came the day in 1943, perhaps the most tragic in the life of Stanisława Kismanowska.

"Mom suddenly closed the shutters on the windows and the door of the store and, holding in her hand the newspaper with the names of those murdered in Katyn, broke down in tears." Halina can see that scene even today. "On the list she found the name of her husband, my father... She sobbed convulsively, so terribly that my sister and I feared for our Mom. We prayed that she wouldn't die on us..."

Captain Jerzy Kismanowski was taken from the camp in Kozelsk to his death in the Katyn Forest as one of the first, already on April 4, 1940, the second day of the transports out. Letters from his wife and other documents were found on his body. Some of them are falling apart and so copies have been made of them. Halina has also kept part of her parents' moving correspondence, from the time of their engagement. She takes in her hand a packet of letters full of intimate expressions. She reads with a trembling voice:

"Skierniewice, January 23, 1933. My dear beloved. What has happened to my Jerzy that he doesn't feel well? I would want to be by him, caress him and surround him with the very best care. For sure you would feel perfect next to me. As you know, my departure to Poronin is approaching. I feel sad and am distraught because we will not be able to see each other soon. I will write to you every day, I swear. I kiss you most dearly. In my thoughts I am always with you, my dear beloved. Stanisława."

"Poznań, February 14, 1933, Tuesday. My dear Stanisława! And so your wishes have come true. You have a lot of snow and can begin learning to ski. I am openly jealous of you, of the one who is teaching you to ski and to those men who are near you! I would like for none of them to be pleasing to you! But what can I do? I have to go along with it since I do desire whole-heartedly that my dear one have a good time, that she be happy and earn the top rank in skiing! Such, however, is fate that I unfortunately can't spend these pleasant times together with you, Stanisława. I will send myself off in my thoughts to Poronin and, if only in my dreams, I am with you. I am healthy and feel quite well. Once again I have a bit of work but too I was at a number of Carnival Balls. I have to admit openly that I feel deeply the loneliness of not being by you. Stanisława, take care that you don't come down with a cold and God forbid that something bad might happen to you. I am enclosing thousands of warm and passionate kisses. Bye! My dearest, sweetest girl! Your Jerzy."

Living through the German and Soviet occupations and then that of the communist regimes was not easy for a woman alone. Stanisława Wyrzutowicz's parents had died earlier before the war and she had to struggle by herself with her two daughters against many reversals of fortune, so humiliating, full of cruelty, undeserving for such a good human being...

Terror and fear reigned in Skierniewice under the Germans. At night, air raids and the wail of sirens and of bombs would harass the city-dwellers. They had to hide in trenches. "Mom had sewn backpacks for us and put hard biscuits and warm clothing in them. We were always in readiness."

Direct from the balcony of their apartment they could see the gallows that had been set up in front of the town hall. The Germans would hang from it Poles caught in street roundups. For each German killed by the Poles, at least ten Poles swept up by chance off the streets would be hung. At night trucks would often drive up to the town hall. Poles shackled in chains would be dragged from them, then imprisoned in the basement of the town hall, interrogated and pushed around. From time to time the Germans would post the list of those murdered and their families could come to claim the bodies...

"Mom was very sensitive to people's hardships. She was very active in giving help, advice and comfort. She would send packages with foodstuffs and warm clothing for Polish POWs and prisoners in German and Soviet camps. More than once she sheltered someone. Poles in the underground, soldiers of the Home Army. We were terribly afraid that the Germans would discover this," she says.

Stanisława Kismanowska also took great care of her daughters.

"Zosia and I always had the most beautifully tied ribbons in our hair and nicely sewn dresses." She smiles in amazement at her mother. "She was solicitous not only for the way we looked, but also for our behavior and education. She was our very best friend and surrounded us with tender care and love."

Their mother taught both Zosia and Halinka how to play the piano, showed them on the map all the countries of the world and spoke to them about each one. She imbued in them a love of literature and esteem for Poland. She placed Poles high on a pedestal, emphasized their gallantry and piety and Polish patriotic deeds. She herself prayed ardently and taught prayers to her girls. They would all three often kneel and beg God for His help for the poor people who were suffering in German and Soviet captivity.

That time of the family together in Skierniewice, of a home without a father, is interspersed for Halina Kozłowska with memories of German columns marching in the streets singing joyfully: haili-hailu-haila... She remembers the German officers in their elegant uniforms and tall, always brightly-shining officer boots. They used to enjoy themselves boisterously and merrily in Polish restaurants as well as on the municipal carousel which she adored. They would often throw candy to the children and pay for horse or carriage rides on the carrousel.

"One day a German officer pulled me out of a group of staring children, got on one of the horses, put me on his lap and we galloped along that way with the music. When the carousel stopped, he asked me if I wanted another ride. I had had enough and terrified ran quickly home. I was afraid of the Germans and went no more to the carousel."

One day Stanisława Kismanowska was notified that she was to be sent as forced labor to Germany. It was a tragedy for her since she didn't know what was to be done with the children. She went therefore to the authorities with this notification. She met there an acquaintance, a Volksdeutscher. It was thanks to her that she was crossed off the list and her notification of forced work in Germany nullified...

Their family home on the Market Square, being one of the prettiest in the city, was soon taken over by the Germans for their use. They threw the entire family out. Stanisława Kismanowska and her daughters had to live with strangers. After the Germans fled, they returned to their apartment house but only for a short while. The Soviet Army had arrived.

"A dirty, drunk and wild horde arrived," recalls Halina. "They threw people out of their houses, us too. They broke the locks, opened the cabinets and in front of our eyes stole almost everything. Those who protested, defended their families or possessions, were often shot."

She remembers that they had to live then in the countryside, near a forest, with tenant farmers. As a child she experienced her own gehenna. She often would hear shots fired in the forest, where the Soviets would take recalcitrant Poles and execute them. They raped women. She and her sister were there alone without their mother because she was running a store in Skierwienice to earn the basic necessities to live. She would return to the village only in the evening.

"I constantly remember how the people were intimidated by the Soviets: what's going to happen tomorrow...? When the bolshevik crimes came out into the open, the massacre of Polish officers in Katyn, the deportations of Poles to Siberia, it seemed that everything was coming to an end... That Poland would again cease existing, that others would tear her down, plunder her, erase her from the map...," Halina says as she recalls the terror-filled mood of the Stalin times. Everyone would listen, secretly, despite the prohibition, to the Voice of America and Radio Free Europe..." It was a such a small thing, a hope that someone was with us, that they wanted to do good for us," she recalls.

But soon enough the authorities confiscated our radio receivers, arrested many of the listeners of this voice from the free world. They would usually jam both of the stations.

She recalls too the later times of socialism in Poland with disgust, as "terrible and hideous." They were thrown out of their apartment on the Market Square by the communist regime of People's Poland as well. It was made the headquarters first of all of the Polish United Workers' Party and then of the League of Women.

"During the communist holidays of May 1st, July 22nd, and the anniversary of the October Revolution, representatives of the government would give their speeches from our balcony," she says remembering it as a farce, not without bitterness.

They never returned to those rooms at the front of the house. Other people were brought there by order of the housing allocation authorities. Other people began to come to Skierniewice. A new worker-peasant class arose and a new "intelligentsia" controlled by the communist government. They accepted a Poland under Soviet occupation and did not like that class of people who had had a "compromising status" in pre-war society.

"They desired to ruin and humiliate us, to plunder us of everything that we still had left. During one of the house searches, the Office of Security (UB), or perhaps the NKVD, seized all my father's medals and decorations, including his Virtuti Militari. I remember the medals. They were arranged securely in a stiff box. They also took from us piles of my father's books, documents of his and letters, and even the banner from "Sokół," of which he had been president. We don't know even today what happened to it all. Why haven't those stolen historical documents and archives been returned to us, even though Poland now calls itself free and independent?" she asks rhetorically, keeping before her eyes the trucks driving off with those precious remembrances of her father. "There were several house searches...," she says, sighing and unwilling to revisit them in memory.

In the 40's, her mother was twice arrested and imprisoned. For what? They had no idea... The girls, only several years old, deprived suddenly of any care or supervision, didn't know what to do but decided to keep up the store. They went to the store, opened it, and became store assistants... They were stalwart in bringing food to their mother in prison.

"It was dreadful. Mom wasn't mistreated physically, but they tormented her with questions about her husband and his political activities. They tried to persuade her of various happenings which had never taken place." She emphasized that her mother didn't want to say much to her daughters as to what had happened. After being released from prison, she taught them certain rules of behavior for when they might be asked a question about their father. They were to answer: "He went off to the war and didn't return."

Following the war, Stanisława Kismanowska managed to create for her daughters a moderately happy home and pleasant childhood despite the deprivation, harassment and historical injustice. Their apartment always shone bright and beautiful with a decorated Christmas tree every Christmas, and the Christmas Eve celebration always began with the sighting of the first star. There were always small presents and tasty home delights.

"In the atmosphere of carols sung in unison, of sparklers on the Christmas tree, our hearts would grow warm and we would feel good together," she says as tears glisten in her eyes...

Likewise at Easter, the girls always had their food blessed, with its butter lamb and Easter cake and poppy-seed cake which their mother would bake often at night. Her youngest daughter still remembers the delectable odor of clean, starched sheets as well of freshly waxed floors... She knows too that her mother had to sell off many valuable things in order to get the money they needed to live on.

"In order to help her, right after graduation my sister and I went to work, I to the Institute of Domology and Zosia to the Department of Health," says Halina. "Earlier, while still in school, and then later when working, we never mentioned that our father had died in Katyn. When asked, we answered in the manner our mother had taught us... We never brought up either my father's only brother, Karol Kismanowski, a lieutenant-legionnaire, who died a hero's death in the battle of Browar near Kiev in May of 1920, or of several other members of our patriotic, gallant family, who gave their lives for Poland as they fought beyond her borders. In those times such family connections would bring only trouble. We would not have been admitted to higher studies or been given a job.

After all these ordeals, Stanisława Kismanowska fell seriously ill. She had a nervous breakdown. She was financially in ruins; she would soon have to close her store since private initiative was persecuted under socialism by the levying of high taxes and through constant inspections. She survived on a very modest widow's pension which she began to receive only after many years.

"Had our father still been alive, our and our mother's fates would have certainly been much different," Halina sighs. Their mother inculcated in her daughters patriotism and Polishness, using their father as example. She loved him to the end of her life. Never did any other man appear at her side.

Stanisława Kismanowska stayed the longest in Skierniewice, at first with Zosia and Halina, and then by herself. She died in 1980. None of her siblings are still living either. It is already subsequent generations, the third, fourth. Besides strangers, dishonest people have taken advantage of the unresolved question of ownership of the house. Newcomers from the regained western lands have come to her house on Market Place, where Halina was born, and settled in and now operate the store.

Halina Kozłowska has been in Poland twice since her departure. She repeats however: "I would very much like to go to Poland before the year is out. I would like to turn over whatever inheritance remains from my mother to charitable purposes. I'm going to try to persuade my sister of this. It is better that our family inheritance would help sick or lonely children, or lonely or old people, the homeless or hungry, than those scoundrels. I think that it would be best if we gave over the part of our Skierniewice inheritance to the Church and it would become owner and could dispose of it as it saw fit."

Can Halina Kozłowska find a way to forgive the wrongs that she and her family experienced in Poland?

"I don't know." Her reply reaches to "all the German and Soviet murderers as well as the Polish thieves and flunkeys of communism. I simply don't want to know them! I don't want to remember them! Let Providence judge them."

Immediately from the Kozłowski house I go to downtown Toronto, to the elegant headquarters of the Association of Polish Combatants, built by old Polonia, on Beverly Street. The many Poles who came are grateful for the present interest in the topic of the the children of Katyn. Questions and demands are numerous.

Lech Żuk, a emigrant of the Solidarity era, says: "Please write that it is time that the words '15 thousand perished officers of the Polish Army' disappear from the Katyn Monument in Toronto. Those words don't tell the truth. What does 'perished' mean? That they left the house and didn't come back? They perished somewhere off by themselves? They didn't perish somehow but were murdered by the Soviets! And also there were seven thousand more!"

Apolonia Kojder, young, born in Canada, whose uncle was killed in Katyn:

"It was hardly a few years ago that I found my father's brother on the lists of the victims of Katyn. On the internet. My father didn't live long enough to know the cruel truth. It is good that the Katyn slaughter is being written about and discussed. Future generations should know the truth and remember the untruths of the past. Your book has to come out in English because in Canada the truth about Katyn is not widely known."

Irena and Krzysztof Zarzecki, writers, translators, who live in Warsaw and Toronto: "Do Polish institutions and the government support the preparation of your book?"

After my reply in the negative ... a collection of money was begun for my ticket. Radio Toronto also joined in later to the same effort... I was given enough for my return trip to Poland...

15

DEVOTEE OF FREEDOM

Chicago, Illinois, USA, July 2002

It is a modern and luxurious forty-two story skyscraper in the very center of Chicago, on the Gold Coast, not far from Lake Michigan, only two years old. Mirosława and Bogdan Horoszowski, the only Poles in this residential tower, occupy a large, comfortable apartment on the twentieth floor. Their apartment is richly furnished with a silver service, crystal chandeliers among golden framed pictures and soft rugs on the natural parquet. A certain coziness is added to their air-conditioned interior by two Persian cats, one white and fluffy like a ball of snow, the other a color reminiscent of coffee cream, both demanding to be petted. And beyond the window, as if in the palm of one's hand, the panorama of Chicago's skyline with one of the world's tallest skyscrapers, the Sears Tower.

It is in the smallest of the rooms of this skyscraper apartment that one finds the world of Bogdan Horoszowski. Over his desk is a picture of Piłsudski, in his magnificent library are mainly Polish books, on the walls are pictures of his family. History and documents are the love and passion of Horoszowski. Our meeting begins by looking at his own English-language film about the fates of the Horoszowski family. Their lives are closely intertwined with the complex history of Poland, with the frequent invasions of the Republic, the wars and battles, for which reason the film is rich in extensive historical commentary.

"I prepared it having in mind my daughter, Ivetka, and grandson. I wanted them to know the true history of Poland and where their family came from," he explains as he starts the projector. The screen is large, wide, and the picture is in color. I make myself comfortable in the sofa, with a Coca-Cola in hand, and feel as if I'm in the movie theater.

The first scenes of the film present his father, Romuald Adolf Horoszowski. He was born in 1894 in Stryj, in the vicinity of Lvov. This is why there are many reminders of Lvov as well as many links to the history of Europe and of the Poland partitioned between its three neighbors. The documentary talks of his childhood in a gentry family, of school in Lvov and of studies in the officers' school at Kormend in Hungary. Capturing the atmosphere of Vienna and Budapest which he visited when on liberty, the camera even caught a glimpse of the watch he wore. There are many other things in the film—horses, maps with the changing borders not only of the Republic but also of the Austro-Hungarian empire, and the music of Strauss. A member of the staff, Romuald Adolf Horoszowski is tall, handsome, as he takes the military oath... His son's voice adds that he was then already an accomplished rider and rifleman.

As a young, barely twenty-two year old lieutenant, he was transferred to Lubaczów. It was the year 1916, and so he went to the front as an Austrian soldier, with the 9th Infantry Regiment. He was shortly thereafter captured by the Russians but was able to escape from the train transporting the prisoners-of-war to Siberia. He had to care for his wounds and return to health over a long period of time after his captivity. After a few months of hospital care, he returned to the 9th Infantry Regiment and immediately afterward found himself at the front. In 1917, he was again wounded and had to return to the hospital. Later he was sent to the Italian front where, in 1918, he was wounded for a third time. Later he joined up with the nascent Polish Army and fought for Lvov.

"My parents met in Lvov but had to separate quickly. My father was transferred to Łańcut where he was the commander of the prisoner-of-war camp for bolsheviks. Later he fought on the Lithuanian-Byelorussian front and participated in the battles for Vilno and Kiev.

In 1920 he visited Stryj. At this moment there appears on the screen his native village, members of his family greeting him. Also the Horoszowski sawmill and the horses that they raised. The young soldier had indeed things to boast of. At the front he had been decorated with the Virtuti Militari cross and other major medals. At a certain moment the film's maker turns to his American daughter:

"I have to tell you, Ivetka, that your grandfather had not merely military talent but also theatrical talent. During his military service he acted in several plays in several cities. He looked everywhere for Helena of the intelligence service whom he had met in Lvov. He saw her again in 1921, as he was performing in a theater in Przemyśl, and almost immediately proposed.

Their wedding took place in August of that same year in the Przemyśl cathedral. Their son filmed the interior of the beautiful church during his sentimental trip there in 1989.

After the wedding the young couple settled in Łańcut. They came to love the city. But hardly a year later Romuald Horoszowski was transferred to Grodno, to the 81st Riflemen's Regiment. In 1927 they took up residence in the former castle of Stefan Batory, right on the Niemen River. The film shows the history of these distant lands, brings close the beautiful old buildings and quaint recesses of Grodno, as well as its present state of devastation and ruin.

"I was born in the Stefan Batory castle, in April 20, 1930. But I haven't done a film about myself yet," jokes Bogdan Horoszowski. He has an exceptionally warm and peaceful face. Diminutive, slender, he gives the impression of always smiling. His grey hair fits perfectly the hue of his suit, harmonizes with his light sport shirt, pants, and shoes.

After lunch, in a restaurant near the skyscraper which, so it seems, serves the best omelets in Chicago, we go to the deck. We talk about Poland against this backdrop, on the comfortable rooftop, in the thick company of neighboring skyscrapers, in the very heart of the second largest city in the United States...

"I lived in Grodno for only three years following my birth." Bogdan Horoszowski expresses each word slowly and carefully, in beautiful Polish, without any trace of an English accent. "I remember the castle and river as if in a mist. There sticks in my memory the image of a faucet strangely fastened to a wall, of weird looking windows in the enormous castle... My sister was born in Grodno two years after me. I called her Ika though her given name is Irena. She had a dark blue baby carriage with large wheels..."

After three years Captain Romuald Horoszowski was again transferred. He became the quartermaster in Grudziądz, over two hundred kilometers from Warsaw. As a small child, Bogdan fell in love with Grudziądz and, as a young boy, adored going to the military march pasts and training maneuvers. His father was an excellent horseman. Bogdan admires Polish officers, but only those from before the war: "They were handsome and wore their uniforms as if brand new. Gentlemen, somewhat gallant in behavior, but always with class. You could recognize a Polish officer at a distance!"

Generally, the social life in the garrisons was a very rich one. In Grudziądz likewise there were balls, various celebrations and social gatherings.

"My father very much enjoyed companionship, and especially beautiful women. And balls too, at which my Mom would complain that he was the last one to leave the dance floor. He also liked theatrical performances, special events, things colorful and showy."

In their house they always spoke of Marshal Piłsudski as Grandfather. He remembers how as a five-year-old everyone was fearful: "Grandfather is ill; what will become of Poland?..."

"I had met Grandfather Piłsudski," says Bogdan animatedly. "My father took me once to Warsaw, where there was a parade on the fields at Mokotów.

Grandfather was on the grandstand; this was in 1935. When he died, I saw people kneeling in the streets and weeping... It was a civil tragedy, a national tragedy, a time of great mourning..."

Bogdan Horoszowski continues his story. In the summer of 1937, his father was transferred again, this time to Sokółka. There Bogdan began to go to school. From school he remembered his well-liked Polish teacher, Mrs. Pawłowska, the director's wife. The Pawłowskis were very much devoted to the school. They themselves met the same fate as many patriots from the circle of the pre-war intelligentsia: he was killed in Katyn, and she survived deportation to Kazakhstan...

In Sokółka, one could feel already a whiff of the coming war. There were increased maneuvers, shooting practice, and other war preparations. One day military gasmasks were handed out to all the residents of the garrison; they were of Polish issue, green, packed in tin tubes. They had to learn how to assemble and use them. Then just before the war they received other masks, English ones.

"Everyone suspected that Hitler would use gas and so we had to be prepared for such an attack."

He learned of the war's outbreak on the radio. He heard that Westerplatte was putting up resistance...

After the first attack of the German air force, the entire garrison in Sokółka received an evacuation order. He remembers the scene exactly: he was sitting in a horse-drawn wagon with his mother, sister Ika, and the nanny. Suddenly he bolted out of the wagon and ran home. There was a photograph album in my father's desk.

"I began to tear pictures out impulsively. I don't know why I did that. They called me but I was packing pictures into my backpack... Thanks to that we have them to look at today," he shows them to us like family relics. They are yellowed now, a bit deteriorated, but that's explained by having survived the war in a small boy's backpack.

He remembers how the civilian columns, of which their wagon was part, followed the army through Sokółka and subsequent towns. His father was on a horse in the front, would often come up to their wagon and ask if everything was in order. After some time, when contact with the military was broken, their wagon turned toward Grodno. The Soviets attacked Grodno a week later.

"I was afraid that they would tie Polish children to their tanks and attack Polish positions." As corroboration of the experiences encoded in his child's memory, Bogdan Horoszowski shows me Jerzy Robert Nowak's book, *Silenced Crime* (*Przemilczane zbrodnie*).

Grodno fought for several days. They had to separate from his father. The son didn't receive specific orders from Captain Horoszowski, but he remembers his father said, as he kissed him good-bye: "Nunek, now you are the sole man in the family. You have to watch over the women."

When his father bent over him, his son managed to unpin from his uniform some of the dangling medals. "Only I couldn't get off the Virtuti Militari. I safeguarded the others in my backpack and they survived the war," he smiles.

Towards the end of September, at the station in Grodno, the Soviets packed Mrs. Horoszowska and her children into a cattle-car. But she knew the bolsheviks from her time in the underground. She placed herself and her children close to the door, obstructing it partially so that it couldn't be entirely closed. She ordered her children:

"Just as the train is leaving the station we have to jump! Each with his backpack. And, after jumping, to remain still in place!"

Her son is still amazed at her courage and determination. And too the discipline of everyone involved, but then they were from a military family. He describes the events emotionlessly:

"As the train was moving along slowly, my mother pushed us out one at a time, my sister, nanny, and me with the dog Żaba. She herself jumped out last..."

He remembers that after jumping out he squeezed himself against the rail embankment and waited for darkness. It seemed an eternity. The train passed on and no one else jumped out besides them. His mother gathered the family into a group and they fled across the fields and roadless areas as far as possible from the train tracks. They hurried on for a long time, in the darkness, his legs already aching. After eating their biscuits, at his Mom's command "Time to sleep," they immediately fell asleep. The next day they went as far as the semaphore. His mother told them to hide in the bushes, and she herself put her ear to the train tracks until a train approached and stopped at the semaphore. After a short conversation with the engineer, she motioned in their direction with her head and ordered: "Come on now. Get in the locomotive!"

Bogdan Horoszowski reaches without difficulty into the rich resources of his memory: "We sat in the engine area on the coal. We were going in the direction of Małkinia, that is, according to the Ribbentrop-Molotov pact, to the border between the parts of Poland partitioned between the Germans and the Soviets. In Małkinia we spent the night in some kind of copse. During our passage to the German side we would fall and rise at a moment's notice. We almost fell into the bolsheviks' hands. Once again my Mom saved us, that time thanks to her knowledge of German."

In Małkinia they had found their first place to stay but danger arose immediately ... from the part of their Polish hosts. They insisted on getting gold. The tireless underground activist did not shut an eye the whole night as she held ready to fire a pistol with an inlaid pearl handle, a present from her father. The then nine-year-old Bogdan remembered perfectly the menacing look of the peasant when in the morning his mother ordered him about, threatening him with the Germans and demanding to be taken to the train station, from which they traveled on to Warsaw.

"The train was full of Huns," says Bogdan Horoszowski. "We were unable to get on it, but once again my mother's knowledge of German helped, and too that she was an attractive woman. German soldiers from one of the compartments pulled us in through the window. After a couple of hours we were in Warsaw."

They looked out over a bombed Warsaw. They were able to go with a cart to 7 May 3rd Street where Hala Iskierkowa, Mrs. Horoszowska's friend from her legionnaire days, lived in a seven-floor building. She welcomed them warmly.

"My Mom took work, as many wives of captured Polish officers did, and she became a waitress in a coffee shop," he says. "Thanks to that we received food coupons. Our nanny Klaudzia decided to find out what was happening to her family in Toruń. She went and we never saw her again. There were only the three of us then with the dog Żaba." They had no information from his father.

He and his sister began to go to Polish school. The Poles, however, were limited in what they could learn; for example, they were forbidden to study history or geography.

At school he made his first contact with an underground resistance organization. Mr. Cieślak, one of the teachers, recruited students to the Grey Ranks. He had, however, to have complete confidence in the ones chosen. He enlisted the twelve-year-old Bogdan Horoszowski for courier work and later for painting in town the Fighting Poland anchors. They would do other things as well: carry over arms, sprinkle with salty kvass the spectators at the movies, tear down German flags.

He remembers Jewish friends who had to go to the ghetto and he didn't understand why. He was in the ghetto, saw the hunger and terrible destitution. Within the activities of the Grey Ranks he would provide Jews with food, from the trolley, through the wall or entering the ghetto area through the Iron Gate.

"In time of war it was normal; people helped each other simply because of human solidarity."

Besides the poverty, he also saw the great wealth of some Jews, owners of factories and workshops. He was unable to understand how they weren't bothered by the annihilation of their people, how they didn't help them. The X Department, that is the Jewish gestapo, was active in the ghetto. Dressed in uniforms of jackets, overcoats, and knee-boots. They had large sticks. These were police cooperating with the Germans. All that was needed was a nod of the head and they would kill one of their own innocent compatriots..."

The ghetto uprising began in 1943. "As part of the activities of the Grey Ranks, we began to unblock the sewer covers so that Jews might be able to escape through them," he recalls. Though death at the occupant's hands threatened them, the then fourteen-year-old Bogdan minimizes his participation in giving help to the Jews: "It was nothing special! The Jews were Poles, only of a different religion! There's nothing to boast of. It was simply a human reflex!"

One day he was taking out the trash from their fourth floor. As he was opening downstairs the container's heavy lid, he suddenly saw a head. Yellowish, with deeply circled eyes. He drew back in terror. It was a Jewish boy, hunted as an animal, hungry. He took him secretly to the boiler room, bathed him under the fire-hose. He brought him some clothes from his home, and fed him.

"I reported this to our outpost of the Grey Ranks. They helped him to get out of Warsaw," Bogdan explains.

Up to 1943 they had no sign from his father. Precisely on April 13 of that year, German radio broadcast a communication concerning the discovery of the graves of Polish officers at Katyn in an area occupied by the Germans. This radio, popularly called "yip-yap," announced that Jewish commissars of the NKVD had committed the murders. Shortly afterward the Germans began to print the lists of the victims. However Captain Horoszowski was not on them.

"While in one of the Warsaw movie theaters during the operation '*wszystkie świnie siedzą w kinie*' ('all the swine sit in the movie theater'), I saw on the screen during a program of "*Wochenschau*" scenes from the exhumation of Polish officers in the Katyn Forest. There was no mention of my father." He says that the film was terrifying.

While living in Warsaw, the Horoszowskis received packages of food from Vilno. The sender was a Roman Kawecki, whom they didn't know. Once while cutting the bacon they had received, a gold ruble fell out of it. It turned out that there were many more of them in the bacon...

"One evening someone knocked at the door. On the doorstep appeared ... my father. It was difficult to describe our joy!"

It turned out that after getting separated in Grodno, Captain Horoszowski and other officers were taken prisoner by the NKVD. They were packed into cattle cars at night but his father succeeded in escaping. His experience from the First World War helped him in his escape, as his wife too had profited from her knowledge of the bolsheviks and their prisons. But the officers who were traveling with him on that transport died about six months later in the Katyn massacre.

After escaping the clutches of the NKVD, Captain Horoszowski made his way to Vilno. There he was active in the Home Army and at the same time worked in a slaughterhouse; it was from there that the packages with gold rubles hidden in the bacon were sent to the family. He knew well that in Warsaw his wife had a good friend from the underground years at May 3rd Street. After his arrival in Warsaw the captain continued his activities in the underground. There was a store with moonshine at 64 Grzybowska Street, a contact point of the Home Army. He worked there officially as a salesclerk under falsified documents with the name Roman Kawecki. He didn't live with the family, only behind the store. He was by this time in poor health since his ordeals in two wars had left its mark on him.

"I would see my father often because at that time I held the concession for the yeast trade," Bogdan Horoszowski remembers cheerfully.

Further discussion of his remembrances is put off to the following day. He has a lot to tell. His remembrances could fill an entire novel.

He observed the German retreat in July 1944 from the Poniatowski Bridge. Because he lived next to it, he was given the order to observe all movement and to make a report to the leadership of the Grey Ranks. "Komar" made it known then that the Germans were hurrying cows, goats, pigs across the bridge. These animals would serve as provisions for the weakening German army. The soldiers of the Wehrmacht went along now without spirit and enthusiasm, dirty, unshaven, bearing lowered rifles.

"It gave us hope that the war would end soon. We were waiting for the order to begin the uprising. It was to have lasted only a short time, its goal being to get control of Warsaw in the course of three days, without Soviet help." He admits, however, that one day he was terrified at the comparison of powerful German tanks with the Molotov cocktails collected by the Grey Ranks which were to destroy those colossi...

The two first orders to take positions at the outposts were retracted. On Tuesday, August 1, there was a light rain. Bogdan Horoszowski, "Komar," received the order to station himself at Grzybowska Street. This area was later called the "Steel Redoubt." On his way he met his sister. She was going with a backpack "to her spot." It was only then that he realized that she too was in the Grey Ranks, in the youngest troop. She had been trained as a nurse.

He ran up to Grzybowska Street out of breath. The boys were already standing in their places and some were loading boxes with weapons and grenades. There was continuous gunfire, many were running in various directions looking for their units or sub-units. The Germans immediately opened fire and at once took command of the bridges. He remembers the barricades, orders, thunder of bursting projectiles, more and more debris, many actions well and poorly organized. His father also took part in the uprising. His mother looked after feeding those fighting. She was living with her daughter in the provisional apartment of a kitchen and two badly damaged rooms. She also believed in victory. Was there then any other option but to fight?

Fourteen-year-old Bogdan often helped in getting supplies. He still remembers the taste of the vegetables from gardens in Warsaw: cucumbers, tomatoes, onions, new potatoes. He would fill sacks full of them.

One day someone noticed that "Komar" was covered in blood. He himself didn't feel it but shrapnel of a projectile had pricked him. No one in his family was wounded in the uprising; even so "Komar" lost many close friends.

He had kept too the amateur pictures he made at the time of the uprising with his Sida camera. He has preserved images of the fighting capital and many friends from the Grey Ranks in the small black and white prints. Bogdan has also in his possession professional photographs, today the only existing ones, of the Warsaw Uprising done by his friend Kris Sylwester Braun, a Warsaw geodesist with a passion for chronicling and photography. These pictures, made by him during the time of the uprising portray the 63 days of struggle for an independent Poland. They are sad, tragic, but at the same time heroic and true. They have already traveled around the world.

The conversation turns back to the uprising. It was a pretty day, the weather too nice to have fallen into the enemy's hands. The Germans, however, surrounded the group of young insurgents, among whom was "Komar," and led them to the Museum of the Polish Army. They placed them in front of a tank that was prepared to attack. The majority looked around, then to heaven, and bid their last good-byes to this world.

"It was my final moment... 'But to be killed at such a young age?' I thought at the time as before me passed by all my fourteen years."

All of a sudden, amidst the din and whistle of projectiles over the tank near them, they were taken and thrown into the basement of the National Museum. They were brought out three days later, having been in the basement without food, even without water. They stood next to a German position firing at places in Warsaw, including the house where he lived. Again they waited, dreading death at any second, mostly from the flame-throwers which were incinerating people. However the Germans led their group under a viaduct and ordered them to cross to the other side of the bridge."

They were taken to the Western station, where electric trains had been positioned, and then on to the camp at Pruszków. They received a bit of food. He remembers that he cooked over a rubbish heap. Two days later the Germans loaded them into a cattle car and, before sealing them in, magnanimously gave them a piece of bread and a bit of water. From behind the cattle car's bars, he carefully made note of the direction. He feared that they were going to Auschwitz but he caught sight of a sign for Breslau, which is Wrocław.

They traveled up to Zoest, a German concentration camp right at the

Belgian border. Their transport had been under severe air attacks by the Allies all along the way.

"For days I had the pleasure of watching how they were battering the Third Reich," he laughs, even though he too was in danger. "During the bombardment the sentries guarding us would run down from their towers and hide themselves in shelters. I decided then to escape."

After weeks of some fortuitous and some heroic travails, he returned to Poland. He searched out the railroad stations, traveled on a lot of trains, primarily on open cars. Finally, he traveled on to Częstochowa where he sought out the relatives of his friends. The Germans were still occupying Częstochowa but they were beginning to withdraw. He joined up again with the resistance movement and took part in destroying German targets, among them a food depot.

He was in Częstochowa at the beginning of 1945. When the weather began to get warmer, he went to Toruń, again by various means of transportation, train, cars, farm-wagons. His mother and sister were living in Toruń in the house bought by his parents before the war.

His father came to Toruń only for a few days. He was already seriously ill and embittered. His dreams for the future, for an independent Poland for which he had fought in both wars, had not materialized. He had lost all his possessions and now had qualms of conscience that he had not secured anything for his children. He had not managed even to bequeath anything at all to his son as he soon found himself in the hospital in Bydgoszcz and from there left the world forever. He died from tuberculosis in 1946, at the age of fifty-two.

After his father's death, Bogdan, his mother and his sister continued to live in Toruń another five years. In 1951 they sold their house which already housed compulsory tenants; nevertheless, they had to pay an enrichment tax. After which, they returned to Warsaw.

They received three rooms with kitchen and bath in one of the villas there. Mrs. Horoszowska was hired to work in a geodesic office and Irena studied dentistry. Bogdan intended to become an engineer and began evening studies at the Engineering College. He worked at the same time.

He joined the "Service to Poland" movement which was chiefly made up of members of the Grey Ranks who wished their country's liberation and the establishment of democracy. Bogdan was a commander in this organization.

"I thought then that something could yet be achieved in Poland." He recalls that he greeted Stanisław Mikołajczyk with a degree of hope. "It soon turned out that the West could not be counted on. The Office of Security (UB) went wild, spreading terror and repression, throwing people in prison, exterminating people in prison, sending them to work camps in the coal mines. A lot of my friends from the uprising were killed. For having done nothing! And I became a class enemy, and my name was on their black list."

He still shudders at the thought of the obligatory parades, carrying red flags, hoisting the hated portraits of Bierut or Stalin. He couldn't bear the servitude, the deceit, the forced communist propaganda. After his return from Germany he had wanted immediately to escape to the West. But his mother had asked: "What will happen to us?"

So he bit his tongue and got a job, initially in Warsaw's Water Works where he did microscopic analyses of the soil, and then in the Ministry of Transportation on Chałubiński Street.

"They soon made me the director of excursions at this resort," he laughs. "I would take our dignitaries all over Poland in special cars with yellow lace curtains, hitched to trains on various routes. I would first of all get my orders and then I would gather everyone at the main station. I noticed that those on official business and on vacation would always have very young wives..."

Though the wages at the ministry were nothing special, he could travel a lot around Poland and was left alone. Even though he didn't hide in a questionnaire at work the fact that he had fought in the Warsaw Uprising and that he was not in the party, he wasn't recruited either for the party or the professional union. And what was most important, he wasn't bothered by the Office of Security (UB). He had already had contact with them on an earlier occasion. They had called him in once to their headquarters in the Mostowski Palace when he was at the time a commander in the "Service to Poland"; someone had denounced him as a class enemy. He remembered the interrogation at the Office of Security (UB) as humiliating and nonsensical.

In 1957 the Ministry of Transportation sent him into the countryside to help in the harvest. He didn't belong to the Polish Youth Association but he preferred the trip to spending his time in meetings. For two months he drove a tractor with sheaf-binder on the state farms. He was congratulated and praised for the work.

"I told myself then: enough of this comedy! I'm not interested in this kind of career. I've got to get out of here!"

An opportunity soon presented itself. In August 1958, he was sent with a group of others from the Ministry to an international exposition of road-construction in Brussels. As with the others, he wasn't given personal possession of his own passport. And he had to leave another document, his military ID, in Poland, at the Military Draft Headquarters. Orbis, the organizer of the trip, supplied them with pocket money, five dollars.

He recalls: "Before leaving, I sold my motorcycle, got my personal affairs in order, all because I planned to remain in the West. I said good-bye to my Mom and sister as I believed that they would now manage without me. I had plans for them to join me later."

In Brussels they stayed at the consulate. Their daily menu consisted of a ham sandwich and a bottle of Coca-Cola.

"Yet the exposition was marvelous! Brussels is a beautiful city. Everything, in comparison with Warsaw, was bright and opulent," he says in admiration.

Bogdan Horoszowski continued going to the exposition right up to the last day but then he didn't get on the return bus. Later he presented himself to the center for political refugees in Brussels and received some basic necessities. He requested political asylum.

Ten days later Bogdan received his political asylum, as proof of which he shows the documentation and even his Belgian passport which was issued in Brussels. He was then twenty-eight years old.

"My dream was America," he explains. "I was raised on Mark Twain and I loved to travel. I looked on Brussels only as a stop on my way to freedom."

Besides there was his fiancée waiting for him in Canada, Mira Kazimier-czak from Warsaw. She had left for the West a year earlier than him, to go to her older sister in Toronto. They had been writing all this time to each other and Mira was waiting for him to arrive.

In April 1960, he left finally to the America of his dreams. From Montreal, where the ship tied up, he went directly to Toronto, into the embrace of his fiancée.

A year later he and Mira were wed. He had been knocking on the US Consulate door all the time. After three years of waiting, he finally received the desired visa to his dreamed-of mainstay of freedom. In 1963, in a Rambler packed primarily with books, which he has always collected, they crossed the border in Detroit. They stopped in Chicago though they had thought of settling in California. However, they rented an apartment on Michigan Avenue, not far from the Museum of Science and Industry. "It was furnished and I remember best of all the bed; it folded up during the day and opened at night. It was fantastic."

Mira, with a mechanical engineering degree from Toronto, got a job in her field at the designing office of U.S.Steel.

Bogdan was employed in the Dietzgen company, selling and repairing surveying tools and geodesy instruments. True to his promises he brought his mother and sister to America. Irena, a dentist, lives in Florida whereas Helena Horoszowska was not able to sink roots in American soil. She didn't feel at ease in Chicago, would leave and then return. She wanted only to be laid at rest in Poland after her death. She is buried in the cemetery at Bydgoszcz, next to her husband.

"Brussels granted me political asylum but the Polish consulate in Chicago would not give me a visa in 1974 for my mother's burial. Therefore I had her body cremated and the urn I sent to Poland," he says not without bitterness.

His drive for freedom and self-reliance didn't permit him to be fully satisfied with his work at the Dietzgen company. After eight years he started up his own company, entirely his own, in his house on the north side of Chicago.

"It was then that our Ivetka was born and I was able to be with her all day long." He says that he has loved her from the time of their only child's birth in 1968. "All the while she was growing up was the happiest time of my life," he smiles delightedly.

The steel mill where his wife was working moved to Pittsburgh. Mira Horoszowska didn't want to go there. Because she was skilled at sewing, she decided to change professions.

"It seems to me that I was always occupied with fashions, from my youngest years. Already as a small girl, I would peek in on women sewing, manage to sit with them for hours at a time, and make note of what their hands created," recalls Mira Horoszowska, who is seven years younger than her husband.

Mira is a beautiful woman. Shapely, tanned, very slim. Her predilection is betrayed by her original and tasteful pink-heather outfit. "I always liked to

Cemetery at Miednoye, Russia, decorated by the families of the victims in 1999, prior to its official opening in 2000. Courtesy of Kazimiera and Janusz Lange, Katyn Family Łódź, Poland.

Miednoye cemetery during the official opening on September 2, 2000. Courtesy of Kazimiera and Janusz Lange, Katyn Family Łódź, Poland.

dress nicely and I simply loved jewelry, but in my family everyone had been engineers and so I followed in their footsteps," she says spiritedly. Later that evening, at suppertime, she added: "My father raised me. My Mom had been killed during the war and her place was taken by a stepmother. I had a brother in Gliwice who is no longer living. In Poland today we have only graves."

When she was pregnant, she sewed a bit and then when the daughter of her dreams was born, she, in order to be close to Ivetka, opened her own shop. She not only sewed but also began to design. Starting up in the 1970's was not so easy. She had a lot to learn.

Today Mira Horoszowski is ranked among the leading fashion designers in the United States. The prices of her designs are on a level with the dresses of Dior or Armani. Their cost runs from two to eight thousand dollars. They are prepared in the workshop of Mira Couture, in the adjoining skyscraper, where over twenty people are at work.

"Ivetka was and is our life." They repeat that she not only fulfilled their expectations but surpassed them. Ivette graduated from Lake Forest College and studied at the Art Institute of Chicago where she received a grant from this renowned school. She has also won beauty contests: twice she was Miss

Illinois, and in 1991 won the title of the Most Beautiful Expatriate Polish Woman. This crowned beauty has traveled a lot, through Poland as well, always appearing in the dresses of the Mira Couture firm. During her student years she was a model then too, one of the best in Chicago. For many years now Ivette has decorated the covers of a large number of American magazines not merely as a model and beauty queen, most recently as Mrs. Illinois 2001, but also as a designer.

The portraits of Mira and Ivette, as successful Polish women, were shown lately in a photographic exhibition at the Polish Museum in Chicago.

Mira: "I am very proud that I am Polish and I underscore that in every interview."

Bogdan: "I always say that I was formed from Polish culture and history. I preserve them not only at home but among American acquaintances. However, the German occupation and then a half century of Soviet occupation took from me my Poland. Not much has changed there today and I don't have much to look back to and yearn for. Despite my parents who couldn't imagine giving up Poland, I was forced to seek out freedom in America."

16

FUGITIVE FROM THE
SAILING VESSEL
"DAR POMORZA"

Pender Island, British Colombia,
Canada, August 2002

I was born in Vilno, the old city of Gedymin, in 1930, exactly 500 years after the death of the great Lithuanian Prince Witold. That's the reason I am named Witold. I was the second of four children of Olympia Zambrzycka, a geography teacher, and Stanisław Swianiewicz, an economics professor at Vilno University. My sister Marylka was two years older than me, Jurek two years younger and Bernadeta nicknamed Dzidzia, four years younger.

We lived at 7 Piaska Street, in a pleasant little house with a large garden. The house was warm and charming but without amenities. We had to get water from a well. I remember that across the street from us lived a Jew. He was short, had a small grocery store and a daughter named Pearl who wanted to play with my sister Marylka. In the period between the wars, the Jews made up one third of the inhabitants of Vilno; most of them lived in terrible poverty. I received my first lessons in anti-semitism from my nanny Jadzia, later these were reinforced at the Jesuit elementary school where I attended the second and third grades. I recall that my father was very upset at that, being always quite tolerant toward all the national minorities.

For vacation we would usually go to Wiazyń, now in Belarus, to the small estate of our grandfather, the father of my mother, Józef Zambrzycki. I know that my uncle Stanisław Zambrzycki also lived there; he perished at age twenty-nine, at the battle of the Niemen River, on September 28, 1920. After his death, he was awarded the Virtuti Militari cross and his wife was given the concession for a store that could sell alcohol. The estate was located in the Mołodeczno District, on the Polish-Russian border of the time. Its location was unfortunate. At the time of the fixing of the borders of the Second Polish Republic, in 1921, fifty hectares remained on the Soviet side, whereas one hundred and fifty, with the building, were on the Polish side. Through the very center of the estate ran the railway connecting Mińsk and Mołodeczno. I remember that the rail station was not functioning because the Soviets had, for all practical purposes, cut themselves off from the world; they had put up a large gate right where the tracks crossed the border. My father's manor house was consequently of military and strategic importance. Half of it was leased to the Border Defense Corps, and the eastern border was guarded by elite detachments of the Polish Army.

Thus I had contact with the Soviets and their communist propaganda right from my earliest days. On September 17, 1939 when they occupied Vilno, I well knew the sort they were even though I was then only nine years old.

Near the end of August 1939, while we were vacationing, my father, uneasy over the events of the preceding days, went to Vilno to see what was going on. When he learned that the worst thing that could befall the Second Republic had happened—namely the negotiation on the night of August 23–24 of the Ribbentrop-Molotov pact—he ordered us on that very same day to return from the Soviet border to Vilno. He informed my mother to wait for his phone call at the post office. My cousin Staś and I almost revolted. Return to Vilno? To School? That was too much. But, what could we do? We had to leave on August 25.

A few days into our stay in Vilno my father was called to the army. I remember his leave-taking very well. First we prayed and then my father said:

"If it comes to war, Vilno will certainly be occupied by the Soviet army." And he added: "Pray that it falls into Lithuanian hands."

My father was attached to the 85th Infantry Regiment stationed in Vilno. My mother, older sister Marylka and I would go out there to see him. On the day before the outbreak of war, the regiment entered the formation of the 19th Infantry Division and left for the front. From the newspapers, though they tried to keep up the nation's spirits, we came to the clear conclusion that the Polish Army was retreating on all fronts. But it was all bearable until September 17 when the Soviets stabbed us in the back.

On the night of September 18–19, we heard that the Polish Officers' Training Corps, which was composed of the students of the upper *gimnazjum* classes, was engaged in fighting. On the morning of September 19, I heard the rumble of motors. We ran out and saw Soviet tanks. To the side of the street there was a bolshevik riding a horse with a revolver in his hand ready to be used. In the afternoon Soviet columns appeared. I noticed that the Soviet soldiers were poorly outfitted, often in rags; even the Soviet officers had non-issue unfinished coats. This was in great contrast to the Polish Army, and especially to the Polish officers, always splendidly uniformed. I remember also that the Jewish population welcomed the Russian troops with enthusiasm.

The remainder of the Polish Army withdrew into Lithuania. Many of the soldiers returned to their homes. Shocking news, which I still shudder at today, reached us a day or two later that the commander-in-chief of Poland, Marshal Edward Rydz-Śmigły left the country and went to Romania...

We were soon able to experience the sad Soviet reality. Soviet soldiers with long bayonets on their rifles were often taking apprehended Poles off into some unknown direction. In spite of the arrests, the Soviets spread a lot of propaganda announcing that they had liberated the poor from the "bourgeoisie." In October 1939, the Soviets transferred Vilno to the Lithuanians — apparently the Lord God had heard the prayers our father had enjoined on us... The Soviet soldiers occupied only the airport. We were glad that an independent Lithuania had come into being.

After the departure of the Soviets, Lithuania was a normal, independent country, one might even say, western. It was easy to move around, people could travel abroad which is why many Poles succeeded in emigrating to England.

Under the Lithuanian regime, supplies of groceries and local transportation improved in Vilno. They introduced the lit, which could be considered hard currency. They required that Lithuanian be used in the schools though we didn't use it, however, because of patriotic feelings, though the language is among the most interesting in Europe.

From my father who ended up in Kozelsk, we had only snippets of information, primarily conveyed by rank and file soldiers who had been released. After March 1940, all information stopped cold.

In the summer of 1940, the Soviets reintroduced Soviet troops to Lithuania and made it one of the Soviet republics. Naturally "at the people's unanimous request." Shortly thereafter began the arrests, deportations to Siberia or, more often, to Kazakhstan.

In the spring of 1941, letters began to arrive from my father in Soviet camps near Archangel in the Komi Republic. Short, laconic, often with the censor's deletions. My sister Bernadeta, today a retired teacher of biology and living in Kraków, has kept some of them that were written in Russian. My father didn't complain against his fate but often asked for food packages, socks, onion, but above all he was concerned about us and the whole family. How moving were the words addressed to my mother, whom he called "Lipka": "Remember Lipka, that the children are the most important, not me. A great duty is before you: raising the children. Whether they become rich or poor, more or less educated is of secondary importance. What is important is that they grow into good and honest people, that they remain faithful in their love of the Highest Good and Truth."

It was only later that we learned that, before our father had actually been transferred to the Archangel camps, he was taken on April 29, 1940 from Kozelsk together with a group of Polish officers to be shot in the Katyn Forest. On April 30, they were unloaded at the Gniezdowo station. But there Lieutenant Stanisław Swianiewicz was separated from the group because of a sudden order from authorities in Moscow. He was taken on to prison in Smoleńsk, and later to the Lubyanka in Moscow. My father spent almost three years in Russian captivity. He was the only one among the interned Polish officers who had happened to be in the vicinity of Katyn Forest at the time of the executions carried out by the NKVD. However it was only in 1943, after the Germans had discovered the Katyn graves, that he found out the full truth about the crime.

During the summer of 1941 the deportations from Vilno to Kazakhstan became very intense. What saved us? Perhaps the fact that, right after the arrival of the bolsheviks in 1939, we had changed our residence. In addition our mother would send us to spend the night at various acquaintances since the deportations always took place under the cover of night and she surmised that sooner or later the NKVD would find us. We would meet again at home in the mornings. We used to go to these nights elsewhere somewhat lightheartedly, not realizing the danger in our situation. One morning as I was returning from a sleepover at a tailor's house, our Jewish acquaintance met me. He was very well dressed, in a suit and not tattered clothes as earlier. I thought that he must be an agent of the NKVD. He conversed with me very pleasantly, constantly asking where we now lived. I was able somehow to evade his questions and not give him our new address. Later we learned that the NKVD had already come for us at 7 Piaska Street where we had earlier been living... The owner of the property, Mr. Żebrowski, did not however give our new address and actually forewarned our mother so she could arrange a hiding place.

When a few days later I was going along the same road, my attention was caught by a squadron of planes that seemed different to me somehow. Soon afterwards, bombs began to fall. It turned out that the Germans were attacking the Soviet Union. Despite that, the NKVD still managed to send off the majority of loaded transports to exile in Kazakhstan...

When the bombing got stronger toward evening, my mother decided to take us four out of the city. At night we traveled to where some Dominican sisters we knew were living. Three days later we returned from their place to Vilno. The Germans were already in the city. The Lithuanians were now joyous, greeting them with flowers.

After the coming of the Germans to Vilno, the Lithuanians established a Lithuanian government and waited for the recognition of autonomy. Hitler of course reneged and made of Lithuania, Latvia, Estonia and Byelorussia one country—Ostland. Even so the Lithuanians cooperated enthusiastically with the Germans.

Right after the occupation of Vilno, the Germans introduced a decree on the strength of which Jews did not have the right to walk on the sidewalks, only in the gutters.

Soon after the arrival of the Germans and our elation that we needn't fear being sent to Kazakhstan any more, it turned out that we simply had nothing to eat. It had been easier during the Soviet times as mother was lecturing at the people's university and some way or other we were able to survive.

After a few weeks Grandfather sent us news that he would return to Wiazyń. He urged us to come too. As I already mentioned, after the reduction of the estate in 1921, Wiazyń was no longer large. Twenty to twenty-five miles from Wiazyń was Kasperowszczyzna, a larger estate whose owner was Mrs. Gnatowska. After the Germans arrived, she removed the peasants and organized a convoy of six wagons. She led the convoy with an iron hand. When one day she came to Vilno for supplies, Grandfather asked her to take our family to Wiazyń. She reluctantly agreed. I remember that a Polish peasant, Władek, came along with her retinue, and the convoy left in the first days of August 1941. We traveled down the main route from Vilno to Mińsk but German military transports would from time to time hurry along down this road. I was sitting in the last wagon. My job was look-out, in case a German motor convoy appeared on the horizon. It was necessary because the Germans did not pull up but overran everything in their path.

BBC had broadcast the news already that, as General Sikorski's government had entered into an agreement with Stalin, the Poles and Soviets were now allies. I remember Mrs. Gnatowska was furious at Sikorski; how could he enter into an alliance with someone like Stalin? She admired the Germans and the power of the Third Reich, and during the trip from Vilno she continually discussed the topic with my mother. I agreed in silence with Mrs. Gnatowska for I was glad that the Soviet deportations to Siberia had ceased.

Our retinue moved ahead very slowly. The trip to Kasperowszczyzna, and it was only a hundred miles from Vilno, took us three or four days. I remember passing through a certain village—I don't remember the name— where the Germans had executed people. After finding two of their soldiers killed, the Germans lined up in a row all the villagers from this village and shot them. After the sharp volley from the machine gun, two villagers remained unhurt and still standing. The German officer allowed these to go home, which Mrs. Gnatowska called magnanimity.

Joyous news about our father reached us in the summer of 1942. Someone in Radoszkowicze had listened illegally to BBC radio and told us the station had broadcast the news that professor Stanisław Swianiewicz had arrived in Tehran from Russia. We were exceedingly glad knowing that our father was now already beyond the reach of the two barbaric governments of the Soviets and the Nazis.

Precisely on April 13, 1943 in the "Goniec Codzienny," a newspaper published in Vilno during the German occupation, there appeared on the first page the headline: "10,000 POLISH OFFICERS MURDERED IN KATYN." Though more than 4400 officers from Kozelsk had been murdered in Katyn Forest, the Germans knew that the Poles had been looking for at least ten thousand more and so they concluded that all of them were buried in the Katyn mound. I've noted that we already knew, for half a year, that our father had miraculously avoided death in Katyn Forest and after a stay in several jails and camps had managed to depart from Russia to Tehran. Even so the shock was indescribable. No matter that from the very outset no one in Vilno believed Soviet propaganda that the Germans had committed this crime. From April 1940, when letters from fathers, husbands and sons stopped coming from Kozelsk—and at that time it was in Soviet hands—everything became tragically clear... Which is why later when I found myself in the West, it irritated me terribly when some continued arguing that the murder in Katyn had been perpetrated by the Germans.

In June 1943, Marylka and I returned to Wiazyń for vacation. In that area Soviet partisans were active and resilient, often putting mines under the trains. I remember that on a ridge immediately overlooking the tracks, the Germans had built a bunker and stationed there a platoon of soldiers for the purpose of guarding the railway. The soldiers of the German army were not only Germans but also people of other nationalities: French from Alsace, Croatians. Only the officers were always Germans.

In the fall of 1943 Marylka and I were again in Vilno and again we began to attend clandestine schools. At that time in the Vilno area the Home Army began to grow larger. At the clandestine classes a school troop was formed— "*Czarna Trzynastka*" ("Black Thirteen")—of which I was a member hoping in that way I would be successful in getting to the forest and becoming a Home Army soldier. We were however kept in the city and given various tasks, primarily the distribution of illegal leaflets. Polish-Lithuanian relations deteriorated greatly. As the Polish Home Army was becoming stronger, the Germans established Lithuanian detachments under the leadership of General Plechavicius to fight against the Home Army. The Poles coped with them effectively and the climax came in May 1944 when the Poles defeated the Lithuanian detachments of General Plechavicius.

Hitler had the talent for calling forth the worst characteristics in each nation. The Germans made use also of Lithuanians to shoot Jews in Ponary near Vilno.

Aunt Lula, at whose residence Marylka and I lived in Vilno, gave help to hiding Jews. She found a place at some acquaintances of hers in the countryside for Cywia Nabożna-Wildsztein, a friend of hers from Vilno University. In the winter of 1944, these acquaintances informed my aunt that they could no longer hide Cywia. Aunt Lula then had to bring her friend to our place in Vilno where outside the window patrols of Lithuanian police, very much German lackeys, used to walk.

I know from my aunt that after the war Cywia and a number of other Jews decided to leave for the Promised Land. They bribed a Soviet pilot who was to transport them out. It turned out that the pilot was an NKVD agent. He took off, circled the airport and landed. The NKVD was already waiting for them. Cywia was imprisoned in the distant north of Russia where she spent ten years. First she worked in a camp at Kolyma. Then, as a forced settler, she was a teacher in a public school in the Yakutsk region where she even became the director of the school. In 1957 she was successful in leaving by way of Poland for Israel. She worked in Tel Aviv at the Historical Institute, knew Hebrew well as her father had been a Hebrew language teacher in a private school. She wrote a book in Hebrew entitled *Ada w ad* (*From Hell to Hell*), treating in it her experience under the Soviet and German yokes. The book was published in Tel Aviv in 1971 but to this day has not been translated into Polish.

Cywia corresponded with my Aunt Lula. In our family archives there is a set of twenty-four letters and cards from the years 1957–1983. In one of them, January 20, 1976, Cywia wrote: "Beloved Marysia, your letters are for me a source of hope and heart, as I have not for a moment forgotten how you and Professor Czeżowski of Stefan Batory University were my angels, you who saved me from death. The most beautiful period of my life is joined with you. Such a thing one never forgets...." And from July 27, 1979: "Beloved Marysia, so often do I wish to have you by my side, for an old friend is better than two new ones. One feels strongly the lack of family, relatives, friends from those past times, of days and years gone by. But then again I have to be content that I survived it all and in a certain degree have been instrumental in building a new-old country...."

My sister Maria has kept also a letter from 1964 with expressions of gratefulness from the Association of Jews from Vilno in Israel. On the twentieth anniversary of the liquidation of the ghetto in Vilno, in this letter the Jews from Vilno thanked Maria Swianiewicz and all her family for the moral and material help extended to them, for their heroism and for delivering their brothers out of the clasp of death. They assure them that they keep in memory those noble deeds, full of dedication, of the Poles.

In the spring of 1944 the Germans had already almost entirely liquidated the Vilno ghetto. They began then to bring in Jews from Western Europe and kill them too at Ponary. This was done openly; the railwaymen told how everyone was driven out of the wagons and shot. One time my Aunt Lula was going along the street not far from a sidetrack and saw the following scene. A train wagon was standing on the tracks. From it every so often a SS-man would come out with a pile of Jewish rags and throw them on the train embankment. Then residents of Vilno would, like hyenas, throw themselves on it and snatch away. At a certain moment a pretty fur article appeared. From one side a certain woman grabbed it and from another a railroad worker (he had a band on his sleeve, Deutsche Reichsbahn). Each of them pulled the fur toward themselves, unwilling to let it go. They danced in this way around the rail embankment until the SS-man noticed; he ran up to those struggling with it, hit each of them on the head with a club, threw the fur on the ground and tramped it into the mud.

In June 1944 the Germans disarmed General Plechavicius' Lithuanian army and sent its soldiers to work in Germany. In the meantime, the clandestine Polish schools had completed the school year and my sister and I had to return to Wiazyń. We had earlier made the acquaintance of Janka, a worker in a German office issuing passes for train travel, who had access to the printed forms. The trains between Vilno and Mińsk were running normally for a while and we received as many travel permits, naturally falsified, as we wanted. At that time, the end of June 1944, Vitebsk was still under German occupation and the arrival of the Russians didn't seem imminent.

Eventually, however, the German front began to break. Junkers (German transport planes) flew very low over the railway, such that at times one could see the pilot's face. I had the impression that they were evacuating Mińsk. The trains also began to run in only one direction, from Mińsk to Mołodeczno, later even on both tracks but in the same direction. Jams cropped up on the railroad, the stops at times were quite long. Remants of the German army would sit on the open platforms. Many of the soldiers moved only with effort, it being clear that they had been marching a long way. At times they would come to the garden and pull up vegetables. When they wanted something better, even only milk, they would pay for it with paper or soap. A non-commissioned officer, a bunker-commander whom we knew, would come with an armed soldier and chase the loitering soldiers back to the train. He would apologize to us for these, as he called them, *"bandit transporten."* One time I saw a German officer appear and look at the soldiers pulling out rhubarb. He had them stand in a line and began to teach them how a soldier ought to behave at the front. I observed all this with curiosity; the German military hierarchy kept even then complete control over the retreating army.

One evening all the trains disappeared. The bunker soldiers on the other side of railroad commandeered two farm wagons, set fire to the bunker, said good-bye to us and left for Mołodeczno. A great quiet settled in all around. After a certain time there appeared a German open field-car with a pair of high-ranking officers. There were non-commissioned officers standing on the running-boards with arms at the ready. Their uniforms were uncommonly full of dust. They asked directions. My mother indicated to them the way and they saluted politely and went on.

That evening we decided to abandon the house and spend the night in the nearby forest. Rumor had it that the retreating Germans would be setting fire to all the houses. In our house was also living Mrs. Romanow, the owner of a nearby chapel in Hurnowicze which was the object of continual predatory raids by Russian partisans. Our own house in Wiazyń had been safe since the Wehrmacht were guarding the railroad and would not allow partisans to approach.

I mentioned earlier on that the Jesuits had taught me anti-semitism, though it was of a different sort than that of the Germans. I know that during the German occupation a Jew fleeing from the ghetto most easily found help from a priest or people connected with the Catholic church. In a radius of less than 12 miles from Wiazyń there were four orphaned parishes as a result of the murder, deportation or mobilization of their pastors. Religious order priests replaced them. These religious pastors saved the lives of at least forty people of Jewish background.

Byelorussia (now Belarus) was immediately considered a part of the Soviet Union. The NKVD set up its own regime and arrested a lot of innocent people though without the massive deportations to Siberia or Kazakhstan. A kolkhoz was established in Wiazyń. Very soon my sister and I had to work on it. We continued to live in the chapel and had about a mile and a half to go to work. The kolkhoz of Wiazyń was given the name of Janka Kupała, a great Byelorussian poet.

In the winter of 1945, I was promoted to "horse-master," which meant caring for the horses. In July 1945, I was sent together with representatives of other kolkhozes to Mińsk for celebrations linked to the anniversary of its liberation. We were taken to the theater, ballet and cinema. We ate at the officers' restaurant. We went even to the government building, the "*Dom Pravityelstva*," the tallest building in Mińsk to survive the wartime operations. Some kind of sessions took place there and some resolutions were taken. Everyone voted; in any case I voted too. The Soviets were experts of propaganda. At times it was enticing but I had, however, been immune to it from childhood. The Katyn crime had had its influence and the sight of prisoners under guard being led down the streets of Mińsk didn't allow me to forget that this was the Soviet Union.

In the fall of 1945, my mother took me out of the kolkhoz and sent me to school in Dubrow, four miles from Wiazyń. In the Soviet Union the kolkhoz couldn't object to education. They accepted me into the fifth class of the Soviet "ten-year program," and since I was then fifteen, I would be twenty by the time I finished school. The Russian school did make a positive enough impression on me. We had a good Russian teacher who, though he upbraided me for my Polish accent, taught me Russian poetry. I can still recite from memory Lermontov and Pushkin.

In the final days of January 1946, we had already all the permits for the next transport from Olechnowicze to Poland. We then boarded a cattle-car together with another family. Each family took half. We had almost nothing with us whereas the other family was traveling loaded down with things taken from a formerly German farm as they had with them a great many sacks of grain. And that's how we traveled to Poland. At the border, the inspection was rather superficial. The NKVD checked only the documents but they didn't do any detailed search.

Władek was traveling on this same transport. Broken-hearted he told us how the SS had arrested Lilka, Mrs. Gnatowska's granddaughter, with whom he had been in love. He had followed the car of the SS at the time and then found a freshly dug grave in the forest...

It was during the first days of July 1946 that we arrived in a totally devastated Warsaw. We made our way from the West station to a barrack of the National Repatriation Administration which was practically empty. After a short time young men in English uniforms appeared. They were Polish Home Army soldiers released from Kaługa who had gotten their uniforms probably as donations from England. It was cold in the barrack because of a lack of fuel for the stove there. It was really fortunate that the young men from Kaługa went around stealing planks and burning them, while shouting joyously: "All for the Polish Army!"

After a month's stay in Warsaw, my mother received work as a geography teacher in Tczew. We went then to that city which is near Gdańsk and again settled in to the Repatriation barracks. I was accepted into the third year of *gimnazjum*. We were assigned a formerly German apartment. My father had sent a few dollars from England, illegally. He was able to do it either through Poles he knew that were returning to Poland or—often enough—through communists, pre-war students of his, who now occupied high positions and traveled on diplomatic passports, thus not subject to strict border controls. Gradually our life was becoming entirely bearable.

In the fall of 1946, November I believe, a secret messenger from my father arrived. He informed us that an escape had been set up for us to England. We had only to get to Szczecin and from there by cars to Berlin. The border guards had already been bought off. Our entire family therefore traveled to Szczecin. We stayed there in different small hotels but our departure was constantly extended. It was only in December that two cars were leaving for Berlin. I remember that the majority of those fleeing were Jews. My older sister Marylka, my younger brother Jurek and my youngest sister Bernadeta were in the first car which had left in the evening. My mother and I were to leave in the second car and so waited in the hotel for the next departure. The next day the escape's organizer came and said that the first car had got into trouble and the Office of Security (UB) had grabbed everyone. The owner of the hotel whispered to my mother: "You have to flee. The Security Police are asking about you!"

We quickly left the hotel. I noticed that some uniformed person was lingering around the entrance gate. We bought tickets for Poznań. My father's repatriated sister, at whose place in Vilno Marylka and I stayed during the German occupation, lived there. I was amazed at my mother, that in the tragic situation of having three children arrested she did not lose her sang-froid...

Marylka, Jurek and Dzidzia came to Poznań a couple of days later. Why did they release them? At that period the Soviets were quietly helping the Jews in their struggle against the Arabs and English. They looked away when Jews were fleeing. Secondly, the head of the Security Police in Szczecin was a former student of my father's and so I believe that he released the children of his Vilno professor together with the Jews.

We returned from Poznań to Tczew. The school director, though he knew of our misadventure to Szczecin, accepted my mother back to her job. However, we lost our apartment.

In the summer of 1947 I graduated from *gimnazjum*. It was possible then, after the fourth year of *gimnazjum,* to go to various technical schools or to the Maritime School in Gdynia though there the competition was incredible. I entered the first year of *liceum.* There I felt a bit lonely and had the impression that the civilized, free world was passing me by. The communists had begun increasingly to turn the screws...

I again began to plan an escape to the West. I sought allies among my friends, and there were many who thought similarly. During our vacation of 1948, Jurek Arski and I scraped together a bit of money. We intended to cross the "green border" with Czechoslovakia, and then go on to Austria. A friend of ours from Warsaw, Jurek, already out of the army but liking to drink, joined up with us. When we were in the so-called neutral band, my friends told me that they would go no further. We returned, to look for a better way, but they had begun to drink. They came to the conclusion that it would be better to go by sea, on to Sweden. I realized that they didn't take such a flight very seriously and so I went back home.

In the winter of 1948 I signed up for a three-week course in navigation. It was open to all but required of candidates to the Maritime School. I went to the course at Darłowo, in August 1948. Our commander and tutor was Captain Niedzielko, from Vilno; he was a big man, bearded, and very severe. He would swear in both Polish and Russian. We were all afraid of this old "Sea Wolf" but we also admired him. One day after the morning report Captain Niedzielko informed us that there were still eight places open in the Maritime School and that supplementary applications could be submitted. I applied at once.

Examinations were organized for us, primarily in mathematics and physics, which happened to be my favorite subjects. Then I had to be approved by a medical committee and to pass a swimming exam. Everything worked out decently well. I was most afraid of the dental exam; the rules allowed only two missing teeth and I was missing three... However the dentist who examined me either didn't notice or didn't want to see, and wrote down two missing. When I was departing from the course, Captain Niedzielko said to me: "I wish you good luck." I returned to Tczew and began to attend second year of *liceum*. I was now living with my mother in the boarding-school which had been transformed into a residence for the teachers. One morning, when I was still sleeping in the attic, my mother ran up excitedly to me holding out a letter. I had been accepted to the Maritime School.

I was to present myself to the National Center of Maritime Education in Gdynia on October 1, 1948. Two weeks remained before I had to leave. Because I had nothing else to do I kept going to the *liceum* though I didn't pay much attention any more to the lessons. It seemed to me that I had a guaranteed career as an officer in the merchant marine, which at that time was one of the best careers. Going along with my head in the clouds, I imagined myself returning shortly in uniform and showing off to the girls. Jurek Arski, the one who attempted the flight with me, called me aside one day and said:

"The Office of Security (UB) has learned that we were escaping to the West and are investigating the matter. That's the end of your career in the Maritime School." I was totally crushed. Only a bit later did he admit it was only a brutal joke.

I went to the National Center for Maritime Education in Gdynia at the appointed time. On the very same day we were taken on board the "Dar Pomorza." Captain Niedzielko was in charge of us. We were first of all to undertake a year-long course at the Maritime Cadet School. The first segment, up to Christmas, was on the "Dar Pomorza" while it was tied up in port, without going out to sea; then afterwards, we were to continue our studies on land taking regular subjects. I remember that Captain Niedzielko taught us signaling.

In late April 1949, as we returned from Easter break, we were immediately sent aboard the "Dar." This time the ship was ready to go out to sea, to Sweden. The Office of Security (UB) interrogated us a couple of weeks before the voyage. The reason was obvious. Each time the "Batory" had sailed to New York, one third of the crew had gone on land and requested asylum. The agent who interrogated me asked about my father. I told him that he had died in the war and he put a cross on the paper. Having parents in England was in those times a crime.

The "Dar Pomorza" sailed out of Gdynia during the first days of May 1949. Initially the wind was weak but we attempted to go under sail. At night the wind ceased almost entirely and so we switched over to the engine. By morning the coast of Sweden was in sight. I was standing on the deck. The day was sunny, without wind. The ship was advancing at a slow pace. Sweden was getting near very slowly. I began to feel uneasy. How to work out an escape? Various thoughts rolled around in my head. The career of an officer in the Polish Merchant Marine was very attractive to me but I had to escape for several reasons. I had a father in London who had been a witness of Katyn. Second, a couple of weeks earlier BBC had recorded an economics lecture of his at the Polish University College and broadcast it in Polish. Third, I frankly couldn't bear communism and its mendacious propaganda. While I was standing there, my tutor Captain Niedzielko came up to me. I snapped to attention.

"At ease!" he said and started up a conversation punctuated as usual with vulgarities. "Are you planning to run off to Sweden?" he asked quite unexpectedly.

"Why, what for! We have here in school a great opportunity for a wonderful career and the government takes such care of us. Who would think of fleeing?" I replied suspecting that he must know something of my father. Captain Niedzielko, who liked me a lot and considered me someone that could be trusted, said:

"You see, I have an enormous responsibility for all of you. If you think that someone is harboring the intention of running off, then let me know," and here his voice became threatening and he added, "and I'll lock him up!"

"Yes, sir!" I saluted, adding that I doubted whether anyone would be so stupid...

We put in to Karlshamn. On the second day in port Swedes were allowed to visit the ship. Swedish sailors came too and on their hats was written KUNGL FLOTTAN which I guessed meant Royal Navy. O, how I envied them! They could serve their king and not some strange "Voice of the Nation" or "Voice of the Proletariat." A number of Poles who lived there also boarded our ship, primarily boys from the Home Army who had succeeded in escaping from Poland. I started talking with one of them; his name, I remember, was Tybursy.

"Are you an ok guy?" I asked directly.

"Ya, for sure," he said.

"I want to escape. What's the best way?"

"It's not that simple. But I'll get some information from other Poles and tomorrow I'll let you know," he said after thinking a bit.

He came the next day and looked for me, and said:

"There are only three policemen here in Karlshamn and they can't defend you if the Poles whisk you back onto the ship. They will look for you too at the railroad station. It's best to run off to the forest; there are a lot of them around Karlshamn. Wait until the ship departs and then present yourself to the police."

There is nothing better in life than to get good advice in a difficult situation... I left the ship during the last shore leave. It was evening, twenty minutes before nine, and we were to be back on the ship promptly at nine. I headed in the direction opposite to that of the rest of my friends returning to the "Dar." No one stopped me. Near the railroad station I crossed the tracks, and right there was the forest. I ran, the woods spread out and I met no one. My sense of time told me that I had run about ten minutes and if I returned, I could still make it back for muster. I continued to run further into the forest until I realized that it must already be ten and no return was possible. It seemed to me the entire time that some hand of Providence was guiding my actions.

I started to feel cold. It was early May and all I had on was a sailor uniform, not even a scarf. The cold was getting even worse than unbearable. I remember that I entered a thicket of bushes hoping that somehow they kept some warmth. Unfortunately, nothing helped, I kept shivering more and more. Later in England, when my father told me that the NKVD tortured people by locking them in a cold room, I understood what kind of torture that was.

All night long I kept walking in the forest, without paying attention where or in which direction I was going. At daybreak I climbed a tree hoping that I might see the port. In the distance I saw the masts of the "Dar Pomorza." They were swaying but I didn't know whether the ship was sailing for Poland or whether it was just moving around the island where there were instruments for demagnetizing ships. After I descended the tree, I remember that the sun warmed up and I fell asleep. I woke up in the afternoon. I thought that I should slowly move toward the port and see if the "Dar" was still there. It was already getting dark and I was walking in a circle, unable to find my way to the port. Every so often I crossed some roads and once I saw some buildings with a well in the yard. I was thirsty and went in that direction but after the menacing bark of a dog I went back. Fortunately the second night was overcast and it wasn't as cold. It began to clear up by the time I managed to reach the port. The slip, where the "Dar Pomorza" had been, was empty! I no longer had to be afraid of the Security Police!

I went off to seek the police and request political asylum. It was a completely empty square at which I met someone and, going up to him, said: *Polisen.* But he used sign language to indicate that he was deaf. I sat down on the bench quite distressed. After about an hour or so an older woman appeared and I approached her with the question about the *Polisen.* She indicated to me a sign next to the building where I was sitting... It was the police station. I entered. The policeman quite calmly handed me a sheet of paper on which my name was written. I acknowledged that it was me and he told me to sit down. Some time later an individual from the KUNGL FLOTTAN was released from arrest. As he left, he gave me a wide smile—it seems that my arrival shortened his arrest. Soon a young girl brought me some breakfast from a nearby hotel.

I was locked in a cell. Gloomy thoughts began to torment me. I didn't fear the Swedish prison, only being sent back to Poland. A few hours later they took me to another room where a Polish woman waited, a translator.

"What are you afraid of?" she asked me.

"On the door it says '*Kriminalpolisen*,' but I am a political refugee," I replied.

"It was the only free room..." She smiled and added, "Please don't be afraid. I'll translate everything so they won't send you back to Poland. I spent the war in a German concentration camp," as she indicated to me the number tattooed on her hand.

I don't remember what she asked me; it wasn't especially difficult. That evening I was allowed visits from some Poles in Karlshamn. They were soldiers from the Home Army. We spent a very pleasant evening together. One of them, a bit older, who it seems spent the entire war in the forest, said:

"I worried a great deal about you. Spending two days without food is nothing, but from the cold one can go mad or hang oneself..." These words gave me great comfort. I was glad that someone understood what I had experienced...

From Karlshamn I was sent to a camp in Landskron. There was a refugee camp there in an old castle. There I met five young Poles from the Home Army. They had gone straight out from the forest, stolen a yacht and fled to Sweden. We drank up together a bottle of wine they had smuggled in and spent the evening in an anti-communist mood.

From there I made contact by letter with my father. Two weeks later I was granted asylum in Sweden. From England my father sent me news that I had already been granted an English visa. Professor Folejewski, who was an acquaintance of my father, was lecturing at the university in Uppsala. I went to his house for a short stay and from there to England on the tourist ship Saga.

The Swedish ship sailed to the English port of Tilbury. After having my visa checked, I was allowed to go ashore. I started looking for my father as I thought that he would come to meet me. A few friendly Swedes, whose acquaintance I had made on board, noticed me looking and explained to me that the price of the ticket included the trip to London. I was almost late for the tourist train.

At Paddington Station in London I recognized my father already from the train window. Nothing had changed since I had seen him ten years before. We threw ourselves into each other's embrace but words failed us. That very day we went to buy some clothes since I couldn't go around in a sailor's uniform. But giving up the uniform was very painful...

I moved into his small room. My father was at the time the dean of the economics department of the Polish University College (PUC), a school opened by the English for Poles who had served in the Polish Army under British command. Its graduates took their examinations at the University of London which would permit them to find work in Great Britain and its possessions throughout the world. My father was earning the same amount as every English person of his position, which was over a thousand pounds yearly. In 1949 that was a large salary.

A few days after my arrival in London our conversation turned to the topic of Katyn.

"How were the Soviets able to wriggle out of the crime before the International Tribunal in Nuremberg?" I asked since I wanted to know. To my surprise I heard my father say:

"The Soviets themselves presented it before the Tribunal, accusing the Germans of the massacre."

"How brazen!" I said.

"In this situation the Nuremberg Tribunal couldn't condemn the Germans because it knew who in fact had committed the Katyn crime. So it did nothing."

"If the western countries accede to the Soviet version, when will the truth about Katyn see the light of day?" I asked. My father considered my question thoroughly and after thinking a while replied:

"I know the Russians well. I came to know them in the prisons, camps, and I went to their schools. Probably sooner or later the Russian historians will dig up the truth and announce it to the world."

Years later I realized that my father was right. Many Russian historians were unable to give their consent to a lie. In particular Natalia Lebiedieva worked for a long time on the Katyn crime and in the end proved that it was the NKVD and not the Germans who perpetrated the murder of Polish officers.

At the Polish University College where I went to visit my father several days after my arrival in England, I met Mr. King. He was teaching English.

He informed me that on the next day the royal cortege would pass through the center of London and he told me how to get there. I went to watch. The royal guard marched by in traditional uniforms, King George VI with the queen passed by in a six-horse carriage and, following them, the princesses Elizabeth and Margaret on horseback. The English crowd reacted without theatrical shouts, simply murmuring their acknowledgement. I came then to the growing conclusion that though I had only recently arrived from regions where traditions and the monarchies had been destroyed and replaced by barbarity, a civilization created in the course of a thousand years had not yet died.

After a few weeks of taking private lessons in English I began to know a completely different, exotic world from beyond the Soviet imperium. Out of curiosity I would go and listen to speakers in nearby Hyde Park. I remember how one of the black inhabitants of Africa—at that time half the continent was in British hands—scolded them terribly for their unjust rule in Africa. I thought that English agents, something of the type of the NKVD or Gestapo, would appear, drag the agitator from his pedestal and deal with him appropriately. Those turned out to be the notions of someone newly arrived from totalitarian countries. The English crowd stood and listened with attention to the arguments of the African. But when he grew wild and began to shout: "The time will come when we will kill all the English in Africa, burn their bodies and use their ashes to fertilize the African soil!" Those gathered round burst into spasmodic laughter. One of the Englishmen politely raised two fingers and simply asked: "Do you think that ashes are good for that?" It was then that I understood that British imperialism functioned completely different from Soviet or Nazi imperialism...

My father and I thought a lot about what I was to do. I was nineteen and candidates to the English maritime schools were accepted only to age sixteen. I very much liked the Maritime School in Gdynia and the "Dar Pomorza" but unfortunately Poland was in communist hands. My father was even then unable to speak the entire truth about Katyn since he had family in Poland and feared that the communists would avenge themselves on mother and the three remaining children.

England had withdrawn recognition of the Polish government in London and had transferred the entire Polish Army under English command to the British Isles. In 1949, when I arrived, there were about 250,000 Poles in Great Britain, and in London itself about 30,000. There were Polish clubs, restaurants and theaters. After the demobilization of the Polish Army, the older military personnel found themselves in a quandary, not having any experience in civilian life. The situation was much better for workers, especially craftsmen. The young Poles who had served under British command had it best because they could study at the Polish University College. The

English paid for their studies and gave them a twenty-pound stipend which was adequate for their upkeep. The graduates were entirely free and could travel to other countries for further studies. I had no way out; I had to give up a career at sea and go back to school.

I acquired technical training at the Portsmouth College of Technology. Later I worked at the Marconi Wireless Telegraph Co. in Chelmsford on projects regarding ocean radar. I would spend all my free time sailing. I bought myself an open boat for ocean sailing and would sail down the eastern, always stormy, English coast. One day at the international club I met a young sailing woman from Holland, Maria (Riet) van Loon. She had come to England to study English. I invited her one day to go sailing. I wanted to impress her with my sea knowledge and we went to the sailing club. My boat was tied up some 100 meters from the shore and the small boat we used to get there wasn't around. A bit patronizingly I asked her if she could swim. When she said she could, we changed into our swim suits and swam to the boat. She outdistanced me by half the distance and with that my patronizing came to an end...

Then Riet left for Paris to study French while working in a French family. I went to see her. Paris has truly a romantic atmosphere and I proposed to her while walking along the Seine. We agreed that we would go to Canada...

I sailed to Canada first, in the summer of 1961, on the M/S Saxonia. My mother was at that time already in England. She had finally received approval to leave Poland and join her husband during the time of Gomułka, in spring 1957, that is, after eighteen years separation. She went first to Indonesia where my father was participating, under the auspices of UNESCO, in a group studying economic issues. A year later they came together to England and my mother became involved in the work of the ethnographic commission of the Polish Ethnographic Society Abroad. I was working then at the Marconi Firm in Chelmsford, on the English eastern shores.

The cruise to Canada across the northern Atlantic was marvelous. However, when land came into sight, fear took hold of me just as it did when I was nearing Sweden. "What am I going to do there?" I wondered. Canada had always interested me. Enormous expanse, forests, mountains, lakes, the ocean. However I had no acquaintances, no work. I arrived in Montreal, and later by train I traveled across the whole of Canada to Vancouver on the Pacific coast. In this beautiful city I experienced my most difficult moment. I felt terribly alone and isolated, not knowing where to turn. At last near a church I found a room in an inexpensive Polish boarding-house which was run by Mr. Buczkowski, who had come from Czerniowce in Romania. It was more difficult finding work. My fiancée had come in the middle of November and it was on that very day that I found work in Calgary, Alberta Province—the wealthiest of all because of its oil deposits. I became an electrical technician, traveling throughout northern Canada servicing the communications equipment on drilling towers. We were married on December 30, 1961, in a Polish church in Calgary.

At that time in Canada medical care was not free. When my wife became pregnant, I had to pay by myself the doctor and maternity hospital. In the course of our first five years in this new country, four children were born to us: Nicholas (television technician), Bernadette (banker), George (bartender), and Edward Gregory (oil industry engineer, computer specialist). Two years later we purchased our own home and that on only one salary. Moreover, I felt good that I had paid off everything without governmental aid. Today free medical care has been introduced into Canada but it is more difficult for young married couples to buy their own home.

After working three years, I learned that the schools in Canada were opening technical departments. Engineering teachers were needed. I submitted my application and was sent to the university in Edmonton where I received a large stipend for the support of my family. After a year of studies at the university I began to teach electronics and mathematics in a Catholic school in Calgary. In 1969 the Ministry of Education introduced the teaching of calculus in the uppermost classes. Teachers of mathematics at that time had not been trained in teaching this subject. The school administration approached me as to whether I, with my engineering qualifications from England, would be able to teach differential and integral calculus. I eagerly assured them I could since differential calculus had been my favorite subject in the College of Technology in Portsmouth. I began to teach it in the upper classes of high school. My liking of mathematics helped me once again as it had years before when I took exams for the Maritime School in Gdynia.

I took my retirement in 1989. Two years later my wife, daughter and I decided to visit Poland and Lithuania. During our visa application, Lithuania became an independent country. We landed in Warsaw on October 22, 1991, which was more than forty-two years from the time of my setting sail from Gdynia on the "Dar Pomorza." First we stayed with my brother Jerzy, a computer specialist in Warsaw, and later in Olsztyn with my sister Marylka, a professor at Olsztyn University. From there we went by bus to Vilno. It was still full of Soviet soldiers around the Wilia River but the Lithuanian national flag already flew from the Góra Zamkowa. I remember many concrete barriers placed near the Parliament building. The Lithuanians put them there against the Soviet tanks. The Soviet Union no loner existed, so there were no border stations on the Lithuanian-Belarus border. We didn't have Soviet visas for the Belarus Republic but my cousin Tomek, a Vilno native, who had been in the Soviet Army in the Far East, persuaded us to go to Wiazyń in Belarus. We set off together with him but with our hearts in our throats. Grandfather had died in 1948. His manor in Wiazyń had long ago been demolished. All that remained were the living quarters of the farm hands which had been made into the Janka Kupała Museum, and we visited that. We met there a couple of old acquaintances. We spent the night at my cousin's, Teresa Dudir, in Radoszkowicze. The following day, not having been arrested for spying on the Soviet Union, we returned to Vilno.

On our return trip to Canada, we visited my father in Chiselhurst in England. He was in the "Antokol" home, living out his final years. He had never stayed long in one place. After returning from Indonesia, he took a position in London as a "Research Fellow" in the London School of Economics. In 1963, he became a professor at St. Mary's University in Halifax, Canada and also lectured in the United States at Notre Dame University in Indiana. My mother worked in ethnography, collected a lot of material on devotion to the dead in Europe and China, and published a lot. We would visit rather rarely as the distances in North America are enormous. My mother died from cancer in 1974 and my father took a very modest retirement. A year later my father was invited to Copenhagen to an inquiry organized by Dr. Sakharov on human rights violations perpetrated by the USSR. Two weeks before the hearings in Copenhagen he was seriously beaten on a street in London. He managed even so to leave the hospital in time to get to the hearings in Copenhagen. In 1982, St. Mary's University honored him with a "Doctor of Laws" degree. He died in May 1997 and is laid next to my mother in Halifax.

My father included his wartime memories in the book *In the Shadow of Katyn* (*W cieniu Katynia*) published in 1976 by the Instytut Literacki in Paris, then by the Oficyna Literatów in 1981 and Czytelnik in 1990. Not long ago I translated it into English and the first English version came out in Canada in spring 2002.

I made my second sentimental trip to the land of my birth in 1997, immediately after my father's death. My youngest son Greg financed my trip. He had been working for several years in an oil firm in Calgary and had flown to eastern Canada to service oil pipelines so often that he had accumulated enough free-flight points to take me all around Europe for free. We went also to my native Vilno. We didn't see Soviet soldiers any more. As we walked down the main street of Gedyminos Gatvie with Tomek's daughter, Ludeczka, and gazed upon the national flag of Lithuania flying on Góra Zamkowa, I let out a deep breath. Vilno was again a city of free people.

From Vilno we went to Poland and as usual had border problems at Lazdijaj. Then on to Gdynia to visit the "Dar Pomorza." I had known Gdynia well but a half century works its will. We exited the train station and I lost my way to the seacoast where the "Dar Pomorza" stood as a museum. My son Greg, who doesn't know a word of Polish, bought a map of Gdynia and that way led me on to the "Dar Pomorza."

17

CHILD OF
TWO CULTURES

Tel Aviv, Israel, October 2002

"Today my fatherland is Israel but I still have emotional ties to Poland. I love Polish literature and language and continue to use it as my own native tongue. Yet Poland is also for me a great disappointment, a disillusion. I feel as if I have been thrust away by it," Wanda Wasserman confides quietly, she who was before the war a resident of Lvov and now lives in Tel Aviv.

It took a long time to arrange our meeting. For months she expressed doubts that she was a fitting subject for the book. Now at last we are meeting at her cousin Janina's, in Warsaw. She has come for only a two-day stay. Decidedly modest and somewhat uncertain of the outcome of our conversation, she lays down the condition that she has to read what I write about her.

She starts off by showing evidence that her father, Robert Dresdner, a medical doctor and second lieutenant of the Polish Army, was a victim of the Katyn massacre. At Katyn Forest, she photographed his very plaque on the cast-iron cemetery wall, then herself next to it, further the Katyn Cross and the Star of David, beneath which she had placed flowers. Though she had been officially invited to the solemn renewal and dedication of the Katyn Forest necropolis in July, 2000, she didn't go because at the time she lacked a visa.

"I felt altogether dreadful that I wasn't able to participate in the ceremony," she repeated on more than one occasion.

That's why she had to visit the cemetery later. When she at last received the visa, she went to Katyn Forest on a pilgrimage organized by the tourist office "Wilejka" and the Katyn Family in Łódź. It was then that she took the pictures she had brought with her to Warsaw. While there, she visited the grounds of the Katyn execution three times, spending time in silence and meditation, linking herself in spirit with her father in the peacefulness... He was a very honest man. It's been said that she is somewhat like him... Surely it's because, like him, her ambition has been to live out her life in honesty and truth. Even though for her the normal supports and securities of life ended at age eleven, at the death of her father. Which is true for her sister, Irena, as well and even more so for her mother, Róża Dresdner.

"Our destinies would certainly have turned out differently if not for the war...," she realized as she stood in the cemetery. Nor was it the first time in her more than seventy years...

Had she not gone to Katyn, she would not have today such peace of mind. And she is content, especially that now surely her strength would not permit her to go there again. Perhaps that is the reason that the pilgrimage made such a strong impression on her...

"I was afraid to go; I'm from Israel." She admits that she personally never experienced any anti-Semitic sentiments on the part of Poles. She has even had many Polish friends. However, from other Jews she heard about the negative feelings of Poles toward her people. "On the other hand I was pleasantly surprised on the pilgrimage to Katyn. Even though I told them right at the start that I was from Israel, I experienced much warmth and welcome from the entire Polish group. The scouts helped me in my walking, even made me a cane of sorts thanks to which it was easier for me to get along on my weak legs. Indeed it was a wonderfully pleasant surprise."

Besides the pictures from Katyn, she brought with her from Tel Aviv "treasured things of my father's."

"He left these with me on September 5, 1939 as he was leaving for the front. It was early morning, I was still sleeping. I remember that I was a bit irritated that Dad was waking me..." She sighed holding with care the precious mementos.

They were things from the year 1920 which he had had with him even earlier in the first war. A small cloth knapsack, yellowed, a bit threadbare and faded, but which still had a red cross on the flap. A tiny, metal box still having intact their address at the time: Lvov, 5 Plac Smolki. Besides these, her father had given her his most recent photograph: in the Polish uniform of a second lieutenant. Bright, beautiful young eyes looked out from under the four-cornered military cap.

"I remember that I asked my dad why he had only one star. He promised me that soon there would be more because the next one had already been awarded...," Wanda Wasserman says, wiping her moist eyes.

She has preserved a document, for its sentimental value, a medical prescription form of a doctor of internal medicine, "office hours from 3:00 to 5:00 at 5 Plac Smolki in Lvov." On it is an authorization written September

5, 1939, by Second Lieutenant Dresdner for his wife Róża. Dr. Robert Dresdner wrote by hand: "I authorize my wife Róża Dresdner to act in my name, in all particulars concerning correspondence, money, wages, the clinic, the transaction of contracts, etc."

"That's all that I have left of him... There were also perhaps two cards from Kozelsk... I remember that I also had written to him but that correspondence has not been preserved." Wanda Wasserman begins with the greatest care to lay out her relics. She doesn't seem tired from her trip to Warsaw though she mentions that she has some health problems. Grey-haired, a bit stout, in a green sweater and a checkered skirt, she is today seventy-four years old.

Robert Dresdner was born on November 9, 1899 in Czerniowce, the capital of the Hapsburgian Bukovina, which is today in Romania. In 1909, which would be still during the Austrian Empire, his own father, Emanuel Dresdner, a doctor of law at the Czerniowski University, was named a ranking official of the highest regional court in Lvov. He moved as a consequence from Czerniowce to the capital of Galicia where he continued in government service for the Austrian Empire. In 1918, he became an advisor at the highest regional court; he was also a member of the lawyer's examination commission. In Lvov he participated not only in hearings related to Bukovina which took place in German but also in those related to Polish affairs. And so it was that Emanuel Dresdner and his family remained in Lvov. He called the beautiful city "little Vienna." After the formation of Poland's Second Republic he continued his service as a judge of the appellate court and a president of the Senate. In 1923, at the age of sixty-four, he took his retirement. He continued, however, to write legal treatises, a large number of which were well regarded in his circles. Some of them, especially the results of his research into executions have enduring scholarly significance today. He was also engaged in social questions, particularly in the Jewish Rescue Committee. In the publication "Jews in Public Service," it was written of Emanuel Dresdner that "He belonged to that infrequently met group of people, today rarely found, who combine in themselves the qualities of a learned, respected, and outstanding judge."

Wanda Wasserman:

"My grandfather was a great man. My father didn't have the opportunity to do the same. He died before he reached forty."

Yet the "Jewish Almanach" had already written about her father, just before World War II, in the chapter "Participants in the Struggle for Polish Independence." It stated that the son of Doctor Emanuel Dresdner, a graduate in medicine from the University of Jan Kazimierz in Lvov, had since 1926 been a doctor at the Cooperative Clinic in Lvov. He announced his services in internal medicine in "Medical News" in the years 1928, 1930 and 1932.

He was one of the co-founders and one of the secretaries of the Academic Circle of the Cooperative Clinic in Lvov and also the resident doctor at the Jewish Business School.

In 1920, he entered the Polish Army as a volunteer, participating in the entire campaign as a battalion doctor. After the war, now in the reserves with the rank of lieutenant doctor, he served on the board of the Fourth Circle of the Reservists' Union. He had been honored with a decoration for his service in the war and with the Cross of the Małopolska Section of the Volunteer Army.

Additional information about Robert Dresdner can be found in Jędrzej Tucholski's book, *Slaughter in Katyn* (*Mord w Katyniu*) published in 1991. After his appointment to the rank of officer, Second Lieutenant Dresdner underwent requisite training and exercises. After one of these—a four-week course at the Center of Health Education at the Officer Cadet School in Warsaw—the official evaluation, written by the head of the battalion school Major J. Piechura, went as follows: "Extremely intelligent, of good physique, adroit. Well-mannered, balanced character. Solid and energetic, very ambitious and dutiful, loyal with a well developed sense of discipline. General grade of excellent."

The name of Second Lieutenant Robert Dresdner appears on the NKVD transport list no. 052/3 of April 1940.

Wanda Wasserman is the second daughter of Robert Dresdner and Róża Landes of Kołomyja. Younger by seven years than her older sister, Irena, she came into the world in Lvov, on January 11, 1928. They lived first on Piekarska Street, then moved to Plac Smolki, to a large tenement. There was a movie theatre, "Marysienka," on the ground floor.

"There were five rooms," she recalls as she adjusts her thick glasses. "But part of the apartment was used for my father's medical office and patient waiting room. Besides his work in the clinic, my father would see patients in his house, thanks to which he was able to support his wife and two daughters in a certain life-style. It was enough for us to have a nice vacation every year, to have household help as well as a quite extensive social life."

Their closest acquaintances were chiefly Poles of Jewish background, but assimilated and emotionally linked to Poland. She explains that she was raised in two cultures and traditions—Polish and Jewish. She gave herself over to both the one and the other culture. Her best friend from childhood was Jan Chorążek, a Polish boy, with whom she played in the sandbox.

"I personally never experienced unpleasantness on the part of Poles," she repeats.

In her youth she didn't frequent either a synagogue or a church. However, she would often go to the Catholic cathedral together with their servant, a Polish woman. Yet every Sunday she would attend Jewish religion classes. It was because God did exist for her though it was difficult to say what kind of God. Even her mother, a great Polish patriot, prayed to God every evening in Lvov, but Wanda didn't know to what kind, perhaps a non-personal God. She does remember also, that up until 1933, which is precisely the accession of Hitler to power, they would decorate a tree at Christmas.

"We were not raised too religiously," she thinks back today with a smile. "At home neither the Sabbath nor other Jewish holidays were observed. Only we didn't go to school on the Day of Atonement, the greatest Jewish holiday." In her opinion what is important is for one to behave decently. It's far worse for someone to pray four times a day and behave reprehensibly.

Wanda attended a state public school located on Sakramentki Street. She was always one of the best pupils, a bit of an intellectual. She recalls however that sometimes she went to the pool, on walks and on trips with friends, and played ping-pong. But most of all she would read. Already as a child she knew the *Trilogy*. She liked very much the humanities, especially foreign languages. Her girls' class was multicultural, just like all of Lvov. The language of teaching was Polish but she learned a few others: German, French, Ukrainian. In her class most of her classmates were Roman-Catholic, a few were Orthodox, and only four of them were from assimilated Jewish families. One of the four, Halinka, soon left to go to a private Jewish school. She was unable to bear the nasty comments on the part of Polish nationalists.

"But my father said that we lived in Lvov, were Poles, and that we had to get used to our group's working within the Republic. I never experienced much unpleasantness, though it did hurt me when I was not allowed to join the scouts. At first in Poland, and then in Romania. It was only in Palestine that I would be welcome to join the ranks of the Polish Scouts' Association, but by then I no longer wanted to."

She loves Lvov to this day though she hasn't seen it again since 1939. Moreover she can't forget her full, happy childhood and the atmosphere of an intellectual, bi-cultural home. And marvelous birthdays! Of the members of her family, of all her friends. She remembers how wonderfully they celebrated them in Lvov. She keeps in her memory too the trips to their grandmother in Drohobycz and to their cousin in Podhajce.

"I loved very much going there. My relatives in Podhajce had a beautiful home with a garden. There was also a lake there, and a kayak on it."

She still has a weakness for the songs of Lvov; she tears up a bit whenever she hears them. She recites from memory the words of the songs of the Lvov cadets, of whom her father was a member, which is why he taught her the text:

> "On a rainy and dismal day
> the children of Lvov go down in ranks
> from the Citadel and the mountain
> wandering over the world..."

She learned of the outbreak of World War II while at the swimming pool. She hurried right home. Her father was to have left for the front that very day, but in the end the date was pushed back until September 5. She remembers that a few days later, when they were already living only in one deliberately darkened room, her dad later contacted her mom. He wanted them to come to a hospital east of Lvov where he was a doctor. And then for a long time afterwards they had no news at all from him.

After several days, about mid-September, Róża Dresdner decided to get out of Lvov. She left everything in the house behind and with only one suitcase headed eastward with her daughters. She crossed the bridge at the village of Zaleszczyki with eleven-year old Wanda and her older sister precisely on September 17, 1939. Wanda remembers:

"When we found ourselves on the famous bridge of gehenna among hundreds of other refugees, someone shouted that it wasn't necessary to flee because the Russians were coming to help. But my mother said: 'Oh! If they're coming, we better go even faster...' She knew many things, and she didn't trust the Soviets."

They managed to reach Romania. They stopped for a while at someone's place in Gałacz, then in the town of Krajowa. There was a Polish school there. Wanda began to attend school. Irene had already completed *liceum*. They lived on the relief aid of the Polish government. It seems that it was in the beginning of 1940 that the first card arrived from the Soviet camp at Kozelsk. The Dresdner women knew then that their second lieutenant was alive and so it was easier for them to bear their own exile. Some people told them that they had seen him, sometimes even on liberty pass; they had urged him to escape from Soviet captivity. Second Lieutenant Dresdner was said to have answered however: "I gave my word as a Polish officer that I would return and I won't break it..."And though the cards from him ceased coming right after, Róża Dresdner explained to her daughters: "The Soviets must not be permitting letters out..."

"It didn't occur to anyone that there existed in the world a country that killed its prisoners of war," she says, repeating the then current opinion. "My cousin, also a Polish officer, was taken captive too after the September campaign, but by the Germans. He lived through it, even though he was a Jew and the Germans had planned the annihilation of our people."

Getting out of Romania wasn't easy. Finally somehow they succeeded. Near the end of 1940 they traveled through Turkey and Syria to Palestine. There they also received help from the Polish government though it was quite meager. In order to survive in Palestine, Róża Dresdner had to do physical work, for the most part in the kitchen, and also by distributing the Polish language newspapers "Nowiny" and "Przegląd." She was not accustomed to that kind of work. Before, as a doctor's wife, she assisted him only during his home practice. She had not finished her legal studies, interrupting them when she married. However, she knew several languages, was well-read, loved Polish literature.

In Palestine the daughters attended Polish school. They began to have their first crushes and romantic encounters. Wanda recalls warmly her own adolescent love for a Polish soldier from General Stanisław Kopański's command. They had arrived in the Near East earlier, and it was only later after their arrival that Gen. Anders' soldiers had come from Russia.

"In 1941, when Russia came over to the Allies' camp, we began to wait for my father," she recalls. "We had expected that he would arrive in the Near East together with General Anders' II Corps. We never questioned whether or not he would, only when."

However, Second Lieutenant Robert Dresdner didn't return. Suddenly, in the columns of the military magazine appearing in the Near East, the "Orzeł Biały," they found his name. He was on the list of those who perished in Katyn Forest at the hands of the NKVD... They experienced a terrible shock.... It was impossible to describe...

Then even more terrible news began to come, of other members of the family killed, of friends and acquaintances, of the extermination of the Jewish people by the Germans.

"My two grandmothers, my aunt, my father's sister, cousins, friends, my closest girlfriends. It is a tragedy beyond description... Mom went completely to pieces. She was no longer that beautiful woman from before the war..." Wanda Wasserman's voice begins to crack as she speaks.

The Dresdner girls greeted the end of the war with indescribable joy. The letters which came to them from Poland were not, however, optimistic. The number of victims of Nazism among their closest ones grew even larger...

Irena was married quickly, to a Polish Jew. She left Tel Aviv for Haifa and gave birth to a son Julian. She helped her lawyer husband in running a company.

Wanda graduated from a *liceum* in Tel Aviv, specializing in the Polish language. She had studied together with Polish refugees.

"In Palestine there began to be talk about creating a Jewish state, Israel. A large number of our own people, Zionists, who had dreamed of this, had been there for some time." Wanda Wasserman had now begun to study English.

In 1946, she left for university studies in Geneva. She studied foreign languages while working for the United Nations, her cherished organization. After her studies, however, she emigrated with her husband, a doctor of medicine, to Sweden. She never returned to her work at the United Nations.

In 1952, she returned to Tel Aviv. She divorced and moved in with her mother. It was a time of euphoria and joy, people danced in the streets.

"The Jewish people were happy and joyous that, after the terrible persecutions and holocaust, the nation Israel had been born. We deceived ourselves that now all of us would live in love and peace. Then I began to study Hebrew, I became a nationalistic patriot of the new Jewish country." She emphasizes, however, that in her family, with her mother, sister and her sister's son, they continued to speak only in Polish. But her patriotic feelings were transferred to the just established, longed-for, independent country of Israel.

She was still not very religious. She went to the synagogue only a few times. She made up her mind, however, to settle in Israel and took a job in a travel bureau in Tel Aviv. She worked there her entire life, and retired when she was sixty. She loved her work, because it was interesting and pleasant though not quite as interesting as her beloved United Nations.

"In life it isn't always possible to realize one's dreams," she explains with great humility and cheerfulness of heart.

Thanks, however, to the reduced tickets she was able to visit the world. She has traveled a great deal, and loves to do so even today. She knows eight languages, five of them very well: Polish, English, French, German, Hebrew. She can get by as well in Swedish, Romanian, and somewhat in Ukrainian.

"And now in Switzerland I am studying Italian," she admits, smiling modestly.

Most recently Wanda Wasserman has spent most of her time in Switzerland. Even though she has her own apartment, her own health insurance and most other affairs in Tel Aviv. But her sister Irena's only son lives in Bern with his family. He had left with his parents right after fifth grade of the public Hebrew school. First to Austria, then his family settled in Switzerland where he did his university studies. Today Julian Igal Mahari is forty-three years old and a professor of economics. His wife, originally from Austria, is a surgeon and together they have two sons, Robert and Rafael.

Julian Igal lost his parents long ago.

"My sister Irena, her married name was Mahari, died young and unexpectedly from a heart attack, before reaching sixty. My mother was still living. That was a further sorrow for us... That's the reason I have treated Julian as a son," explains Wanda Wasserman. Julian Igal Mahari was raised in a Polish-speaking home and still considers Polish his mother tongue. He reads and writes in Polish. Because of his feelings toward his grandmother Róża Dresdner and his extended family, he has asked his mother's sister to teach Polish to his own sons. It's for this reason that Wanda Wasserman presently spends more time in Bern than in Tel Aviv.

"Seven-year-old Robert is eager to learn. He already knows Polish verses, especially those of Tuwim and Brzechwa; we have read together Henryk Sienkiewicz's *W pustyni i w puszczy*. Whereas four-year-old Rafael, though a sweet and lovable child, is not as attracted by the language of his grandparents. At least for now." Wanda Wasserman laughs that her nephew Julian is a bit disappointed in her, even upset, that his younger son doesn't want to read children's books with her. At their home in Bern they have a large Polish library which many a child in Poland would envy.

Julian Igal Mahari has high regard for traditions and inculcates them in his sons. He goes to synagogue with them even though he himself isn't especially religious or practicing. It is something that he shares with her; of late she has been more often to synagogue and is beginning to observe the holidays and fasts. The economics professor attaches a great deal of weight, and much feeling and respect, to the bi-cultural past of his family. It is out of that sentiment and respect for history that Julian Igal Mahali would like for his sons too to know the Polish language. Wanda Wasserman shows me the pictures of her favorite, named after her father, the seven-year-old Robert.

"He goes to English school but at home he speaks German and Polish." She points at the handsome face of the boy. "And besides once a week he attends Jewish religious classes. O! in this picture he is even in the yarmulke," she says, happily. Wanda Wasserman also has always with her photographs of her own mother, her father, her sister Irena as well as Julian Igal's whole family.

Róża, the mother of Irena and Wanda, the wife of the second lieutenant of the Polish Army murdered at Katyn, Dr. Robert Dresdner, died in 1986. She was eighty-four years old. To the final moments she was heart and soul in Poland, living in the past, and speaking a great deal about it. Despite her talent for foreign languages, she never learned Hebrew very well. She never visited Poland again. She was afraid. Nor did she ever remarry. She lived only for her daughters, Irena and Wanda, and then also for her only grandson, Julian Igal. She is primarily the one who taught him Polish and instilled in him his feeling for the first fatherland.

"Had she lived, she would have been thrilled that Igal travels today all around the world, writes books, and above all, that he lectures in economics at a number of universities, including in Polish at the University of Maria Curie-Skłodowska in Lublin," says Wanda Wasserman, proud of her nephew.

Róża Dresdner didn't wait for the official acknowledgement of the Soviets to the slaughter in Katyn.

"Even so Mama always knew, one hundred, even one thousand percent by whose hands her husband had died," asserts Wanda. "She never had the slightest doubt of it because in Israel the truth of it had always been spoken and written. We have saved many articles on the topic, in Hebrew and English. She was however never able to go to the place of execution."

This is why her daughter, Wanda, has not only been to Katyn Forest but also keeps contact with the old country. Her first visit to Poland in 1991 was for her a great experience. Her only cousin, Janka, also from Lvov, lives in Warsaw. Unfortunately they were unable to keep contact for many years, even by letters. In Communist times, having family in Israel was not very welcome in Poland. It was only after the overthrow of the totalitarian system, at the beginning of the nineties, that her cousin Janka sought out Wanda in Tel Aviv. Now they visit each other yearly.

"I come now quite gladly," avers Wanda Wasserman. "It is pleasant to hear the language so dear to me, which I consider yet my native tongue. A love for all Polish literature has also endured. I know Polish better than Hebrew and English. And I continue to think in Polish, count, feel poetry, even though the Poland of my feelings is for me the pre-war one. I can't change all that even if today my homeland is Israel."

She is glad that Poland has so many noble, marvelous people. At the same time she is sad that not all Poles are exactly that way...

After retiring, Wanda Wasserman began to be socially active at the University in Tel Aviv. She conducts research on anti-semitism in the world, searches for and gathers together articles appearing in various languages written against Jews. On this basis she can say that anti-semitism continues to exist in the world.

"Why? Where, in your opinion, reside the causes of anti-semitism?"

"I don't know. Earlier I had the hope that it had died out after the end of the war, that the times of cruelty and of the suffering of the Jewish people had passed forever. And that the Jewish faith would be respected just as every other one. Our religion is for sure beautiful, it doesn't allow murder, it has a positive stance toward the world and people. Perhaps anti-semitism carries over from the fact that Jews have for so long lived without their own country. I don't know... I don't want even to think about it... I'm far too old..."

"And how do the Poles emerge in your research? Are they indeed anti-semitic?"

"They aren't in the best place, although I would gladly much rather say that they weren't on the list at all; that would be dear to my heart. It hurt me a lot when once the libel, that it was Jews who murdered the Polish officers at Katyn, was printed in Poland... Even so, I don't believe that the Poles occupy the first place in terms of negative attitudes to Jews. They are located in the middle."

"Even during my preparation of this book some Poles, living witnesses of history, reproach Jews for cooperation with the NKVD... The majority of families of Polish officers, prisoners in prisoner-of-war camps in Kozelsk, Starobelsk as well as Ostashkov, were sent into the depths of Russia and assert that it was in large measure with the help of Jews from the Polish *kresy*...

"Is that so? But how many Jews were there among the exiled? One cannot generalize. My very best friend together with her family was also deported into Siberia, she lost all her teeth there being only twelve years old. There were despicable people and communists equally among Jews and among Poles, a good example being Feliks Dzierżyński. One cannot judge collectively. Sure, Jews have always been eager for new ideologies, they have always sought justice. Never did they imagine that communism would evolve so badly... Jews too have cause for grievance against Poles, for more than one gave them over to death, sometimes a neighbor, often for money."

"However many Poles helped Jews, often at the cost of their own lives saved them from annihilation. Even the forest at Yad Vashem is witness to this; most of the olive trees there were planted by Poles decorated with the Medal of the Just among the Nations of the World..."

"That fact is recognized in Israel. There are Jews who recall the Poles with great respect and love. They are grateful to the Polish people for their survival. Unfortunately they are in the minority."

A Katyn Family Association exists too in Tel Aviv. It hasn't numbered many persons, hardly even twenty, and today the number of members is even less. But it was at the initiative and fundraising of this association that on the 60th anniversary of the Katyn massacre a memorial plaque was unveiled, dedicated to the Jewish officers of the Polish Army murdered by the NKVD. Wanda Wasserman, a member of the Katyn Family Association in Tel Aviv, shows me the picture of the ceremony in the forest at Beit Shemesh near Jerusalem.

"It was a great ceremony. The Polish Consul in Israel took part in it as did officers of the Polish Army." Wanda Wasserman shows color photographs from the ceremony. Polish and Israeli flags were fluttering; there were beautiful red and white wreaths. The Israeli press wrote about the ceremony even though the truth about the crime had always been known and preserved. In Israel there was even a collection of poems about Katyn.

The President of the Katyn Family Association, Janina Ziemian, today quite seriously ill, made great efforts that the plaque be placed in Yad Vashem. The Institute thought, however, that it was a place of reverence dedicated to the victims of Hitler and the Nazis, not of Stalin. Too, funds were lacking for a genuine monument, which is why only a plaque was placed near Jerusalem. Even so, what is important is that the memory of Katyn is kept likewise in the Holy Land.

Wanda Wasserman has not given much thought as to where she would wish to be buried.

"That doesn't have a lot of meaning for me. I don't much believe in an after-life. I rather want to believe that if I have tried to be a decent person through my entire life and will have been of help to people and to my family, then the Lord God will account me as having done good, and not evil.

In my opinion a positive testimony of life is more important than prayers and the external forms of faith."

Her mother and sister are at rest in the Holon cemetery in Tel Aviv. But there is no longer any room there for her as the adjacent plots have been sold. Her nephew doesn't want to discuss the topic. He is much too busy, and besides he believes that his aunt will live quite a bit longer.

For the present, Wanda Wasserman is mulling whether to go in October with Julian and his family to North America. It's hard for her to decide, because she fears that due to her age and leg problems she won't bear well the difficulties of the trip. But at the same time she would very much like to see again some members of their distant family from New York, Washington, Buffalo...

"In Israel the fashion is to change one's name into Hebrew. I have remained Wanda. I like the name, my parents chose it for me and so I think that I ought not to change it." She bids me farewell warmly, as a Polish woman.

18

KATYN PILGRIMS

Łódź, Poland and Kharkov, Ukraine,
October 2002

As recently as twelve years go, Janusz Lange of Łódź thought that his father rested in the Katyn Forest, but during the exhumation his father's remains were never found. He knew for sure that Oskar Lange, a medical doctor and a captain in the Polish Army, had been a prisoner in Starobelsk, but he had no idea what had happened to him subsequently. Which is why in April 1990 he set off on a pilgrimage to Katyn Forest. He didn't find there, however, any traces of Oskar Lange.

In 1991, Moscow handed over to Warsaw the lists of Polish prisoners-of-war from the three camps: Kozelsk, Starobelsk and Ostashkov. It was then that Janusz Lange was able to learn that his father had been murdered in the basement of the NKVD at the very center of Kharkov and buried on the property of the resort at Piatichatki in a forested park, ten miles from town.

He went to Kharkov in 1991. He recalls:

"That August 11 will remain in my memory until the end of my life. Together with a group of thirty-two people: widows, daughters and sons of the prisoners-of-war murdered in Kharkov, I flew to Kharkov for the funeral service of the remains from the first exhumation."

The ceremony was a state occasion with an honor guard and orchestra of the Polish Army. Even the terrible downpour, a veritable cloud-burst, with a strong wind snapping tree branches, one of them striking the head of a high Russian military official, was unable to mar the solemn, patriotic mood. The forest in Piatichatki made a disheartening impression. The marked depression of the heavily leafed, wooded land, overgrown with bushes hinted that, beyond the single uncovered grave at which they stood and placed flowers, the remains of further victims would be found.

"As I was standing at this first pit of death, I felt that finally, after fifty years, I was burying my father. It was painfully moving. I couldn't rid myself of the sorrow, of my hatred toward the perpetrators, that they had deprived me of the possibility of knowing my father, of being with him. That they took from me the full joy of childhood."

He left this place shaken but with a great desire to return again. He went back to Poland with the greatest treasure of all, some earth from the tomb of death. At the same time skulls marked with bullet holes, taken during the initial exhumation, also went to Poland with this first excursion, for more detailed examination.

Destiny had it that Janusz Lange would visit Kharkov once more in this same year of 1991. He went again with his family: his wife Kazimiera, his only brother Tadeusz and his wife Zuzanna.

"We wanted to see the necropolis as well, and also the NKVD building where the Polish officers were killed under the cover of night. We intended to go also 135 miles further eastward, to Starobelsk and to visit the cloister from which in the spring of 1940 3,820 Polish officers were transported by train to Kharkov."

They went by train together with almost one hundred people from all over Poland. The majority of them were children of Polish officers lost at Kharkov. They were all extremely excited at this first opportunity of seeing the final road and the place of internment of their fathers...

Traveling accommodations were spartan. They traveled first to Brześć in Belarus, and there waited some hours at night in a dirty and cold Ukrainian train to Kharkov. They weren't able to see a thing through the grimy windows. In the four-person sleepers, the temperature didn't get much above freezing. The exceptionally difficult trip lasted more than two days. Despite the fact that they arrived in Kharkov chilled to the bone and hungry, they went immediately in their rented Ukrainian buses to the cemetery. In Piatichatki, with the forest now naked of leaves, there were already several mounds after the exhumation conducted by the team of Professor Andrzej Nadolski of Łódź. Father Stanisław Wróblewski, chaplain of the garrison church in Łódź, said Mass at the first raised mound. His briefcase served as an altar. Just behind the mound there stood already the Prymasowski cross, with the metal plaque of the Katyn Family affixed to it. A December wind howled around them.

"That Mass was an enormous experience for all of us. We were standing in a dark stillness, in snow and hard cold, in a black wild forest overgrown with thicket. It seemed to us then that we could hear the voices of all those who had died. At the end of the Mass, we sang in a loud, almost unnatural voice, with deep concentration and full of tears, 'Jeszcze Polska nie zginęła...' [Poland's national anthem: 'Poland will not perish as long as we live...'].'" The Langes remember that the road of death, now darker because cinders had been sprinkled over it since 1940, was all that could be seen in the light of the night and the candles. It was on this road that the vehicles from the NKVD building came and threw into the two pits on both sides of the road of death the bodies of those killed with a shot to the back of the head... The Langes promised to themselves then that they would do all possible to have a cemetery there that would worthily commemorate the murdered Polish officers.

After the difficult experiences of travel and visiting the burial site of the officers, the pilgrims attempted to calm their emotions in the Kharkov hotel, Intertourist. However, the accommodations there were terrible. The toilets had no seats, the flushing devices were broken, the hotel food abominable, and the stores empty. It's under such conditions that Ukraine experienced the shock of freedom... And the Katyn children—the retrieval of their fathers' resting place...

On the following day they left in the morning for Starobelsk. The motor coach broke down a few times and they only reached the cloister in the twilight of the setting sun. Meanwhile soldiers were being quartered in it. At the gate there was a guardhouse: they were allowed to proceed onto the fenced-in terrain as an exception and magnanimously permitted to take photographs. The Lange's remember that everyone was battered emotionally, agitated, and they wanted very badly to see it and to preserve the memory. Someone had a map of the Starobelsk camp sketched by a former prisoner ... someone else had the roads of the monastery sketched out....

"The possibility of our moving around however was severely limited. We were under careful observation by the soldiers. An enormous lock hung on the doors of the Orthodox church. It was only at the exit that we managed to hoist the national flags of the Katyn Families and to affix the plaque brought with us from Łódź: 'To the memory of the officers of the Polish Army imprisoned in Starobelsk 1939–1940, murdered by the NKVD. The families from Łódź, Dec. 4, 1991.'"

They also lit a votive candle beneath the plaque and said a prayer. The bewildered authorities of the Starobelsk unit placed an honor guard by it. Just in case... And to the great delight of the pilgrims...

There was no lock a large building not far from the great Orthodox church. They already knew that the captains of the Polish Army had been imprisoned in it. Imperceptibly several of them went into the "captains' quarters," quickly passed by the green-tiled stove and went up the stairs to the first floor. This is where the prison slat-beds had formerly been.

"When we entered, there were soldiers lying on beds. Young men, the majority of them of eastern facial features. They were relaxing. They were taken back at our presence. We were immediately asked to leave the 'captains' quarters.'"

All told, they spent only a bit less than an hour on the premises of the Starobelsk cloister. Even so, they did succeed in seeing that the structure was badly ruined. The stucco was falling from all the buildings, bricks from the cloisters, the stairs were crumbling, shrubs were growing on the roofs. The Orthodox crosses were missing from the towers.

The first Starobelsk pilgrims had wanted also to find the burial place of the forty-eight Polish officers who had died earlier, before the executions at Kharkov in the spring of 1940.

"As we searched for their graves, we went along Kirowa street, bore left and entered the Ukrainian cemetery. However, it was already dark and it was getting time for us to return. Our train was leaving Kharkov that evening at nine." Janusz Lange said.

In Kharkov they were able to go also to the former NKVD building where the executions took place. The director of the town hotel Intertourist was with them. When they came up to the building she began to shout hysterically: " Don't go in to the NKVD, no one has ever come out of that building alive! Kazimiera Lange had to stay with her in the bus while the rest of the pilgrims went up to the building. There at the gate through which the living entered and the dead departed, they started to light votive-candles and place flowers. A watchman came out... He began to trample on the candles and wreaths, and then threw the "desecrated memorial" over the fence. The indignant members of the pilgrimage put down other candles... But he did the same to them...

The Poles asked for someone to show them the basement where their fathers had been tortured. The Ukrainians were amazed at this and told them to get the proper papers. The pilgrims, however, had to leave the city within the hour. The return trip was passed in equally difficult circumstances. Of cold and hunger.

"We felt happy even so that we had been able to see the final resting place of our closest ones and the place where they had been imprisoned and murdered," Janusz and Kazimiera Lange said in unison.

We are conversing in their apartment, in the Retkinia complex in Łódź. With coffee and home baked sweets. Their living room is being redecorated and so Kazimiera Lange has set a small table in a small room, among piles of books, documents and packages. One part of the library is dedicated to the regions of Vilno and Lvov, a second part to the Katyn massacre. The first group belongs to Kazimiera, the second to Janusz. Among their things is their cat "Kicia."

"Since that pilgrimage we hadn't gone for four years to Katyn Forest or to Kharkov," says Kazimiera Lange. She is a lively, energetic brunette, four years younger than her sixty-three-year-old husband Janusz. She calls herself "a distant child" of Katyn. The issue of Katyn has so taken hold of them that their retirement has been completely consumed by it. Janusz Lange is the chairperson of the Governing Council of the Federation of Katyn Families in Warsaw, and too the president of the Katyn Family Association of Łódź. His wife Kazimiera is his "right hand."

"In 1996 we organized together a general pilgrimage of the Katyn Families to the Vatican. We had an audience with the Pope on April 13," chimes in Kazimiera, assisting her reticent husband. "The Pope's blessing, our conversation with him, brought us all to tears. It was not only a great moment in our lives but also a call to further commitment."

It was on the way back from Rome that the Langes decided to organize a group and go that September to Kharkov, at the conclusion of the ongoing exhumation. After their return home they linked up with the tourist agency "Wilejka" in Łódź and under the title of Katyn Family organized with them the excursion. They traveled to Kharkov by motor coach. Kazimiera and Janusz Lange were the guides of the expedition. They took lodgings in the same Intertourist hotel.

"In September 1996, the forest in Kharkov had already been somewhat thinned out. Beautiful, pine crosses now stood at the tombs marked with red and white ribbons, there where the remains of officers had been discovered during the exhumation. Our joy was great because it was no longer the valley of death, but simply tombs. Even so, as before, the black path of death was evident. But walking on the clay ground was difficult; it wasn't possible to free one's shoes from the clammy soil."

That pilgrimage was once again an enormous experience, especially for those who had come for the very first time. The solemn ceremony was modest. An ecumenical prayer was said. Present were Włodzimierz Dusiewicz, president of the Federation of Katyn Families, Andrzej Przewoźnik, secretary general of the Council for the Preservation of the Memory of Struggle and Suffering, Father Tadeusz Dłubacz, and representatives of the Polish Army.

Two months later Janusz Lange found himself in the official government delegation of Włodzimierz Cimoszewicz. In Kharkov he signed with the Ukrainians an agreement regarding the establishment of the future cemetery.

"I on the other hand decided that I would be traveling there with pilgrims. In order to place candles at the graves, as ikons of sorts. And to tell in the east finally the truth about this tragic crime," said Kazimiera as she poured the coffee.

She brought the first forty-person group of pilgrims to the cemetery at Kharkov in 1997. It was then that she had a shock. There in the ground raised over the tombs after the exhumation, in the cracks and fissure of the dried-up earth, she saw the white remnants of human bones. They most likely came from the remains destroyed by the special Soviet machines, the so-called "meat-grinders," which in the seventies ground up the bones to conceal traces of the crime. She burst into tears...

Janusz Lange with his wife Kazimiera at a memorial wall in the Kharkov cemetery, near the tablet of his father, Dr. Oskar Lange, in Kharkov, Ukraine (previously USSR), 2002. Courtesy of Kazimiera and Janusz Lange, Katyn Family Łódź, Poland.

"I was afraid to show this to the pilgrims!" she said.

She immediately informed the consul Zdzisław Nowicki and the graves were then sprinkled with white sand. Those human bones became the driving force behind an intense activity in the Katyn circles (there are twenty-five Katyn Families in Poland as well as several outside the country). Kazimiera Lange and her husband began to exert pressure for the establishment of a worthy and permanent cemetery. After all it wasn't possible that the bones of heroes should be so dishonored...

It was a year later, on June 27, 1998, that there took place in Kharkov the solemn dedication and setting of the cornerstone at the necropolis. The presidents of Poland and Ukraine, Aleksander Kwaśniewski and Leonid Kuczma, took part in the ceremony but the official charter of the cemetery was signed only by Janusz Lange, in his capacity as lead of the Council of the Federation of Katyn Families...

"The signing of this document, so significant for the future cemetery, by someone outside the ranks of the official governments, was an acknowledgement of the importance of the work of the Katyn Families. The document for the

Katyn Forest had been signed in 1995 by Lech Wałęsa, and the one at Miednoye by Andrzej Milczanowski," recalls Janusz Lange. When he visits the Kharkov cemetery he always stops near this tablet. To this day his signature remains the only one.

In 2000, at the sixtieth anniversary of the Katyn massacre, despite many obstacles, three cemeteries were solemnly opened and dedicated: in Kharkov (June 17), in Katyn Forest (July 28) and in Miednoye (September 2).

"It was an enormous effort of many people; it's impossible to name all of them," said the Langes with emotion as they recalled those celebrations. The cemeteries are for them the places where a terrible past meets the present. They are the eloquent witnesses to the life and accomplishments of a previous generation of Poles. "When we saw 'our' cemetery decently cared for, tastefully arranged, beautiful, where the epitaphs containing the history of the Polish intelligentsia were clad in iron, we were filled with happiness."

They looked for his epitaph: "śp. kpt. dr. med. Oskar Lange." They knelt and said a fervent prayer. This was for them the symbolical tomb of their father and father-in-law. They laid flowers and lit candles in remembrance.

"At last my father ceased being an anonymous, unknown soldier. He had attained his own soldier's resting place among his colleagues, with whom he had fought and worked for the fatherland." Even today Janusz Lange is deeply moved when he recalls the moment that the necropolis was opened. He thanked God then on his knees. "And when we heard the exceedingly beautiful sound of the bell that had been placed there, that symbol that joined us, the living, with those interred in that place, we feared that our hearts would burst! From emotion and joy!"

Kazimiera Lange, who was pouring coffee, joined in:

"Janusz was white as a sheet during the dedication of the necropolis at Kharkov. He was unable to speak. After ten years of complete devotion to exposing this crime and to preserving its memory, he could finally weep over his father's grave, which he had sought out for such a long time."

It was after this, recalls Kazimiera, that her husband stood up and, looking at the graves, said:

"We aren't permitted to forget them. We must surround this place with appropriate reverence and remembrance. Such honor as befits the great national heroes must be rendered to those lying here. Even if they were not permitted to die with arms in their hands."

Both the Lange's smilingly add: "Since then we continue to make pilgrimages. In conjunction with the Tourist Agency 'Wilejka,' we have taken already more than 1500 persons to the three Katyn cemeteries."

It is Sunday, September 15, 2002, at the Main Station in Warsaw. Pilgrims are gathering in front of window number 1, at 8:00 in the evening. In one hour the train will leave for Kiev and from there, another train to Kharkov.

Some of the people are returning directly from the Military Ordinate of the Polish Army on Długa Street in Warsaw. Two hours ago the chapel of Our Lady of Katyn was opened. In this chapel there is the icon of Our Lady of the Victims of Katyn, which had been carved by the Polish lieutenant Henryk Gorzechowski into a plank of a camp bed in the Soviet camp at Kozelsk. He had given it to his son, also Henryk, on February 28, 1940, as a present on his nineteenth birthday before he himself died a few months later in Katyn Forest. Thanks to having consigned his son to the protection of the Holy Lady, the son Henryk escaped execution not only at Katyn Forest. Several times he evaded death and, by some miracle, survived the entire war. Today the holy relic, together with fragments from the three wartime cemeteries of Katyn Forest, Kharkov and Miednoye, is again among the soldiers. It has been bestowed upon the cathedral as a national memorial by the sculptor's grandson, also Henryk Gorzechowski, now living in Gdańsk. On the walls of the newly opened chapel in Warsaw are the names of twenty-two thousand Poles who were murdered in the east in 1940 at the hands of the NKVD, of which seven thousand are nameless, buried most likely chiefly in Bykovnia and Kuropaty.

Each participant in a trip to Kharkov is welcomed by guides Kazimiera and Janusz Lange. Each receives a folder and the circular badge of pilgrim. The guides emphasize that they are going on a pilgrimage, not a tour. The composition of the group consists chiefly of families of officers lost in Kharkov, and so for them the place itself is holy.

The Langes inform the group: "We have 800 miles to Kharkov and an additional 135 further to Starobelsk."

The characteristic smell of the east greets us in the Ukrainian train, but it is clean and warm in the four-passenger sleeper cars. The Ukrainian train officials in their grey uniforms help us find our places, arrange the white bed linens, offer us warm and cold drinks. In the lounge of each car boiling water is available. The pilgrims can fix for themselves coffee or tea, and hot soup. Some have already traveled by train, know the routine and are adequately prepared for a trip of almost two days. The border formalities at five in the morning take a long time in Dorohusk. The under-carriages of the train are changed since the rails in all of the former Soviet Union are of a different gage than in the rest of Europe.

We won't get to Kiev until six in the evening. I seat myself therefore next to Kazimiera and Janusz Lange. Their narrative is punctuated by the characteristic clatter of the wheels on the rails... Slow, regular, monotonous... The train speeds eastward no faster than forty miles an hour...

Janusz Lange is convinced that his father was a great Polish patriot. Even though he never knew him. He was barely eight months old when, in August 1939, his father, a doctor of the 4th Regiment of Heavy Artillery in Łódź, Captain Oskar Emil Lange was mobilized and ordered to go to the defense of Warsaw. Even so he knows his father from his mother's and his older brother's stories ... as well as from one photograph. He shows it to us: in it his father is holding him, an infant, in his arms standing next to his wife, Halina Lange.

"For a long time I didn't know that my father had died at the hands of the NKVD in the Katyn massacre. My mother, fearing that it would make our lives more difficult, kept the fact from me and my brother. Even so she always remembered him with love as a good husband and father," Janusz Lange tells us. He is thin, tall, unassuming. Of late he has been ailing and has spent a number of weeks the last year in the hospital.

Oskar Emil Lange was born in 1893 in Łódź. He studied medicine first in Dorpat, then in Warsaw. After independence was regained in 1918, he signed on as a volunteer to the Polish Army while still a student. Later he served as a doctor in various garrisons and military units. His wife, Halina, was eleven years younger than him. She was born in Mohylów on the Dnieper, in present-day Belarus, into a family of the gentry. She was an only child. Early on, at age two, she was orphaned of her father, Walerian Furowicz, a lawyer, and up to 1917 she studied in the *liceum* in Mohylów. However, the bolshevik revolution took place and threw her life into turmoil. The Soviets took possession of and plundered her family estate, drove her and her mother from Mohylów, and sentenced them into homeless wandering. In 1920 both of them arrived in Poland. She did not have the opportunity to attend university. She became an accountant, and then in 1925 was hired to work in the municipal court in Vilno. In that same year, at the New Year's ball, she met Lieutenant Oskar Lange.

"Their marriage took place three years later," says Janusz Lange. Halina and Oskar had a happy home in Łódź. They took part in military celebrations and social gatherings, had guests over, and took relaxing trips to the mountains. Besides his duties in the 4th Regiment of Heavy Artillery, Oskar Lange was a doctor at the local Józef Piłsudski Liceum. Intermittently he would work also at the military hospital in Ciechocinek. He was active as well in the Medical Association and paramilitary organizations.

Unfortunately, September 1939 intervened...

"My father's regiment was dispatched to the defense of Warsaw. Aunt Anna, with me in her arms, reached the capital on one transport whereas my mother, brother and grandmother were to come on a later transport. But the train on which they were traveling was bombed in Skierniewice. They had to return to Łódź. They found that their apartment had already been occupied by the Germans. For almost a full month, my mother, brother and grandmother wandered about the covered market in 'Górniak,' waiting with several hundred others for some kind of shelter."

It was only in the beginning of 1940 that the Lange family was reunited in Łódź, but now without the head of the family, Doctor Oskar Lange. His wife, Halina, succeeded in finding work in a German firm; she and her mother also supplemented their income by knitting and ... telling fortunes. They had learned fortune telling while still in Russia, after their expulsion from Mohylów by the bolsheviks. More than once their knowledge of the art of fortune telling with cards saved their lives...

"We received two cards from my father during that time, both filled with a deep love and care for the family. He wrote from the camp in Starobelsk. He was convinced that because he was a POW he would return soon." Janusz Lange still has those cards in his possession and showed them to me earlier when we were in his apartment in Łódź.

In one of them, from November 29, 1939, Captain Oskar Lange wrote with tiny letters: "Dear loved ones! I am alive. Please don't worry about me. My only distress is lack of news from you and what has been happening to you, inasmuch as I don't know exactly where you are and whether, as I suppose, you returned safely from that bombed evacuation transport from Skierniewice to Łódź. Halina, my dear, please don't give up, only wait patiently. We will be together! Kisses."

On the second card, from March 8, 1940, Dr. Oskar Lange said: "I'm writing to all of you, to my brothers and sisters as well. Put together some kind of minimal finances for Halina and my beloved children, to keep them from dying from hunger." Also: "I authorize Halina, Grandma and all of you to take out loans in my name in whatever shape and form."

"Unfortunately, that short-lived contact with him was suddenly broken off; the letters we sent came back to us. A flicker of hope that father was alive and would return began slowly to die in us. My mother, grandmother and aunt knew the bolsheviks well..." Janusz Lange knew the family narratives, how the bolsheviks had murdered Aunt Anna's six sisters right before her eyes at their family estate...

These women from the *kresy* joined the underground conspiracy. For a time there was even a contact point in their own home for the Home Army; both of them also participated in the secret education of young people.

They would send letters to Moscow via the International Red Cross and other organizations, always in search of Captain Oskar Lange. "He doesn't appear in the rolls," was the reply that they received several times.

In 1945, precisely on March 13, a card came to them from the cavalry officer Tarnowski who had been the adjutant of the commander of the military in the Lublin region. Janusz Lange has this card today as well: "At the order of citizen General Bukojemski, I wish to inform you that Captain Oskar Lange was in the camp at Starobelsk, but where he was transferred to or where one might look for him, the General does not know. For this reason he is unable to give any information."

Lieutenant-Colonel Leon Bukojemski (later General) was also a prisoner-of-war in Starobelsk. He, however, had been transferred to the temporary camps of Pavlishchev-Bor and Griazowiec, and from there made his way to the Polish Army being formed in the USSR.

"My father, due to his German sounding last name, and I remind you that the Soviets were then allies of Hitler, had also the possibility of being freed. Even so he didn't break his oath. He didn't betray the Polish Army and remained faithful to the end," his son emphasizes.

It was January 19, 1945, the day of Łódź's liberation from German occupation. Those who were charged with raising Janusz Lange, Grandmother Eugenia, mother and Aunt Anna, did not much trust the recovered freedom. They foresaw merely the change of a German occupation to a Soviet one...

"Then began the following phase of our lives, requiring a reorganization and accommodation to the new circumstances of the Polish People's Republic," Janusz Lange says of his fate.

After many attempts his mother found work in the General Consumers' Cooperative "Społem." This work, and also other odds jobs, as well as packages from the UNRA and emergency relief on the part of some of his father's friends and colleagues, allowed them a meager survival. However, police inspections began. The Office of Security (UB) was searching for things belonging to Captain Lange.

"Mother had to hide away everything that had been my father's. She concealed some things deeply in nooks and corners, spread others among acquaintances," Janusz recalled. "She altered her longing for her husband into a concern about our health, upbringing, progress in school."

Unconsciously she waited for her husband's return, despite the fact that all the efforts made to find him had come up empty. Janusz wipes his glasses:

"Mother deluded herself into thinking that as a doctor nothing bad should come to him, even in wartime. She persuaded us that he would probably fall under the special protection of international law. However, the years passed without him returning. Despite that, mother conjectured that he had perhaps been sent into the depths of Russia, that being a doctor he was helping other exiles... So she waited..."

Halina Lange did her best to be both father and mother. She was the great friend of her sons, often their buddy, and at the same time the person who guided them into their independent, adult lives.

"It is thanks to her that I look back on my childhood as a happy time, one with the smell of Sunday cakes and jams, and though fatherless, one filled with love." He emphasizes that he will never forget the warm occasions with friends around a Lithuanian dinner dish, often with fortune-telling and card playing, and the visits of "aunts and friends" from Vilno.

In 1953, Janusz's grandmother, Eugenia Furowicz, died after a long illness.

"That was a blow. Mother lost not only her own beloved mother, but her best friend. This affected her own health." At the time Janusz Lange was fourteen years old.

Despite heart problems, Halina Lange continued to work to keep up her spirits and to live for her sons. She was yet able to rejoice that her older son, Tadeusz, became an engineer, a graduate in electrical engineering from the Łódź Institute of Technology. In 1962, a son, Jerzy, was born to him, and he was her only grandchild. She further was pleased that her younger son Janusz had begun studies in law at the University of Łódź, and later worked at the same place she was working, the "Społem," where for almost forty years he would be engaged in organizational and administrative affairs.

Halina Lange retired after twenty years of work. But hardly a year and a half later, her heart gave out under the strain of a life governed by so many hardships. On November 6, 1966, she had her fourth infarct. At the age of not quite sixty-two, she was laid to rest in the cemetery of Zarzew in Łódź.

"Right up to her death, she believed that her husband, with whom she had spent twelve happy years, was still living somewhere. Practically to the very end, she was convinced that they would meet each other again," her son says.

He too kept trying to believe the same. It was not until 1968 when he left for London, and six years later for several months to the United States, that he became acquainted with publications concerning Katyn. Finally he gave up hope... He lost himself only in his speculations as to where his father's grave might be...

Halina Lange was the first Katyn widow that Kazimiera came to know. It was Kazimiera's destiny to make the acquaintance of more such women who had been required for decades to bear the bitterness of silence and lies concerning the death of their husbands. She met their children, grandchildren, their entire families.

"I have the satisfaction of being able to help these people today," she says with tears in her eyes. "I return from each subsequent pilgrimage richer because of the unforgettable experiences. I have the privilege of experiencing together with them their emotions, and to draw from them a wisdom that is so needed today and strength in their patient expectation for the truth of this crime."

Kharkov, just as Kiev some three hundred miles away, greets us with a fall rain. Waiting for us in the station, also a magnificent edifice, are representatives of the Association of Polish Culture, Polish reporters, and a motor coach. About four thousand Poles, today ever more courageously acknowledging their roots, live in this city of a million and a half, the largest in eastern Ukraine. Unfortunately more than ten thousand Poles were murdered in 1938, and then over the following decades it became better not to mention one's Polish background.

Presently, according to the latest census, 145,000 Poles, including a significant number of the intelligentsia, live in Ukraine. An ever greater number of citizens admit their Polish roots.

"Today I feel as if I have broken out of the eggshell in which I was suffocating and have begun to breathe freely," is how the vice-president of the Association of Polish Culture, Janina Mieńszowa, describes her feelings and those of others of Polish heritage in Kharkov.

We continue on our way to the "Kharkov" hotel, formerly the "Metropol." It is situated on one of the largest plazas in Europe—the Plaza of Freedom. There is also a gigantic, shining statue of Vladimir Lenin. On one side of this plaza there is a large and colorful amusement park which is noisy far into the night. Lenin seems paranoid as he looks onto the colorful, brilliant carousels, going round and round to the rhythm of resounding English music...

After settling in and having something to eat, our pilgrimage pays a visit to the municipal consulate of the Polish Republic. It has been in Kharkov for six years; a second one is active in Lvov.

"The Cemetery of the Victims of Totalitarianism, constructed by Poland in 2000, has been handed over to the control of the city," the Consul General of Poland in Kharkov, Michał Żórawski, tells us over tea and cakes. It is well taken care of, inspected and cleaned daily, the paths being cleared even in the winter. The necropolis is slowly growing into part of the landscape of the city; even young couples visit it and place flowers. Not long ago members of the II International Motorcycle Katyn Rally rendered special homage to the murdered Polish officers.

The Polish officers who were buried in the spring of 1940 in the Kharkov Piatichatki cemetery had been imprisoned since the fall of 1939 in the Starobelsk monastery.

It is 135 miles to Starobelsk. The road is narrow, bumpy, long past any repairs. The traffic on the road is almost nonexistent, and our aging bus, moving along at more than forty miles an hour, is barely able to handle the higher ridges. We are almost in another time, another world...

Starobelsk, quiet, constructed of wood, still having a statue of Lenin, was founded in 1686 and now has almost twenty thousand inhabitants. A cloister for women in the center of town was closed down by the bolsheviks in 1923 and turned into a prison. It was after the war that the army stationed soldiers here in the desecrated environs of the church and ruined monastery; they even placed a storehouse here. It was ten years ago that the entire property was returned to the nuns.

There are young sisters here now in Starobelsk, numbering twenty-five. The nuns are slowly rebuilding both the church and the monastery, with only the offerings of the faithful. The small church of Holy Trinity, called also the Winter Church, is now open; the painters are at this very time covering the

Teresa Kaczorowska, the author, in the Kharkov cemetery, Kharkov, Ukraine (previously USSR), 2002.

last walls. Now it is possible to pray here, place votive candles, admire the brilliant gold iconostasis, purchase icons made by the sisters. The interior of the large church under the name of Our Lady of Divine Help, called the Summer Church, is entirely ruined; at the moment there is some work being done on the elevation. There is a cross among the ruins and torn up floor planks. We place lighted candles before it.

Some of the pilgrims, among whom was Janusz Lange, succeeded in entreating Sister Ekatermina to let them into the "captain's room." Work was in progress there also.

"Oh, the stove with the golden tiles is not here any more," notes Janusz Lange. "I am always moved when I am here and would like to have asked my father so many questions."

The internment place of forty-eight officers has been discovered here, these POWs of the Starobelsk camp who died during their imprisonment, before the executions in Kharkov. In the forest, at the municipal cemetery, we visit their section, prepared by the Polish Republic. The graves have been put in order, decorated with flowers, red and white flags. Much help in this has been given by the local Association of Devotees of Polish Culture and Language under the name of "Bridge of Hope." Their members invite our group to their center. We are overwhelmed at their reception of us. There are Polish songs sung by children. They express acquaintance with Polish literature, are full of warmth and hospitality, and have a table rich in food. The Lange's are on friendly terms with many of them, ask about relatives, exchange small gifts. Other pilgrims give small presents, money and books to the children.

The prisoners-of-war were taken by train from the monastery in Starobelsk to Kharkov. They were led from the train station to the NKVD headquarters. A huge, terrifying, rebuilt structure stands in that very spot. We don't even ask to be allowed to enter because we already know the answer. Today the Ukrainian special service occupies the building which is why we hurriedly take only a few pictures.

We move toward the Kharkov cemetery, along a road that is straight as an arrow, lined with slender poplars. I think to myself, "Strange how the poplars recall the night transports of dead Polish officers killed by a bullet to the back of the head in the basement headquarters of the NKVD?" After about six miles we stop in a parking area, on the right side of the roadway.

Two monuments with crosses greet us at the cemetery gates, a Catholic one with a poem from Asnyk and an Orthodox one dedicated to the victims of bolshevism in the years 1938–1941. Across from them there is a black, marble tablet in three languages, Russian, Ukrainian, and Polish, dedicated to those Soviet and Polish citizens who were murdered here in the years 1939–1941; the tablet was placed here in 1991 by the Kharkov KGB.

The necropolis, located here among leafy trees, on land that was not long ago a center for the NKVD, encircled by a fence, now bears the name "Kharkov Cemetery of the Victims of Totalitarianism." It is indeed beautiful and well cared-for, at this time especially adorned by fall. It covers in Piatichatki exactly 5016 acres. Two emblems, of Poland and of Ukraine, hang at the entrance gate. Testifying to the different faiths and nationalities of the victims here are the symbols of four faiths, each placed on its own plinth: a Catholic cross, an Orthodox cross, a Star of David, and a Muslim crescent.

"There are various religious services here," we are informed by the vice-president of the Association of Polish Culture Janina Mieńszowa. She herself can serve as an example of the different religious groups inasmuch as she is Catholic and her husband Orthodox.

We begin at the asphalt, poplar-lined street and proceed down the path of death. Paved with black cobblestones of granite, it makes a loop around the necropolis. Along it had been dropped the murdered bodies, tossed onto both sides of the path into holes that had been dug earlier.

Two huge cast-iron altars crown the extremities of the cemetery, one dedicated to Polish officers and the other—across from the first—to the inhabitants of Kharkov. The names of the victims have been engraved on the altars.

There is an aesthetic walkway connecting the two. At the entrance to the walkway are two castings: one of the Cross of the September Campaign of 1939 and the other of the Virtuti Militari, and on both sides 3800 plaques inscribed in Polish.

The pilgrims are visibly moved. They search out the names of their relatives on the plaques and the Catholic altar, pray and lay flowers. They light the votive candles they have brought along with them and take pictures. All of them in their thoughts join to their relatives and consider their lives. They find the plaques dedicated to the fathers of those in this book: Jan Adamczyk, Julian Gruner, Zdzisław Spanily, Oskar Lange, Józef Wasilewski...

"I have been here ten times, but the more often I come, the more willingly do I return," sighs Janusz Lange. "This cemetery is close to me and always beautiful, though it has a different look at each different season of the year."

The great-grandson of Dr. Oskar Lange, eighteen-year-old Michał, Tadeusz Lange's grandson, is on pilgrimage also. Another of Michał's great-grandfathers, from his mother's side, Eugeniusz Smoliński, also died at the hands of the Soviets and lies at Katyn Forest. "The preservation of the memory of these people who are interred here forever strengthens generational ties and should be official Polish policy," says the young man with emotion. He is surprised that the schools teach very little on the topic of this crime, which is why the young people know so little about it.

Kazimiera Lange explains:

"Eight generals murdered at Kharkov lie here: Stanisław Haller, Leonard Siekierski, Leon Bilewicz, Aleksander Kowalewski, Kazimierz Orlik-Łukowski, Franciszek Sikorski, Konstanty Flisowski and Piotr Skuratowicz. Likewise there are 55 colonels, 127 lieutenant-colonels, 230 majors, around 1000 captains and cavalry captains, 2400 lieutenants and second lieutenants.

The bell placed on the ground near the altars begins to sound, beautifully and piercingly. Today is precisely the 17th of September. We are to take part in a special Mass celebrated at the cemetery altar, now decorated with flowers. A Polish priest will lead this service on the anniversary of the Soviet invasion of Poland.

"On earth death will always remain a mystery," he says with the accent of the *kresy*.

In the evening we have some time for conversation even though almost everyone has a cold of sorts and is coughing. It is quite a bit colder in Ukraine than in Poland.

"Kharkov and Starobelsk are two very distant places joined together by the Katyn massacre. The road is the most difficult one to traverse which is why the least number of pilgrims come here," the Lange's explain. Throughout our journey I continue to be amazed at their fortitude and their zeal for the Katyn affair.

They bring out photographs from earlier pilgrimages, not only those to Kharkov and Starobelsk, but also those to Kozelsk, to Ostashkov and Miednoye, even to Kuropaty and Bykovnia.

"Every Pole should know these places as well as they know Monte Cassino," they affirm. "Otherwise the truth about Katyn will never be fully penetrated. First there was silence for a half century, then the opening of these cemeteries was not adequately publicized to the world, to Poles, Russians, Ukrainians."

It happened that we even met two young Ukrainians on the train, traveling students who knew nothing either of the Soviet aggression against Poland on Sept. 17, 1939, or of the establishment of these three Katyn necropoli.

"Almost all the Ukrainians and Russians whom we meet in the cemeteries are convinced that they relate to the victims of the totalitarianism of Hitler and not of Stalin," explains Kazimiera Lange.

Before leaving Kharkov, we visit once again the necropolis in Piatichatki. The families of the officers take leave of their fathers, uncles, grandfathers... Most of them are advanced in years, and don't know if they would be able to come here again...

"Everyone who makes the pilgrimage to the Polish military cemeteries in Kharkov, Katyn Forest, or Miednoye, returns to Poland a changed person, richer because of the unforgettable emotions, understanding better himself and others. Many come back here again, but we have perhaps been here the most," whisper the Langes.

They are aware that there remains much work for the Katyn movement. The families of those murdered continue to await from Russia acceptance of official involvement in this crime, acknowledgment of responsibility for it, apologies. The families also count on access to and the release to Poles of all documents connected to the Katyn crime, including names and places of internment for the over 7,300 citizens of the Polish Republic also murdered as a result of the decision of March 5, 1940.

"The stagnation in the investigation conducted by the Russian military prosecutor is upsetting to those in our circle. We are hopeful that the investigation conducted by the Institute of National Memory will conclude with an acknowledgement of the Katyn murder as a war crime and genocide," says Janusz Lange as he shares his thoughts and goals concerning further work.

It begins raining, and the wind starts blowing. The first leaves of fall begin to sprinkle down from the trees... As if the spirits of the Polish officers were signaling their existence... I gaze at the meditative faces of the pilgrims so linked with those who had died ... and hear the silent whisper:

when you are here
it hurts less

INDEX

Adam Mickiewicz University (Poznań) 81
Adamczyk (née Schinagiel), Anna 61, 67
Adamczyk (née Doerr), Barbara 78
Adamczyk, Eric 78
Adamczyk, George 75–76, 78
Adamczyk, Capt. Jan Franciszek 59–61, 64, 75–76, 248
Adamczyk, Jerzy (Jurek) 61, 63, 65–70, 73, 78
Adamczyk (née Żebrowska), Józefina 78
Adamczyk, Wesley (Wiesław) 59–80
Adamczyk, Zofia (Zosia) 61, 63, 65–66, 69–73, 78
Ahvaz 71
Aleksander, Mr. 179
Allies 3, 4, 49, 131, 195, 227
Alma-Ata 67
Amsterdam 158
Anders, Gen. Władysław 67, 69, 131, 227
Andropov, Yuri 133
Archangel 203, 204
Arski, Jurek 211–12
Asnyk, Adam 247
Augustowski 26
Augustowskie Lakes 113
Auschwitz 42, 113, 121, 125–26, 150, 194

Babynin 98
Baranowicze 18
Beit Shemesh 231
Belarus 16, 46, 128, 139, 201, 209, 219, 234, 241
Berdówka 24
Beria, Lavrenti 16, 42
Berlin 158, 210–1
Bern 228–29
Biała Podlaska 102
Biała Waka 148
Biehler, Professor 25
Biernatki 34–35

Bierut, Bolesław 196
Bieszczady Mountains 82
Bilewicz, Gen. Leon 248
Blochin, NKVD agent 104
Boguszewski, Kazimierz 143
Bohatyrowicz, Gen. 89
Braun, Kris Sylwester 194
Breslau 194; see also Wrocław
Brezhnev, Leonid 132
Browar, battle of 183
Brussels 196, 197
Brzechwa, Jan 228
Brześć 95, 97, 101, 234
Brzeżany 152, 157
Brzozowski, Stanisław 26
Budapest 187
Bukojemski, Gen. Leon 242, 243
Bukovina 223
Buzek, Jerzy 47, 48, 57
Bydgoszcz 195, 197
Bykovnia 240, 249

Calgary 218, 219, 220
Cambridge University 73
Canada 5, 55, 57, 62, 73, 162–64, 169–70, 173–76, 185, 197, 201, 218–20
Caspian Sea 68
Cemetery of the Lvovian Eaglet-Cadets 13, 22
Chełm Lubelski 95
Chelmsford 218
Chicago 6, 51, 54–57, 59–60, 62, 70–75, 78–79, 152, 186, 188, 197–198, 200
Chiselhurst 220
Chodzież 87
Chojnów 153, 156, 157
Churchill, PM Winston 3
Ciechanów (Zichenau) 106, 109–11, 113–17
Ciechocinek 241
Ciesiul, Mr. 142, 144

Cieślak, Mr. 191
Ciężkowice 60
Cimoszewicz, Włodzimierz 137
Ciula, Mr. 15
conspiracy of silence 3–4, 22, 38, 46–47, 49, 89–90, 115, 132, 150, 161, 172, 184–85, 216, 249; see also cover-up of the Katyn massacre
Copenhagen 220
Council for the Preservation of the Memory of Struggle and Suffering 47, 90, 128, 159, 237
cover-up of the Katyn massacre 3–4, 6, 22, 28–29, 37–39, 41, 45–47, 49, 75, 90, 92, 115–116, 119, 122–24, 126, 132–33, 139, 146–47, 150, 160–61, 172, 177, 182–84, 185, 206, 213, 216–17, 237, 242, 244; see also conspiracy of silence; oppression
Czeczot, Jan 143
Czerniowce 218, 223
Częstochowa (Jasna Góra) 42–43, 165, 195
Cieżowski, Prof. 207

Dachau 108
Darewo 15
Darłowo 212
Dec, Lt. Ignacy 150–154
Dec (née Głodzik), Julia 151–56
Dec, Stanisława; see Sojowa, Stanisława
Dec, Wisława (Wisia) 151–56, 159
Dec, Zosia 151–56, 160
Deerfield 59
Dembiński, Adam 111–113
Dembińska (née Korzybska), Ewa 115
Dembiński, Jacek 115
Dembiński, Janulek 111–13, 115
Dembińska, Laura 111–113
DePaul University 74
Detroit 197
discovery of Katyn Forest massacre 3, 17, 45, 54, 85, 104, 122, 129, 166, 179, 192, 204, 206
Dłubacz, Fr. Tadeusz 237
Dnieper River 88, 241
Dorohusk 240
Dorpat 241
Dresdner, Emanuel 223
Dresdner, 2nd Lt. Dr. Robert 221–27
Dresdner (née Landes), Róża 222–29
Drohobycz 225
Drwęca River 28
Dubrow 210
Dudir, Teresa 220
Dukla 82
Dulap cemetery (Tehran) 69
Dusiewicz, Włodzimierz 237
Działdowo 109
Dzierżyński, Feliks 143, 231

Eastern Prussia 109–10, 113
Ebensee, Lake 167

Edinburgh 55
Egypt 73, 162
Ekatermina, Sister 246
England 30, 73, 86, 131–32, 168–69, 203, 210, 213–20; see also Great Britain
execution of Katyn massacre POWs 16–17, 39, 41, 88, 103–04, 116, 204, 236, 247
execution order of Polish POWs 3
exhumation of Katyn victims 33–49, 54, 78, 85, 103–05, 122, 154, 192, 233–34, 237

First Polish Corps 55, 93, 128
Flisowski, Gen. Konstanty 248
Folejewski, Prof. 215
A Forgotten Odyssey 60
Foxley 168
France 4, 141
Frenkiel, Olenka 75
Furowicz, Eugenia 243, 244
Furowicz, Walerian 241

Gałacz 226
Garwolin 95
Gdańsk 170, 210, 240
Gdynia 23–24, 30–32, 146, 211–13, 217, 219–20
Geneva 227
Geneva conventions 16
genocide 1, 3–4, 17, 57–58, 80, 92, 249
George VI, King 217
Germany 3, 54, 56–57, 83, 155, 181, 196, 208
Gestapo 27, 42, 53, 84, 109, 111, 113, 141, 153, 191, 217
Giedymin Tower 130
Gliwice 199
Głódź, Bishop Sławój Leszek 31
Głodzik, Roman 157
Głodzik family 151
Gmunden 167
Gnatowska, Lilka 210
Gnatowska, Mrs. 205
Gniezdowo 17, 88, 204
Golgotha of the East 49, 160
Gomułka, Władysław 218
Góra Zamkowa 130, 219–20
Gorbachev, Mikhail 4, 45, 103, 124
Gorzechowski, Lt. Henryk 30, 240
Gorzechowski, Henryk (grandson) 31, 240
Gorzechowski, Henryk (son) 30, 240
Grabowska (Patey-Grabowska), Alicja 118–126
Grabowska, Stanisława 120, 121
Grabowski, 2nd Lt. Kazimierz Roman 120, 122–23
Grabowski, Mariusz 125
Grabowski, Wojciech (Wojtek) 120–21
Granowska 163
Great Britain 4, 60, 70, 216–17; see also England
Grey Ranks 6, 191–95

Griazowiec 243
Grodno 143, 188–90, 192
Grodzisko 158
Grudziądz 52, 164, 188
Gruner, Ewa 33–50
Gruner, Dr. Julian (Lucjanowicz) 33, 45, 49, 248
Gruner (née Mittelstaedt), Maria 33
Grybów 60
Grześkowiak, Mr. 28
Gulag Archipelago (Solzhenitsyn) 20

Haifa 227
Halifax 73, 220
Haller, Gen. Stanisław 248
Hanus, Józef 82, 86
Hanus, Kazimierz 81
Hanus, (Babunia) Maria 82–86
Hanus, Tadeusz 85
Heiland, Frau 156–58
Hirsh, Anthony Marcin 53–54
Hitler, Adolf 1, 58, 76, 108, 158, 189, 205–06, 225, 231, 243, 249
Holon cemetery (Tel Aviv) 232
Hołub (née Reutów), Alina 128
Hołub, Maj. Bronisław (Bronek) 127–31, 135
Hołub, (Halina's sister) Jadwiga (Jadzia) 128–35
Hołub, Józef 128
Hołub (née Gródek), Maria 128–30, 134
Holubno 83
Home Army 6, 111, 113, 116, 120, 130–31, 141, 143, 145, 153, 166, 171, 181, 193, 206, 210, 213, 215, 242
Horoszowska, Helena 187–97
Horoszowska, Irena (Ika) 188–96
Horoszowska, Ivette (Ivetka) 186–87, 198–200
Horoszowska (née Kazimierczak), Mirosława (Mira) 186–87, 197–200
Horoszowski, Bogdan ("Komar") 186–200
Horoszowski, Capt. Romuald Adolf (pseud. Roman Kawecki) 186–95
Hryniawo 25
Hurnowicze 209

Inflanty 33
Innsbruck 175
International Red Cross 3, 242
Iran 68, 70, 162; *see also* Persia
Iskierkowa, Hala 191
Israel 5, 207, 221–22, 227–32

Jan Kazimierz University (Lvov) 12, 223
Janina (Janka; cousin of Wanda Wassserman) 221, 230
Janowski, Tadeusz 163
Jaruzelski,Wojciech 45, 103, 124
Jasionek 155
Jeleński 140
Jerusalem 153, 231

John Paul II 31, 163, 170, 173
Junikowski cemetery (Poznań) 24
Juszkiewicz, Ryszard 85

Kacprzak, Józef 101–02
Kaganovich (ship) 68
Kaleta, Prof. 159
Kalinin (presently Tver) 103–04
Kalisz 34–35, 37–38, 41, 43–44
Kaługa 210
Kalwajt (Née Hołub), Halina (Halinka) 127–137
Kalwajt, Mirosława (Mira) 128, 132–37
Kalwajt, Ryszard 131–32
Kamińska, Halina 52–53, 56
Kamińska (née Ruchniewicz), Jadwiga 51, 58
Kamińska (née Karpińska), Krystyna 55–57
Kamiński, Prof. Edward 51–58
Kamiński, Ivone 55–56
Kamiński, Jerzy 52–53
Kamiński, Capt. Marcin 51–54, 58
Kamiński, Norbert 55–56
Kamionka 111–12
Karlshamn 213–15
Karpiński, Major Władysław 55
Karun River 71
Kasperowszczyzna 205
Kaszuba, Andrzej 169
Kaszuba, Jan (Janek) 167–71
Kaszuba, Jan (son) 168
Kaszuba, (Maria Lidia) Maja 162–172
Kaszuba, Marek 169
Kaszuba, Mirosław 164, 169, 171
Kaszuba, Zbigniew 169
Kaszuba, Zdzisław 169
Katowice 85, 156
Katyn (Katyń) (symbolic title for all topics related to the entire massacre) 3–6, 19–22, 29–32, 43–44, 46–51, 54, 56–58, 60, 72, 75–78, 80, 84, 87–90, 92, 104, 115–16, 119, 122–25, 128, 132–34, 159–61, 163–64, 166, 170–73, 175–77, 179, 182–85, 189, 192, 204, 206, 209, 213, 216–17, 220–21, 224, 229–31, 234–40, 244–45, 247–49
Katyn Cross 22, 48, 160, 221
Katyn Families, Association of 48–49, 160
Katyn Families, Federation of 57, 237–38
Katyn Family(ies) 6, 22, 24, 30–31, 34–35, 46, 48–49, 56–57, 75, 77–80, 96, 104–05, 134, 137, 160, 162, 171, 198–99, 221, 231, 234–35, 237–38,
Katyn Family Association 6, 30, 134, 162, 231, 237
Katyn Forest (site of one of three massacres) 2–3, 5, 16–17, 21, 31, 34–35, 41, 46, 57–58, 77–80, 84, 86, 88–90, 103–04, 116, 119, 124–25, 129, 132–34, 161–62, 171, 179, 192, 204, 206, 221, 227, 229, 233, 236, 239–40, 248–49

Katyn Forest massacre (refers specifically to the massacre at the Katyn Forest site) 4, 81, 85, 89, 122, 127, 132
Katyn Madonna of Gdynia 32
Katyn massacre (refers to the combined massacres at three sites) 4, 5, 11, 14, 20, 60, 90, 91, 115, 119, 123–24, 126, 146, 192, 221, 231, 236, 241, 248
Katyn Monument 31, 104, 163, 170–71, 176, 184
Katyn Museum 44
Kawecki, Roman 192–93; see also Horoszowski, Capt. Romuald Adolf
Kazakhstan 17, 65–67, 189, 203–05, 209
Kazań 34
KGB 36, 41, 247
Kharkov (Charków) 3, 5, 16, 24, 26, 30–31, 34–35, 37–41, 44, 46–48, 50, 57, 59, 64, 75–77, 90, 116, 137, 139, 171, 233–40, 244–49
Kielce 110
Kiev 183, 187, 239, 240, 244
King, Mr. 216–17
Kismanowska (née Wyrzutowicz), Stanisława 175, 178–84
Kismanowska, Zosia 177–78, 181, 184
Kismanowski, Capt. Jerzy 176–180
Kismanowski, Karol 183
Koch, Erich 109
Kohn, Dr. 20
Kojder, Apolonia 185
Kołomyja 224
Kolyma 20–21, 207
Komi Republic 203
Konopnicka, Maria 117
Końskie 110
Kopański, Gen. Stanisław 55, 227
Kormend 187
Korzybska, Aurelia 115
Korzybska (née Okoniewska), Maria 107–11, 114–15
Korzybski, Adam 115
Korzybski, Sgt. Aleksander 106–08, 116
Korzybski, Jan (Jaś) 106–117
Korzybski, Michał 111
Kościerzyna 53–54
Kościuszko, Tadeusz 62, 74
Kościuszko Foundation 6
Kowalewski, Gen. Aleksander 248
Kowel 95
Kowno 143
Kozelsk (Kozielsk) 1, 3, 9, 16–17, 19, 30, 53, 84, 88, 103, 119–20, 122, 124, 129, 153, 162, 166, 179, 203–04, 206, 223, 226, 230, 233, 240, 249
Kozelsk Mother of God 162
Kozśowska (née Kismanowska), Halina 173–185
Kozśowski, Jacek 174–77
Kozśowski, Tadeusz 174

Krajowa 226
Kraków 9, 48, 63, 75, 84, 105, 139, 155–56, 171, 203
Krasiński, Count Edward 107–08
Krasiński, Zygmunt 106, 108, 117
Krasiński estate 108
Krasiński library 107
Krasnovodsk 68
Kraszewski 44
Kresy 9, 15–16, 24–26, 31, 89, 103, 127–28, 130, 135, 138, 145, 148, 230, 242, 248
Krushchev, Nikita 20, 45
Krzyżanowski, Gen. Aleksander ("Wilk") 130
Krzyżanowski, Prof. Jerzy 119
Kuczma, Pres. Leonid 238
Kuczyński, Fr. 25
Kuhaje 19
Kupała, Janka 209, 220
Kuropaty 240, 249
Kustanai 65
Kwaśniewski, Pres. Aleksander 238

Lambianowice-Opole 92
Łańcucki, Father Adam 152–53, 156
Łańcut 82–83, 187
Landskron 215
Lange (née Furowicz), Halina 241–44
Lange, Janusz 233–249
Lange, Jerzy 244
Lange, Kazimiera 234–49
Lange, Michał 248
Lange, Capt. Dr. Oskar 233, 239–43, 248
Lange, Tadeusz 234, 248
Lange, Zuzanna 234
Lazdijaj 220
Łążyń 52
Łeba River 114
Lebanon 72
Legnica 156
Lenin, Vladimir 58, 76, 100, 147, 245
Lermontov, Mikhail 210
Leśnik, Ewa 81–90
Leśnik, Marian 81, 87–90
Leszno 122
letters from Soviet POW camps 16, 26, 45, 53, 63, 84, 108, 122, 129, 139, 153–54, 166, 179, 203, 206, 223, 226, 242,
Lewandowski cemetery (Lvov) 21
Lipsk 158
Lithuania 5, 127, 132, 134–35, 138–41, 145–46, 203, 205, 219–20
Liverpool 73
Łódź 6, 29, 91–94, 98, 101–102, 104, 165, 221, 233–37, 240–44
London 4, 27, 29, 55, 69, 75, 113, 131, 162, 168–69, 176, 213, 216–17, 220, 244
Lubaczów 187
Lublin 38, 85, 95, 229, 242
Lubyanka prison 204

Łuck 25, 61–62, 79
Łuński, Czesław 85
Lvov 9, 11–13, 18–22, 83, 92, 152, 165, 171,
    178, 187, 221–26, 230, 236, 245
Lvov University 21
LVR 130
Lyons 158

Maciejowice 95
Maczek, Gen. Stanisław 30, 55
Madejska (née Hanus), Janina 82–85
Madejski, Franciszek 81, 86
Madejski, Judge Stanisław 83–85, 88
Madonna of Katyn 31
Mahari (née Dresdner), Irena 222–228
Mahari, Julian Igal 227–29
Mahari, Rafael 228
Mahari, Robert 228
Malinowski, Major 99
Małkinia 190
Małopolska 12, 60–61, 224
Mariampol 33, 42–43
Maryhill cemetery (Chicago) 57
Mauthausen camp 167
Medreli, Father Antoni 162
Melak, Stefan 119
Michotek, Jerzy 11, 19
Mickiewicz, Adam 25, 143, 159
Miednoye (Miednoje) 3, 5, 30–31, 34–35, 41,
    46, 57, 77, 90, 92, 96, 103–05, 116–17, 171,
    198–99, 239–40, 249
Międzyrzecki, Artur 118
Mieńszowa, Janina 245, 247
Mikołajczyk, Stanisław 195
Mikoyan, Anastas 16
Milczanowski, Andrzej 239
Milewska, Jadzia 112
Ministry of Education 147, 158, 219
Ministry of Foreign Affairs 81, 87
Ministry of National Defense 12
Ministry of Transportation 196
Mińsk 128, 202, 205, 208–09
Mississauga 173
Mława 83–84, 111
Mohylów 241–42
Mokotów 165–66, 188
Mołodeczno 202, 208–09
Molotov, Vyecheslav 16, 193
Monte Cassino, battle of 70, 249
Montreal 60, 197, 218
Moscow 18, 44–45, 82, 98, 101, 147, 204, 233,
    242
Mosul-Kirkuk 69
Moszyński, Adam 176
Munich 54
Murowana Oszmianka 130

Nabożna-Wildsztein, Cywia 207
Nadolski, Prof. Andrzej 234

Narew River 110
Nastarowicz (née Słowik), Barbara 105
Nastarowicz (née Spychała), Helena 93
Nastarowicz, Jadzia 93, 98, 102, 104
Nastarowicz, Krystyna 105
Nastarowicz, Marcin 93
Nastarowicz, Michał (policeman) 93–104
Nastarowicz, Stefan 91–105
Nastarowicz, (Uncle) Stefan 92
Nastarowicz, Włodzimierz 105
Nicholas Copernicus University (Toruń) 36
Niedzielko, Capt. 212–13
Niemen River 188, 201
Niłowa Pustyń 100
NKVD 1, 2, 4–5, 14–20, 26–28, 30, 39, 46,
    63–65, 67, 75, 85, 88, 92, 100, 103–05, 108,
    122, 129, 131, 142, 166, 182, 192–93, 204,
    207, 209–10, 214, 216–17, 224, 227, 230–31,
    233–36, 240–41, 247
Northwestern Medical and Dental Schools 55
Nova Scotia 73
Nowa Wieś (Neudorf Groditzberg) 156–58
Nowa Wilejka 146
Nowak, Jerzy Robert 189
Nowe Miasto Lubawskie (Pomorze) 26–28
Nowicki, Zdzisław 238
Nowogródek 24–26, 30–32
Nuremberg 3, 216

Odessa 131
Office of Security (UB) 29, 182, 195–96,
    211–13, 243
Okólnik 107–08
Olechnowicze 210
Olkusz 75
Olsztyn 219
Olsztyn University 219
Omsk region 45
Opinogóra 106–10, 115, 117
oppression of Katyn families: by Polish com-
    munist government 4, 5, 29, 37–38, 43–44,
    49, 55, 60, 81, 92, 115, 118–126, 150, 159–
    160, 172, 177, 179, 182–83, 195–96, 213, 217,
    244, 249; by Soviet Lithuania 127–30,
    132–34, 139–40, 143, 147, 241; by Soviet
    Ukraine 19–22; *see also* cover up of Katyn
    massacre
Orchard Lake (USA) 162
Orenburg 178
Orlik-Łukowski, Gen. Kazimierz 248
O'Rourke, Count Karol 24–26, 32
Ościsłów 112
Ostashkov (Ostaszków) 1, 3, 16, 91–92, 99,
    100–04, 108, 116, 119, 230, 233, 249
Ostrołęka 113
Our Lady of Katyn 32, 76, 240
Our Lady of Kozielsk 9, 48, 162–63
Our Lady of the Victims of Katyn 30–31,
    240

Pahlevi 68–70
Pavilnys 127, 134; see also Vilno Colony
Pavlishchev-Bor (Pawliszczew Bór) 98, 100, 243
Pawłowska 189
Pelczarski 171
Pender Island, British Columbia 201
Persia 67–72; see also Iran
Petersburg 82
Piastów 115
Piatichatki cemetery (Kharkov) 59, 233–34, 245, 247, 249
Piatnica 171
Piechura, Major J. 224
Piedemonte 70
pilgrimages to mass grave sites 21, 31, 50, 59, 64, 75–76, 88–89, 103, 116–17, 124–25, 132–33, 135, 160, 171, 221–22, 233–50
Piłsudski, Marshal Józef 15, 62, 74, 130, 143, 146, 186, 188
Piłsudski's Legion(s) 60, 106, 150–51
Piotrkowski, Krystyna and Ryszard 173
Plater (family) 13
Plechavicius, Gen. Povilas 130, 206, 208
Płock 85
Płomyk 27
Podhajce 225
Podkarpacie 82, 88–89, 150–51
Podlesiejki 13
Pogwizdów 84–85
Polan 157
Polish Army 1, 16, 19, 23, 27, 31, 34, 54, 59, 67, 69, 127, 130, 133, 140, 150, 162, 178, 184, 194, 202–03, 210, 216–17, 221, 224, 229, 231, 233, 235, 237, 240–41, 243
Polish-Bolshevik War 150
Polish Free University (Warsaw) 14
Polish Red Cross 3, 46, 51, 110, 116
Polish University College (PUC) 213, 216–17
Pomorze 26, 48–50, 52
Ponary 140–46, 148, 207–08
Poronin 180
Portsmouth 218–19
Positivism Museum (Ciechanów) 116
Powodowo 28
Poznań 24–25, 28–29, 42–43, 81, 87, 177–78, 180, 211
Poznań University 25
Prosna River 37
Prusiek 164
Pruszków 122, 166, 194
Przemyśl 83–84, 87, 187
Przewoźnik, Andrzej 47, 237
Ptak family 156
Puchalik (née Pelczarska), Jadwiga 164–69
Puchalik, Capt. Zygmunt 164–66
Pułaski, Kazimierz 62, 74
Pushkin 210

Quebec 169

Radio Free Europe 28, 146, 182
Radomsko 122
Radoszkowicze 206, 220
Radoszyce 110
Rakańce (Rakonis) 138, 147–48
Ratno 95
Reczek, Prof. 159
Redłowo 31
Rembertów 171
Rexdale 169
Ribbentrop-Molotov pact vi 47, 95, 190, 202
Romanow, Mrs. 209
Romanticism Museum (Ciechanów) 116
Rome 31, 105, 162, 170, 237
Roosevelt, Pres. Franklin Delano 3
Rossi cemetery (Vilno) 130, 134
Równe 64
Ruchniewicz, Jan 51, 53–54
Ruchniewicz, Konstancja 51, 53–54
Russia 15, 26, 33–34, 46, 57, 65, 78, 80, 86, 90, 96–97, 100, 104, 128, 133–34, 143, 162, 198–99, 206–07, 227, 230, 242–43, 249
Rutkowska 108
Rydz-Śmigły, Marshal Edward 203
Rymszewicz (grandfather) 30
Rymszewicz (grandmother) 25
Rymszewicz, Hala 26
Rymszewicz (holdings) 32
Rymszewicz, Piotr 24, 25
Rymszewicz, Teresa (sister to Maria Karolina Spanily) 26
Rynkowski, Ryszard 129
Rzeszów 150–56, 159–60

St. Bonaventure High School (Wisconsin) 74
Sajewicz, Jan 140, 144
Sajewicz (née Wasilewska), (Aunt) Lola 140–46
Sakharov, Mr. 220
Sakowicz, Kazimierz 142
Santa Rosa, Mexico 71
Sarny 61, 63
Schlage 110
Scotland 54
Sea of Okhotsk 20
Second Polish Corps 69, 168, 227
Secret Service (SB) 177
Seliger (Lake Seliger) 99, 103, 108, 116
Semiozersk 66, 73
Sharmamulzak 65
Shelepin, Aleksandr 16
Siberia 14, 24, 26, 29, 39, 42–43, 57, 60, 65, 72, 81, 98, 130, 140, 142–43, 146, 182, 187, 203, 205, 209, 231
Sidor, Andrzej 14, 21
Sidor, Józef 12
Sidor, Maria 12
Sidor, Ola 21
Sidor (née Mendykówna), Olga 13–21

Sidor, Roman 11–22
Sidor, Lt. Władysław Antoni 11–19
Siedlanowski, Andrzej 102
Siedlce 120
Siekierski, Gen. Leonard 248
Sieniawa 151
Sienkiewicz, Henryk 44, 228
Siepak, Gerry 62–63, 71, 79
Siepak, Lt. USNC Jean 71, 79
Siepak, Aunt Maria 62, 71, 73–74, 79–80
Sikorski, Gen. Franciszek 248
Sikorski, Gen. Władysław 205
Skiel, Fritz 107
Skierniewice 174, 178–82, 184, 241–42
Skóra, Michał 110
Skrzyński, Count 82
Skuratowicz, Gen. Piotr 248
Śliżewski, Andrzej 140
Słupsk 114
Smoleńsk 17, 88–89, 132, 204
Smoliński, Eugeniusz 248
Smorawiński, Gen. 89
Śnieżko, Stefan 46–47
Soja, Gabriela 160
Soja, Zenon 159
Sojowa, Barbara 159
Sojowa, Małgorzata 159
Sojowa, Marek 159
Sojowa (née Dec), Stanisława 150–161
Sokółka 189
Sokolnicki 109
Sokołów Małopolski 150–52, 160
Solzhenitsyn, Aleksandr 20
Sopot 52
Soprunienko, Pyotr 16, 39
Sosabowski, Col. 120
Soviet Union 1, 4, 16, 37, 45, 65, 67, 98, 100,
    115, 120, 130, 143, 153, 204, 209–10, 219–20,
    240; *see also* USSR
Spanily (née Rymszewicz), Karolina Maria
    23–30
Spanily, Andrzej 23–32
Spanily, 2nd Lt. Zdzisław 23–29, 248
Spychała 93, 104
SS 113, 125, 131, 141, 144, 157, 208, 210
Stalin, Jozeph 2–3, 16, 28, 55, 60, 98, 102,
    168, 177, 182, 196, 205, 231, 249
Stalingrad 155
Stanisławów 38
Stankiewicz, (Uncle) 132
Stankiewicz (née Hołub), Zofia 128–29, 131,
    132
Stara Wieś 120, 123
Starobelsk (Starobielsk) 1, 3, 16, 23, 26, 35,
    39, 41, 44–45, 49, 63, 75, 103, 119, 139,
    146–147, 230, 233–36, 240, 242–243,
    245–49
Stefan Batory University (Vilno) 139, 201, 207
Stołbnyj Island 99, 103, 116

Stryj 187
Strzegowo 111
Styr River 62–63
Świaniewicz, Bernadeta (Dzidzia) 201–11
Świaniewicz, Bernadette 219
Świaniewicz, Edward Gregory 219–20
Świaniewicz, George 219
Świaniewicz, Jurek 201, 211
Świaniewicz, Lula (Świaniewicz family), Aunt
    (Marysia) 207–08
Świaniewicz, Maria (Marylka) 201–11
Świaniewicz, Nicholas 219
Świaniewicz (née Zambrzycka), Olympia
    (Lipka) 201–11
Świaniewicz, Lt. Stanisław 201–06, 213–216,
    220
Świaniewicz, Witold 201–220
Świerzna 49
Święty Jerzy cemetery (Toruń) 58
Święty Józef cemetery (Łódź) 93
Swojatycze 13–15
Szczecin 33, 40, 43, 46, 48–49, 210–11
Szlachtowicz, (née Kalwajt), (Halina's
    daughter) Jadwiga 128, 132–37
Sztutowo 53

Tarnopol 83, 164
Tarnowski 242
Tashkent 178
Tczew 210–12
Tehran 68–72, 206
Tel Aviv 207, 221–22, 227–28, 230–32
Terespol 102
Tilbury 215
Tomaszów Mazowiecki 41–42
Toronto 55–56, 60, 162–64, 168–71, 173–76,
    178, 184–85, 197
Toruń 36, 40, 51–56, 58, 191, 195
Troki 143
Tucholski, Jędrzej 224
Tunisia 103
Turkmenistan 67–68
Tuwim, Julian 228
Tver 16, 103–04, 116
Tybursy 213
Tyszkiewicz 24, 148

Ukraine 5, 11, 16, 61, 64, 70, 76, 137, 233,
    235, 238, 244–48
UNESCO 218
United States (USA) 4–6, 51, 57, 59, 60, 70,
    72–73, 119, 162, 186, 188, 199, 220, 244
University of Maria Curie-Skłodowska
    (Lublin) 229
Uppsala 215
USSR 16–17, 20, 34–35, 38, 53, 64–68,
    76–80, 86, 96, 103, 137, 198–99, 220, 238,
    243, 246; *see also* Soviet Union
Uzbekistan 67

Vancouver 218
van Loon, Maria (Riet) 218
Vatican 237
Vienna 172, 187
Vilno 9, 13–14, 33, 127–35, 138–48, 178, 187,
    192–93, 201–08, 211–12, 219–20, 236, 241,
    243
Vilno Colony 127, 130–32, 135; see also Pavil-
    nys
Virtuti Militari 35, 51, 73, 128, 178, 182, 187,
    190, 202, 248
Vitebsk 208
Vladivostok 93
Voice of America 182
Vorkuta 11
Voroshilov, Kliment 16

Wajda, Andrzej 124
Waka River 148
Wałęsa, Pres. Lech 88, 170, 239
Warsaw 9, 14, 26, 29, 31, 34, 41, 44, 52, 54,
    57, 60–61, 81–83, 87, 94, 102, 107–08,
    115–16, 118, 120–22, 124–25, 128–29,
    132–34, 164–66, 170–72, 175, 177–78, 185,
    188, 191–97, 210–11, 219, 221, 223–24, 230,
    233, 237, 239, 240, 241
Warsaw Ghetto Uprising 192
Warsaw University 38, 115, 118, 175
Warsaw Uprising 6, 120, 122, 166, 194, 196
Wasilewska (née Siemierikowa), Freda 138,
    144, 148
Wasilewska (née Rebkowska), Helena (Lila)
    139–46
Wasilewska, Mania 140
Wasilewski, Józef 138–149
Wasilewski, 2nd Lt. Józef (father) 138–40, 248
Wasilewski, Józef (grandfather) 138
Wasilewski, Józef (son) 139, 147
Wasserman (née Dresdner), Wanda 221–232
West 3–4, 25, 90, 113, 131, 146, 156, 158,
    175–76, 195–97, 206, 210–12
Westerplatte 189
Wiazyń 201, 205–06, 208–10, 219
Wieczorkowski, Ryszard 162
Wilejka River 127
Wilia River 219
Wisconsin 56, 74
Wisłok River 154–55
Wisztoka 139
Witold, Prince 201
Wizytki 165

Władek 205, 210
Wodzyński 107
Wojtecki, Officer Cadet 124
Wolodia (née Wasilewska), Jolanta (Jola) 147
Wolsztyn 28
Wołyń 61–62, 72, 82–83
Wołyński, Włodzimierz 128
World War I 51, 60, 93, 178, 192
World War II 1, 9, 32, 47, 75, 89, 118, 223,
    226
Wróblewski, Fr. Stanisław 234
Wrocław 156, 158–59, 194; see also Breslau
Wrocławek 52
Wsielubie 24–26, 32
Wyrzutowicz, Stanisław 174
Wyszyński, Stefan Cardinal (Primate of
    Poland) 43, 170–71

Yad Vashem 153, 231
Yakutsk 207
Yalta 130–31, 142
Ypatingas, Burys 141

Zagórze 19
Zakopane 83–84
Zaleszczyki 226
Zamarstynów 12
Zambrzycki, Józef 201
Zambrzycki, Stanisław 201
Zan, Tomasz 143
Zarnoch, Andrzej 43, 49–50
Zaryte 80
Zarzecki, Irena 185
Zarzecki, Krzysztof 185
Zarzew cemetery (Łódź) 244
Zawistanowicz, Hela 152
Żebrowski, Mr. 204
Zełemianka 152
Zgierz 105
Zieliński, Tadeusz 162
Ziemian, Janina 231
Ziomek, Prof. 159
Złoczów 92
Żodziszki 147
Zoest 194
Żórawski, Michał 245
Żuk, Lech 184
Żukow 141
Zulauf 27
Żuromin 129, 131